Whole School Health Through Psychosocial Emotional Learning

Whole School Health Through Psychosocial Emotional Learning

Jared Scherz

Foreword by Esther Wojcicki

FOR INFORMATION:

Corwin

A SAGE Company

2455 Teller Road

Thousand Oaks, California 91320

(800) 233-9936

www.corwin.com

SAGE Publications Ltd.

1 Oliver's Yard

55 City Road

London, EC1Y 1SP

United Kingdom

SAGE Publications India Pvt. Ltd.

B 1/I 1 Mohan Cooperative Industrial Area

Mathura Road, New Delhi 110 044

India

SAGE Publications Asia-Pacific Pte. Ltd.

18 Cross Street #10-10/11/12

China Square Central

Singapore 048423

Publisher: Jessica Allan

Senior Content Development

  Editor: Lucas Schleicher

Associate Content Development

  Editor: Mia Rodriguez

Product Manager: Francesca Dutra Africano

Production Editor: Amy Schroller

Copy Editor: Megan Markanich

Typesetter: Hurix Digital

Proofreader: Sue Irwin

Indexer: Integra

Cover Designer: Karine Hovsepian

Marketing Manager: Sharon Pendergast

Printed in the United States of America.

ISBN 978-1-0718-2363-7

This book is printed on acid-free paper.

21 22 23 24 25 10 9 8 7 6 5 4 3 2 1

Contents

· ·

Foreword

· ·

At no time has education been in more disarray. Many are clinging to an old model where teachers are the primary authority figures, controlling learning through force-fed instruction. Through Zoom and other virtual mediums, control is more illusory, increasing the stress from a conscientious but antiquated mindset. Those responsible for directing education, including administrators and school boards, also feel helpless, with limited options for reaching the multitude of remote learners with quality instruction and lacking the data to measure the efficacy of this approach.

Finding new ways to empower both student voice and educator volition are among the greatest challenges of modern academia. New avenues for promoting intellectual and social emotional learning (SEL) are needed, including methods available to urban and rural learners with limited technology access. Without a new paradigm we will simply be staying afloat, overtaken by the increasingly volatile rapids.

Important questions about K–12 education need to be posed in order to pioneer a meaningful shift. For example, does education mean memorizing facts about history? And if so, which history? And who wrote it? Is it learning about the plant world or the human body? Is it learning how to write? Is it reading the classics or just reading? We also need to consider how kids learn today, including the helpful and harmful consequences of technology-driven learning. And just as importantly, we need to consider how the mental health of our students and school communities impact academic success.

In the 1950s, I memorized what they told me to memorize. If I didn't, I failed. My number one goal was to follow instructions. By the time I was a senior in high school I was great at following instructions. But was I great at critical thinking? Or creativity? Probably not, but it didn't matter as much then. Today it matters—a lot. Employers want people who can think critically, be creative, communicate well both verbally and online, and collaborate well with everyone. With the growing complexity of our professional and personal lives, the stakes, and the pressure to succeed, could not be higher.

In the current survival mode of COVID-19, the objective is having continuity of education and minimizing disruption to maintain some semblance of normalcy for students. The dilemma, however, is incidental depravation of control, leading to students who feel even less in charge of their learning. The potential long-term academic and emotional consequences will not be known for some time, but it's reasonable to assume the deleterious consequences of chronic trauma. One of my students said this about a class: "They forced us into groups with people we didn't know or, worse, didn't want to know, and they told us to work together. We were never consulted, never asked what we thought." This attitude may reflect the growing impotence felt by students and educators who are living in an uncertain world where health is not a given.

As long as students and teachers are excluded from decision-making and treated as vessels to be "filled with knowledge" (as the film *Waiting for "Superman"* showed), we are in trouble. As I've written in my book *How to Raise Successful People*, we need to focus on trust, respect, independence, collaboration, and kindness. My classrooms are organized this way: Trust the students, and they will learn to trust themselves and their peers. Respect their ideas, and they will, in turn, believe in those ideas and will feel confident discussing them. They will respect themselves and their community if their teachers model how to behave this way, and teachers will be able to model this behavior if administrators do.

I am concerned about diminishing respect and independence in the present online model. It can feel overly directive, with administrator agendas leaving teachers and subsequently students with less autonomy. It can also be skewed toward too much freedom with a lack of accountability. These extremes leave educators feeling more frustrated, which is concerning for a system already struggling with recruitment and retention.

Helping students become the CEOs of their own learning means empowering educators to facilitate the transition toward greater ownership through self-determined learning. Just as there are incredible resources available for students and teachers, we have to know how to disseminate information through well-established and credible mediums, determine what has value, understand how to ensure veracity, and evidence multiple sources to become discerning learners. This is the gift that Jared Scherz gives us.

Expecting educators to adopt a new paradigm means they need to feel valued and supported in their work, a daunting challenge amidst the chaos. With the increased recognition that without teachers this country comes to a standstill, we need to add the caveat that quality follows training. Our future hinges on the success of our teachers, so it stands to reason that the physical and mental health of our most important professionals needs to be a top priority.

The psychological well-being of our teachers is imperative because, next to parents, they are the primary modelers of social emotional skills. Individuals cannot teach or learn if they are stressed out or sick or if they are struggling to meet basic needs. We need a national effort to improve the lives of our teachers and attract more young, talented people to the profession. Teachers are critical to the future of our economy, the quality of our health care system, and the morality of our leadership.

Change our teaching and change the future. Empower our teachers to nurture our students to solve the complex challenges in our community so we can all feel safe. Support the millions of educators, paraprofessionals, administrators, and support professionals with personal and professional tools to do their jobs well.

As you will read in this book, the intersection of organizational health and individual wellness is a starting point for our new conversations about whole school health. Dr. Scherz introduces us to fifteen educators whose incredible journeys reflect the critical importance of this movement to embody a new paradigm around psychosocial emotional learning (PSEL) and how it relates to school success.

—Esther Wojcicki, Founder
Palo Alto High Media Arts Program and
Cofounder of Tract.App, an afterschool program
to engage and empower kids

Acknowledgments

· ·

Writing this book was unlike any of my previous efforts. Instead of exerting to articulate one coherent voice, I attempted to integrate multiple perspectives while wrapping my own ideas around each. None of the contributors viewed my text in advance so as not to influence them; they were only given parameters for theme and depth. I didn't know what I would be receiving or whether it would support my premise that embodying principles of social emotional learning (SEL) was the ideal approach to whole school health.

And so, we set out to find fifteen educators willing to share their most intimate personal and professional life experiences with the world. The request was sizable: to deliver four plus pages of poignant memories, tribulations, and reflections, both inside and outside the classroom. This is a difficult task on a regular day, but when you layer the impact of a pandemic with educators struggling to adjust to this radical shift toward virtual instruction, the challenge felt more like first-time pearl or oyster diving during a fierce storm.

My TeacherCoach team helped to scour the country looking for candidates to contribute their educator narratives, interviewing countless classroom teachers looking for that "right" person. I'm grateful to this group who took on this essential task without hesitation while juggling our other top priorities that seemed to multiply like gremlins.

Our key criteria were to be highly self-reflective, transparent, authentic, and a willingness to be raw. If you consider your own life, I suspect you might have a difficult time finding many who fit this description. There were many promising applicants who graciously offered their help, allowing us to sift through representatives of small and large districts within urban, rural, and suburban areas.

Our contributors were challenged beyond what they expected, digging into their past at a time when the present felt most unstable. Many provided intimate moments of their lives, never before shared with friends or family. Together, they provide a rare glimpse into the psychological life journeys of the most important and unsung professionals on the planet.

I feel privileged to bring you these stories, hoping you appreciate the risks each took to exemplify the concepts within. Through continued courage and ongoing sacrifice, I imagine their vulnerability will inspire new and existing educators to grow our resiliency and unity.

To ground the theoretical with the applied, we enlisted the help of a company to help provide data-driven results. I would also like to acknowledge the work of John Ciolkosz from C Solutions, LLC, who helped to synthesize the data, making meaning of my research sample. As an educator and a statistician, John offered his valuable lens to enrich the often-ambiguous concepts being postulated.

And finally, I'd like to thank the district leaders from around the country who provided meaningful quotes and insights in support of our work. Their and the other leaders' near impossible work to safely reopen schools in the midst of the pandemic, without any respite or restoration from the previous year, makes their efforts nothing short of heroic.

Publisher's Acknowledgments

Corwin gratefully acknowledges the contributions of the following reviewers:

Ray Boyd
Principal
West Beechboro Independent Primary School
Western Australia, Australia

Marianne L. Lescher
Principal
Kyrene Traditional Academy
Chandler, AZ

Christopher Thurber
Psychologist
Phillips Exeter Academy
Exeter, NH

About the Author

Jared Scherz is a clinical psychologist, author, and consultant who has worked with educators for over 30 years. He earned his MEd from Penn State University and became an elementary school counselor before gaining his PhD in psychology. He has created innovative prevention and intervention programs in both rural and inner-city schools.

Dr. Scherz believes that by supporting educator wellness and organizational health, schools will be better equipped for the challenges of modern-day education. He also believes that self-reflective practitioners who can recognize and meet their own needs are the keys to cultivating environments where both academic and psychosocial emotional learning can flourish.

As the CEO of TeacherCoach, Jared's mission is to develop educational ecosystems that bring new revenue streams into school districts, make schools the hub of wellness in their community, and blend personal growth and professional development for faculty. Through the first ever Learning Engagement System (LES), districts can meet the needs of both the individual and the organization. For more information about TeacherCoach, email coach@teachercoach.com or visit us at www.teachercoach.com.

Introduction

....

When I first wrote this introduction in January of 2020, I referred to our nation as "in peril," polarized with mounting tension resulting from an inability or unwillingness to successfully negotiate our differences. Like shaking up an old-fashioned soda bottle but keeping the lid on tight, unresolved differences create trapped energy and can spawn implosions like anxiety or depression or explosions such as violence.

I had no idea that when I revisited this introduction in March 2020 that we would be facing a new crisis, superimposed on a social justice revolution, unparalleled in our nation's recent history. The magnitude of a global pandemic, disproportionately sickening those with weakened immunities and our minority populations, captured our collective focus and continues to be our top priority. COVID-19 has taken the lives of many people, made innumerable others ill, bankrupted businesses, and abruptly halted traditional education.

Since 1635 when the first schoolhouse was built, we perceive school as a brick-and-mortar institution, a place where students would first leave their homes and be tended to by adults other than the child's parents. Whether it was the certainty of a meal or the hope of a better future, schools represented the second home for academic learning.

It's now March 22, 2020, and in states all across the country school districts have been shut down, with fifty-four million students experiencing something new in our nation's history—a large-scale transition to virtual instruction, with widespread uncertainty about next steps.

While this book will be complete long before the conclusion of this global emergency, without a sense for how education may be forever changed, there is one vital piece of learning that will endure. Our health is our most precious commodity, requiring both prevention and intervention at home and in our educational organizations.

We spend too little time anticipating problems or misreading warning signs, with divergent views keeping us stuck. We are better served by a collective vision and well-measured strategies to replace the iterative fire extinguishing process that is public education.

While a global pandemic may not be easy to predict, the perennial threats schools face certainly are. School violence is preventable, as is our surge in mental health problems, addictions, and dropouts. A rush to implementation and divided philosophy leads to shortsighted solutions that miss the etiology of these social issues.

Fortifying infrastructure, such as policies or physical deterrents, while ignoring deep internal fissures only provides a single prevention layer against school violence. Substance abuse education will improve knowledge but overlook the critical element of tolerating distress. Training educators around suicide may alert them to the warning signs but discount the cause of underlying mental health problems.

Replacing single solution models with a multilayered prevention paradigm, plotting warning signs like an X-Y axis coordinate system, allow quadrants of influence to expand our assessment dimensionally. In a multitiered system, we treat warning signs as the epicenter of a complex set of issues, searching for patterns and etiology.

An example of this early warning detection and prevention paradigm would certainly include the alarming numbers around teacher engagement as reported by Gallup. While there is high complexity for interpreting this statistic, the idea that only 30 percent of the educator workforce are engaged in their work is an indicator of breakdown, much like soil erosion producing vitamin-deficient fruits and vegetables (Hastings & Agrawal, 2015).

A depletion of personal investment in one's profession is predictive instructional efficacy. With a decline in motivation of teachers to nurture their students, we can estimate the challenge of teaching life skills that go far beyond the realm of academia. It takes ethically intimate relationships between teachers and students to promote social and emotional growth—perhaps even more so than academic achievement.

Professionally intimate relationships between teachers and students represents the gut in our immune system, where at least 80 percent of our physical health is protected. If weakened, we may be at risk for a host of threats that compromise our well-being. Strong relationships, in contrast, supporting children through their individual journeys while minimizing harm can only be accomplished by educators who feel excited and supported to face new challenges.

For the teacher-student relationship to be strong, it requires other layers of support for the educator from his or her professional community, parent community, and personal network. These outer layers seem to be compromised in many instances, putting pressure on the educator rather than infusing them with positive energy.

Society is vacillating between cohesion, where neighborhoods come together to exercise, and fragmentation, as seen through hoarding and price gouging. Through a global threat of illness, financial deviation, and psychological turmoil, we breed acts of kindness shadowed by ones of indifference. Perhaps a growing instinct for self-preservation, a decline in our moral fabric, or the dehumanization of our personhood, hastened by technology, is destabilizing our school system by eroding the layers of support that teachers need to invest in their work.

As a microcosm of society, schools can be more than preparatory academies for careers; they can be incubators for solving polarizing social problems. As we begin to appreciate how the erosion of our collective personhood is a cause and catalyst for many of the threats we are working to solve, we need to treat psychosocial emotional learning

(PSEL) as a paradigm beyond a solution. Developing the whole person, capable of deep dives into the etiology of life's largest threats, is a modality that encompasses prevention, intervention, and pedagogy.

We are increasingly aware of how academic success may be limited by psychological impediments but are only in our infancy when it comes to developing a whole child approach. Constraints of time, training, and finance are just a few of the barriers hindering the understanding of and the need for social emotional learning (SEL) in schools. With time and a lack of training identified as major barriers by an *Education Week* survey (Schwartz, 2019), a curriculum- or skill-building approach would strain our already taxed system. This approach may be burdensome and suboptimal for sustainable growth.

In this same *Education Week* survey, 78 percent of teachers recognize its part of their job to help students develop strong social and emotional skills (Schwartz, 2019), but less than half felt prepared to do so. It is encouraging that a majority recognize the value of SEL, indicating they view their work extending beyond academics. Educators appreciate we are developing students at the intersection of their personal and professional lives.

Whole child education integrates life inside and outside of school, viewing problems as an opportunity for learning. By delving deep into the complexity of obstacles, we take ownership for our environment, whether a group, workplace, or society. Whole child education means viewing the school as a garden where we learn lessons of ecology that every organism has a function and every challenge invites possibility for evolution.

Instead of spraying chemicals onto weeds, absorbed by the root system of the desired plant, we consider what this dandelion has to offer. Life is busy, and haste makes for poorly reasoned decisions. Soil erosion runs parallel to the degradation of human life, with the effects of technology, social and traditional media, helping us to depersonalize our neighbors. Efficiency has a price, and for our children the decline of empathy and our shrinking capacity for distress are the hidden consequences buried deep where we need to excavate. See Figure Intro 1.

While technology provides access and vicarious experiences to people lacking opportunity, it also instills a growing expectation to have what we want, when we want it. Our natural desire to get wants met faster may mean a growing neglect for our needs. If we can access Google on our phones to learn how the beautiful swallowtail butterfly pollinates the sweet citrus scented nectar of verbena, then we may not go outside to experience it firsthand. And these are the experiences that bring peace, joy, and love into our lives—some fairly important needs.

Educators try to keep learning stimulating and enjoyable, competing with the expectation of immediate gratification. Capturing student attention by inserting technology into instruction is the quick fix but risks further skewing students into their brains and away from their bodies.

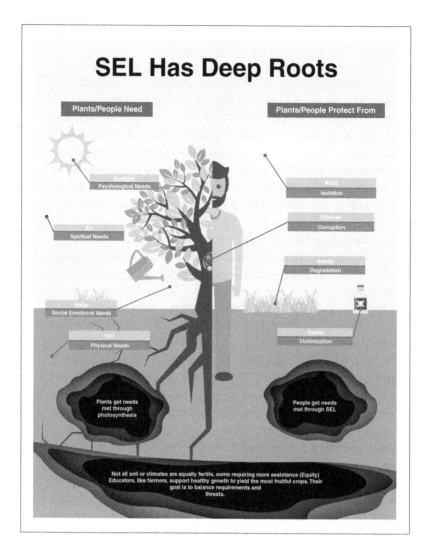

Transitioning into a whole child paradigm means balancing brain and body, where sensations and feelings become the building blocks to identify and meet our needs. Our bodies also provide the medium for intimacy, which is ultimately how engagement, an emerging concept in education, is made possible. Engagement is not simply about gaining or sustaining somebody's attention, a modern concept perpetuated by companies branding their product or service. Stimulating interest is a shallow measure of engagement, as it can also be used to describe the enticement a child has to drugs and alcohol. Full engagement requires free will, intentionality, and discernment.

For individuals to be engaged, we balance our own wants and needs with that of the organization, generating a mutual reciprocity. Engaged educational ecosystems are ones where all levels of the organization within a larger community are interdependently but transparently influencing each other to improve. Thus, our work is at the intersection of individual wellness, organizational health, and community partnership. Each individual works on personhood or character, improving the overall fabric of organizational climate, infused with resources from the larger community.

Our starting point, personal growth, is accomplished through PSEL that embraces all levels of the system. Most SEL programs are simply skill building, not cognizant of the greater context. Whole child education means preparing students to become productive members of society, appreciating the influence of self in relation to others and the large community.

Through our integrated lens, we can expand from a model of skill building to embodied learning. Educators will appreciate both the macro and micro prevention efforts through a paradigm that integrates PSEL into curriculum and classroom activity. The macro is the health of the organization, and the micro is the specific tools to help each student with strengths and limitations for each of the learning elements.

Fifteen PSELs will be explored in this book, developed through an iterative process, emulated by the adults, and actualized through the culture of the school and the achievement of the students. Read this book with your faculty, and together prepare for the challenges of incorporating these ideas into whole school success.

PART I

CURRENT STATE OF EDUCATION

Learning often means asking the right questions to help us think critically, consider our myopia, and expand our perspective. Inquiries have helped to ignite debate around our health care, food system, climate changes, and long-standing inequality and equity disparities.

Questions are the tools by which a democratic society evolves, providing checks and balances to prevent skews empowering selective beliefs. While questions may elicit threat for those who promote sameness over change, the absence of questions is a scarier proposition. Placing our faith in a few people to make decisions for the whole, without a healthy degree of challenge, can keep us stuck—or worse, drive us to devolve.

We now recognize food deserts, label foods as non-GMO, curtail our carbon emissions, and discuss reparations to those we have oppressed. But are we doing enough to improve the education system these social, political, and economic challenges hinge upon? *Endangering Prosperity* authors wrote, "It will take more than small steps and timid actions abetted by general confusion as to whether serious policy changes are worth their political costs" (Hanushek, Peterson, & Woessmann, 2013).

True transformational change requires attention to processes over outcomes, that is, *how* we are doing something over the end we are striving toward. Asking questions that are both measured and measurable in order to improve our educational system begins this exploration.

Is the U.S. education system moving in the right direction? Are tests a viable measure of achievement, aptitude, or teacher performance, and what importance should they have? If educators are satisfied but approaching burnout, are we doing enough to support them? How do social emotional and moral development impact learning, and whose responsibility is it to teach those skills?

How we measure efficacy and interpret the results inform our academic health. The answers may vary, however, depending on the source. The self-report of educators, national comparisons of academics, graduation rates, the experience of safety for students, teacher-child engagement, or any number of variables can be used.

Even if we could agree upon the variables and how to make sense of the data, the results will not necessarily extrapolate to the whole. If we can agree, for instance, that educators are experiencing elevated stress levels requiring greater support, the causes and hence solutions will vary. A small district in Kentucky, for instance, rates student behavior as the primary cause of stress (72 percent), while work-life balance is reported as the top cause in a small New Jersey district.

While blanket statements about our educational system aren't fair to those excelling districts, we will have difficulty embracing a growth mindset as long as our educators and institutions are in survival mode—the extent to which helps determine every other indicator for success, making a shared lens for examining the issues our first step in problem-solving.

Those on the front lines of education require an active voice, helping to inform decisions and measure outcomes, designed through feedback loops for real-time reporting. With input, educators can help shape our experiments to translate data into decision-making. Educators and administrators will be more vested in implementing change, knowing their input is considered and utilized.

Too often, changes reflect the excitement of a new idea or the temporary abatement of a problem, often to benefit a person or campaign. Creating change, whether incremental, transitional, or transformational, without fully understanding the existing issue we are trying to fix, can worsen a situation. We may increase dependency or reduce self-reliance, add to the burden of those implementing the change, and obscure measurements of cause and effect.

Our medical system is a prime example, treating symptoms more than underlying issues. Fevers, headaches, and hypertension have become problems to solve instead of indicators of possible lifestyle issues. Our overuse of antibiotics to treat bacterial infections reduce the good flora in the intestine for up to a year, depressing immunity and creating more complex problems.

Identifying cause through the lens of systemic influences is a more time consuming first step but allows us to look thoroughly at an issue, to take measured action. Without hypothesis generation and testing, we may compound a problem, creating more pressure on an already taxed system with the added consequence of lost time.

As with any organization — service or product focused — we can optimize by first considering barriers to success. In education, that involves questions about our workforce. Why are we having difficulty recruiting and retaining educators? What are the teachers' obstacles to success? What inhibits educators investing fully in their work? Would we be facing the same challenges of improving student success if they were more engaged?

CHAPTER 1

Teacher Recruitment and Retention

Rachel is a special education teacher entering her seventh year in the same suburban middle school. It was her third year in therapy, and as a veteran of personal growth work, she did a good job identifying distress that wasn't ordinary and owning those factors that were self-imposed.

When Rachel first began therapy, three years prior, she felt out of control, which was true when it came to her eating, but it was also a product of misperception. Her eating included continuous binges of unhealthy foods throughout the day, followed by periods of starvation and excessive exercise to purge herself of the calories and guilt. The more weight she gained, the more the cycle of guilt and self-annihilation intensified.

On this pivotal day, Rachel admitted a shameful regression—one she had worked so hard to overcome just two years prior. Through challenging group therapy, she described a destructive pattern of rushing to the daily display of cookies, cakes, and other sweet treats in the teacher's lounge and gobbling them down quickly before anybody knew she was there. Rachel quickly identified the escapism, a common protective mechanism, to cope with a moderately stressful class.

During this year, Rachel had three disruptive students who accounted for 95 percent of her time, a familiar ratio for teachers in all types of wealthy, poor, urban, and rural schools. One of these three boys was the ringleader who incited the other two into a frenzy of microaggressions that incited the class and devolved the lessons.

Rachel's primary concern was for the other students whom she knew were being deprived of a quality education and perhaps feeling unsafe. School is the one place she knew children were supposed to feel emotionally safe and physically secure. She took her job seriously, and when she was unable to regain control of her class, a combination of guilt and remorse flooded her body.

Rachel shared all her creative attempts to address this growing concern, but it was to no avail. When she sought help, her principal's response was this: "Send him out on an errand." Rachel resented the apathy of her school leader but also felt dismissed and discounted, much the way she did growing up in a family where alcohol and gambling took precedence over child-rearing.

What surprised Rachel more than the response from her principal was the fact that there were two other adult males in her class, assigned there as one-on-ones for other students, whose attitudes seemed to show more blame than concern. She felt judged by them, although she could not quite identify what specifically they did or said to cause that feeling. She wondered if she projected this judgment onto them or whether she was picking up on something real.

Between the perceived judgment, feeling dismissed, her worry for the students, and her own erosion of efficacy, Rachel began to spiral downward. Losing control at work brought her to a familiar but terrifying place, on edge as she embraced the ineptness. She began consuming foods high in carbohydrates, a serotonin boost, to help with the impending depression. The elation she felt in those few moments after consuming the high fat and sugary products provided an immediate escape from stress.

She felt relieved in the moment but knew all too well about the long-term consequences of overeating. She knew intellectually that she would regret the binge, even feeling shame for losing control, but the momentary benefits of her escapism prevailed. She couldn't stop her self-sabotage as long as the intensity of her feelings remained buried.

Through a process-oriented group, she considered her options, acknowledging what she already knew from her experiences in those weekly sessions. Confronting her principal was necessary; otherwise, the resentment she pushed down would keep surfacing as anxiety, which she knew the food provided a distraction from. While she feared conflict and being seen incompetent, she knew that continuing on her current trajectory was going to further compromise her health and potentially jeopardize her work. She also knew that addressing several racially disparaging statements he was alleged to have said when angry contributed to her reluctance.

We can extrapolate what a suburban special education teacher can teach us about the growing national problem of recruitment and retention. To do this we will need to look at this situationally within the larger context, pulling from this scenario.

We need to understand the underlying causes for microaggressions and what the actions the administration takes have on the community. A lack of impact can land just as hard as any blatant discriminatory attitudes or behaviors perpetrated by leadership. Being proactive in appreciating diversity sends a strong message to the community that every person is valued.

Professional learning needs to prioritize social justice, diversity, equity, equality, and the dangers of ethnocentricity and racism. Rachel is Caucasian but feels strongly about cultural sensitivity, wanting to work in a school with greater diversity to stimulate her own learning. She learned through private coaching that contrasting differences promotes deeper learning and intimacy than the pseudo-intimacy of sameness. She never had school-sponsored professional development (PD) around equity and equality other than a boring PowerPoint two years prior.

Our current system is guided by the principle of accountability but may be leaning away from autonomy, creativity, and personal investment. When we hold everybody to the same standard, we limit creativity and autonomy, lessening our emphasis on the creative processes that drive organizational health. We endanger teacher empowerment and fuel the problem of engagement, to which every other issue in education can be linked. According to Gallup and Gary Gordon, the author of *Building Engaged Schools,* engagement is a critical concern for education (Hastings & Agrawal, 2015).

Educator stress stemming from pressure, unrealistic expectations, lack of work-life balance, and diminished voice can reduce longevity for existing educators and discourage new recruits. We want educators to feel supported inside and outside the classroom because this is the most personal of all professions, extending educators well outside the school day.

Accountability is well intended but can be implemented with more process-oriented strategies that enhance all types of learning. Standardized curriculums that limit creativity may increase resentment as teachers feel more like factory workers, impacting student treatment.

A familiar pattern is playing out across schools nationwide. A student misbehaves. Perhaps some unmet need, such as belonging, triggers being disruptive in class. The teacher responds, influenced by the fear that there will be no support from the administration, who is focused on bigger issues. When the teacher interacts with the disruptive student in an avoidant or hostile manner, based on the anticipation of resentment for not having backup, the parent gets involved. The backlash from the angry parent myopically focuses on how unfair the teacher treated the child, garnering support from the school leadership who doesn't want public relationship problems.

When the teacher feels let down by the school leader or anticipates the same, a move is made toward protective mode. The teacher's self-interest becomes paramount over the well-being of the students, which for most educators is ego-dystonic or not aligned with the teacher's beliefs. The intrinsic passion of the educator is slowly replaced by a more self-serving agenda. As teachers become less invested in their work, student outcomes decline. Legislators looking to save the system and advance their careers come up with pragmatic, well-branded solutions. The No Child Left Behind Act (NCLB) and Every Child Succeeds Act sound important but do not address the complexity of engagement. Teachers react to dramatic policy shifts in part due to their skepticism and resistance to change but also with a sense of futility that their input matters. When those on the front line don't have a say in what's best for students, their frustration turns to futility. Their interactions with students are shaped by their attitude toward the system and the cycle begins again—only this time with greater intensity.

According to the paradoxical theory of change, before anything can be different, we first need to fully understand what already is. Why is this issue a problem now? Has it been a problem for a long while, or are we are just recognizing it? Have our solutions not worked, and why? Is the problem indicative of more complex dynamics we aren't appreciating?

Most important to solving this or any other problem is recognizing our previous model wasn't working and then examining the lens through which we are viewing the issue. To accomplish this more easily, we begin with the forces for sameness and change that are serving to keep us stuck. Sameness and change are perennial influences exerting their pressure on us throughout the day although we seldom give attention to it.

When we fail to consider our reasons for holding back or rushing to action, especially when our decisions lack a deeper appreciation of the etiology of the issue, we scaffold new problems on top of old. Stopgap measures, ill-conceived quick fix solutions (a product of our prescriptive society), and general reactivity will make it harder to understand why the issue became problematic to begin with.

Using social emotional learning (SEL) as an example, we might add in a new expectation for educators to embed social skills training into a subject area as a result of increased reports for cutting, a specific form of adolescent self-harm. Teaching students how to communicate more clearly around their feelings seems at the surface to be straightforward and helpful. If we can consider that the increase in cutting originates from increased pressure students are feeling academically—holding their teachers responsible for their burden—expecting them to communicate feelings they aren't ready to share may increase pressure rather than decrease it.

With current challenges making attracting and sustaining new teachers even more complex, the macro and micro levels of system yields important data. Understanding the state or federal policy shifts and the role of the individual district as well as the dynamics created between the two is where solutions begin to form. The level of funding, consumption of resources on mandates, and priority setting will determine how the intersection of individual wellness and organizational health helps or hinders support for new educators.

While we are waiting on those decisions from policy makers, who often lack the ground level perspective to establish meaningful initiatives, we can design and test our own solutions to present for endorsement. We know the existing issues identified by educators who rank student behavior, work-life balance, and an absence of input into decision-making as important areas to address, but we don't yet know what will be added or reprioritized on that list.

To initiate bottom-up change, we will need to examine how policies and procedures balance protection with oppression, so volition isn't compromised in the service of safety. As our focus will be physical safety, especially for students, we must ensure the psychological welfare of all levels of the system and beyond to restore teaching as the most valued profession. To do this we will need to move out of survival mode, where adverse working conditions are improved.

Without enough qualified teachers entering the profession—and depending upon the actual rate of attrition—we may be depleting our system to dangerous levels. Between 2009 and 2014, the most recent years of data available, teacher education enrollments dropped from 691,000 to 451,000, a 35 percent reduction. This amounts to a decrease of almost 240,000 professionals on their way to the classroom in the year 2014, as compared to 2009 (Sutcher, Darling-Hammond, & Carver-Thomas, 2016).

While it may be unfair to contrast the U.S. with other countries, it's difficult to ignore the discrepancy. "Compared to high-achieving jurisdictions like Finland, Singapore, and Ontario, Canada—where only about 3 to 4% of teachers leave in a given year—U.S. attrition rates are quite high, hovering near 8% over the last decade, and are much higher for beginners and teachers in high-poverty schools and districts" (Sutcher, 2015).

Recruitment efforts are sometimes hampered by poor teacher orientation or onboarding, mismatches between candidate and district, inadequate funding (especially poorly represented minority communities), and a lack of administrator support. Schools may also lack the attention to an educator's needs for personal support, believing professionals should separate their work and home lives. With the new complexity of stressors brought on by the pandemic, our lens may be widening to include creative supports new teachers would value.

The study also found a high association between a lack of administrative support, the quality of school leadership, professional learning opportunities, instructional leadership, time for collaboration and planning, collegial relationships, and decision-making input—all influencing the degree of educator engagement. The safety mechanism being put into place and resulting changes in how educators manage their classrooms may influence the nature of engagement, possibly increasing the burden.

Engagement is a broad term with deep meaning, necessitating a closer look in this new era of instruction. With the temporary shift toward virtual instruction and possibly longer-term use of a hybrid model, engagement between all levels of the system needs rethinking. If we can better understand how contact is made and maintained between different subsets of the system, we may learn where and how to strengthen those connections. In doing so we may find creative ways to attract and sustain more qualified educators who wish to rise to the challenge.

Key Points

▸ Our effort to raise accountability has potentially lessened autonomy, creativity, and investment. Balancing these polarities is an important task for district leaders.

▸ Accountability is important, but an overemphasis can shift us toward an outcome focus, neglecting important processes.

▸ SEL can be a way to support educator well-being while improving student achievement, including addressing social justice issues.

▸ Recruitment and retention are even more critical to sustain our schools, requiring more in-depth appreciation of individual wellness and organizational health.

CHAPTER 2

Engagement

In 1635, the one-room schoolhouse was born in Dedham, Massachusetts. It was a simpler life but still with challenges, including a persistent threat of attack from the displaced Native Americans, power imbalance toward white males, and no electricity. Barriers in our modern educational system, by contrast, include the lack of qualified teachers entering the profession, turnover, school violence, the debate over charter schools, the controversy around methodology, and an outcome-focused and evaluation-based curriculum.

Job satisfaction stretches across many of these issues, with reported lows in 2012, a drop of twenty-three percentage points since 2008 (Strauss, 2013). Principals also reported a nine percentage point drop during this time period. A small research sample conducted by this author of approximately 350 respondents in three states, however, found nearly 87 percent of educators reporting moderate to very high job satisfaction (Scherz, 2019). Thus, it may be helpful to drill down to determine what we are measuring: how demographics and work conditions factor in.

While job satisfaction concerns are not unique to the U.S., with more than a third of U.K. education professionals feeling stressed, compared to 18 percent of their workforce overall (Speck, 2018), there are some factors we can prioritize. Salaries might be low on this list, with nearly half the teachers in this country reporting satisfaction with their salaries (less so for rural educators).

Less tangible aspects of satisfaction, such as well-being, are more difficult to define and measure but may be a higher-priority investigation. The insidious nature of apathy, detachment, and diminished investment can strip a system of rigor like a processed-foods diet strips the body of nutrients. As we navigate dietary challenges within the context of the food industry, so, too, are we exploring engagement in the context of our educational system.

Engaged teachers like what they do, but we do not know that disengaged teachers dislike their work or perhaps what aspects of their work they are less satisfied with. Are disengaged teachers lacking investment due to the nature of teaching in this current climate or the circumstances surrounding their specific employment? It is less likely a person enters the profession if they do not want to work with students, although subject matter expertise, industry job availability, and scheduling may certainly account for some.

The appeal of shaping lives has likely been compromised by something within the educator or their environment. Job responsibilities or the receptivity of students may detract from enjoyment. For principals,

75 percent reported their job became too complex, reflecting the speed, quantity, and diversity of work tasks all educators are pressured by (Will, 2018).

Relationships are hampered when students are enabled by parents, within systems that emphasize grading over learning. The pressure families face to compete for college admissions or the lack of collaboration from parents who provide too much freedom to their children, lacking intrinsic motivation, create animosity where compassion would normally exist. Educators become angry at the system they didn't help to create, enervating them from fully vesting in their work. The danger, as we are increasingly aware, is the dilution of these relationships impacting student success. Protective factors such as self-esteem, determination, and grit in young people are fostered through relationships with caring adults, teachers, and mentors. And yet, teachers' well-being, the engine for this work, is often at best an afterthought to professional development (PD)—and more often dismissed entirely.

When teachers feel healthy and happy, bringing their whole selves to work, they can foster the kinds of relationships necessary for student development. To help students learn how to meet their own needs, becoming more self-sufficient, requires effective role models, not simply more skills. As we better appreciate this relationship and the implications for student success, we will devote more resources to this area.

While engagement may well be emerging as the single most important barrier in education, we can't change it unless we understand its meaning. Engagement is an often used but poorly understood term that is generally linked to motivation and attention as well as inferentially tied to learning and behavior. Without clear consensus on the use and definition of this concept, we are easily manipulated by those who capitalize on our uncertainty.

Engagement Defined

Professional engagement is often underappreciated as an aspect of professional learning. Other aspects of PD, including mastery of skills, application of theory, and refreshers on fundamental knowledge are all important but less effective if engagement is compromised.

Engagement, a measure of work investment, is a derivative of skill building but mostly proceeds it. It is analogous to a baseball player who isn't happy with the team he is playing for but is going for extra batting practice. Sometimes integrity alone will allow the player to maximize output, but more often maximum learning saturation is reached too early without absorbing the full benefit of the skills.

When we get engaged to be married, we make a formal commitment to our partner, symbolized through a ring or some other form of investment. We've announced our intent to share life forever with another person, giving up much of what we consider to be *our* possessions, wishes, needs in favor of ours (as in mine and yours). Our money, material collections, time, and energy are all (prenuptial agreements notwithstanding) divided in half with this commitment. We agree to make decisions together; to live in the same house; and, for many, to start a family. The engagement is the process by which we prepare to be less self-focused.

Gallup defines *engaged* teachers as involved with, enthusiastic about, and committed to their work. They know the scope of their jobs and constantly look for new and better ways to achieve outcomes. *Not engaged* teachers may be satisfied with their jobs, but they are not emotionally connected to their workplaces and are unlikely to devote much discretionary effort to their work. *Actively disengaged* teachers are not only unhappy but also act out their unhappiness in ways that undermine what their coworkers accomplish.

These terms may be overly simplistic, not considering the stages of development for intellectual and social emotional learning (SEL). With fluid stages, we increase our depth of understanding and investment based on our intellectual and psychological capacities. A more enhanced view on engagement may be borrowed from a branch of psychology called Gestalt.

In Gestalt therapy, we use the term *contact* to signify how awareness is used to take actions around meeting our needs. Contact is a process where two distinct entities come together to form something new, like the ocean and sand, forming a changing shoreline. Contact or contact boundary is where entities exchange information, define themselves, and form their process for negotiation and intimacy. Engagement can be thought of as the way in which we make contact. Engagement is the early action(s) we take to explore newness or the ongoing method by which we navigate ourselves in relation to others or the world.

Stages of Relational Engagement

Reaction: My attention is aroused through sensory awareness prior to figure formation. My senses elicit feelings, and feelings trigger needs. My alarm sounds at the potential threat to needs being compromised and excitement around other needs being met.

Resistance: My forces for sameness and change are activated, triggering my protective mechanisms. I notice my hesitation and begin looking inward at motivation and/or intent.

Reflection: I form images, associations, and memories. Instinctive reactions give way to more deliberate recognition of self in relation to others. As I own my "stuff," I can more easily navigate the challenges of taking in the other while maintaining my sense of self.

Receptivity: My protective mechanisms dissipate as I identify how to meet my wants and needs, aware of my style of manipulation. Fear is leaned into helping to grow excitement.

Reworking: As I recognize my needs, I more closely consider the other. We begin to explore and negotiate differences, considering where change or acceptance is needed to make better contact.

Stages of Academic Engagement

Curiosity: My attention has been sparked, the degree to which is based on my innate level of intellectual hunger, how the content resonates, my current state of mind, and the delivery method.

Consideration: I continue to think after the stimulus is removed. I want to learn more. I'm influenced by rigidity, mood, and external conditions (relationship, context, investment). I wonder how this stimulus generates information that applies to my world. Discernment is key.

Capacity: My ability and willingness to apply this information leads to acceptance, rejection, or ambivalence. Success with applying this information will also determine my attitude.

Commitment: I begin planning and/or implementing how to use this new information. The strength of the data or delivery is mixed with my receptivity and cemented by my experience.

Confluence: I'm incorporating this new belief, thought, method, or perspective into my existing identity. I have determined how this new learning fits in my schema. Obstacles to success do not derail but enhance my new learning.

Engagement and Leadership

Leaders engage with their faculty through consistency of follow-through—adhering to the mission or vision, providing support in times of distress, holding faculty accountable, and creating a culture of cohesion. The full investment of oneself into the modeling, motivating, and orchestrating for the purpose of bringing out the best in each person is the job of the leader.

Leaders also engage as ordinary people, removed of title and role, leaving only organic care and concern. In these moments of contact, a leader remembers that everybody is on the same team with the shared interest of nurturing student growth. Beyond affirmation, engagement can also be accomplished through meaningful differencing and intense curiosity. Dr. Michael Salvatore, New Jersey Superintendent of the Year (2019), shared the following:

> Connectedness has become a living essential for educators and school leaders as they navigate the changing landscape of remote teaching, leading, and learning. Some may envision personal digital tools, which allow access to information, shopping, and work; whether it be a laptop, wireless router, or tablet. These engineered devices provide a basic network connection, but the opportunities to deeply affect others go far beyond the virtual *Brady Bunch* images flooding social media. Connectedness

begins by exploring the experiences and circumstances of those we encounter. Further, seeking to understand how life events shape individual perspective heightens this connection. Great teachers and leaders leverage these processes, identified as social emotional leadership, to build healthy relationships aimed at elevating thought and inspiring action.

Technology and Engagement

If you ask a technology company, engagement may be used to describe the focus and sustained attention of the end user. "Eyeballs," commonly used to measure the effect of an advertisement, determines the growth of that marketing effort to convert and retain customers. These branding specialists know that engagement represents an emerging need in education, which they are capitalizing on.

With the increased use of technology in this country, it seems evident that the nature of engagement is inextricably tied to the mediums by which we relate and learn. We are essentially helping the marketing companies through use of these products and services, becoming their sales conduit to students. Without considering efficacy of impact, we are complicit in escalating unintended consequences.

The ISTE (International Society for Technology in Education) Conference is one of the largest in the country, attracting all the major brands, including IBM, Apple, AT&T and more. If you attend this conference, you may be struck by the number of taglines promoting *engagement* as a selling tool. These companies research student engagement, which according to Gallup decreases every year after fifth grade.

Office Depot has one of the larger signs that reads Engaging Students, Inspiring Success, a powerful message and a huge promise. Success is a catchy word, but it does not clearly articulate what this looks like or how their product or service contributes to the outcome. Is success academic achievement accomplished through student engagement promoting critical thinking or other social emotional skills?

Using the term *engagement* in one's brand signals to the parent or educator that this service or product is going to be well received and even adopted as part of the overall learning campaign. For the millions of parents and educators who struggle to get and keep the attention of this younger generation, this sounds highly appealing.

Engagement has been used to describe the phenomenon of linking students in the classroom through interactive media, teachers with other teachers through resource sharing, and even schools with the community through parent-teacher software. There is no shortage of apps, software, and devices that bridge connections through technological innovation.

We aren't questioning, however, the quality and depth of these connections. Are we truly linking people with each other, and if so, how? Are we connecting people to the device, software, or app as a medium, and what impact does that have on the interaction? We don't know whether the results of this engagement will impact the classroom culture, the student's ability to make meaningful contact with others, or even improve the way we negotiate.

Tristan Harris, a former Google project manager, wrote a manifesto that warned the public of large tech companies attempting to capture and sustain attention without regard to misleading advertising and potentially harmful consequences. In spite of the attention he received from the general public and even the founder of Google, nothing evident came as a result of his warning.

Engagement, according to the large tech companies, and apparently a growing number of smaller tech companies wanting in on the action, is about leveraging the interest of the end user. If a tech company cites student engagement via their cool math app that kids love, we must read that as generating interest and recidivism with their product or service.

By this definition of engagement, we could also include crack, heroin, and sugar as effective engagement tools because they, too, stimulate interest and long-term use. People are motivated to use these substances, but perhaps more accurately, they are extrinsically motivated. That means the reward is coming from the outside and not from within. This is an important distinction because externally driven reinforcers create dependencies and not sustainability.

If every time little Johnny is given a piece of candy for cooperating, he will learn to look for the reward. He does not necessarily feel good about his action but rather the brain stimulation derived from the sugary substance. This temporary euphoria can also trigger tantrums when the reward is not quick enough, frequent, or proportional in his mind to the action.

In essence, we are creating a child who may lack empathy, self-regulation, and internally generated motivation if we rely too heavily on external stimuli. Children who seem spoiled, entitled, and impulsive are ones who are used to getting something, never fully appreciating themselves in relation to others, the foundation for relational engagement.

This same child who is fed candy and sugary desserts every night ultimately loses appreciation for the natural sweetness of fruits, requiring higher levels of stimulation to keep interest. If we replace sugar with computer math games to learn arithmetic, consider what happens when we remove the game.

We want to feed the mind the same way we do the body, with organic material that promotes long-acting nourishment, the fuel for intellectual and emotional health. Learning environments are rich in nutrients grown from a collaborative team of parents and educators.

Technology isn't a threat until we make innovation the driving force absent of measuring consequences. If we lose sight of the harmful impact of technological advances, we diminish the incredible progress of access and equity. Without considering these limitations, they can easily blossom into full-fledged dangers, both for the students and educators.

Examples of this unfettered technological progress can be found in other industries, but the lessons have not translated into the present. Consider how opium led to the production and use of morphine during the Civil War (1861–1865). Army surgeons desperately needed to treat field wounds of soldiers, making the substance highly effective. Now, opioids are the leading cause of death for people under fifty.

The same example is found in our food industry, revolutionizing longer shelf life for foods during wartime rationing. Now we use artificial ingredients and processed foods that require less frequent visits to the supermarket, producing food deserts that keep low-income families unhealthy and unable to elevate their quality of living. This disparity became more obvious during the early phase of the pandemic, with so many immune compromised people becoming ill and not recuperating.

While there needs to be further research to consider all the extraneous variables, the United States with 4.25 percent of the population accounted for 29 percent of the world's confirmed deaths by mid-May. Health and Human Services secretary Alex Azar suggested that underlying health conditions, including among minorities, were one reason for the high American death toll (Collinson, 2020).

As we recover, we might also consider what the next major health crisis will encompass. If we don't pay close attention to the consequences of innovation, if we don't examine and even measure the impact of technology, we are inviting both known and unknown dangers into our classrooms. Already, we see research informing us that up to half our children are addicted to their cell phones (Felt, Robb, & Gardner, 2016). Cortisol levels rise when we put our phones down; children and adults alike are glued to our social media, altering our neuropathways.

As additional research may reflect addictions, anxiety, attention deficits, behavioral problems, and declining student success is related to technology, we may have a dilemma. If we continue to introduce new technologies that promote engagement but rather stimulates dependency with declines in attention and tolerance for distress, then we could be heading toward a crisis that dwarfs the pharmaceutical and food industries combined.

Socially responsible technology, the type that promotes interdependence and not reliance on constant stimulation, is the responsibility of every educator to monitor. Through dedicated teams, we can assess the inherent limitations of our tech use before it causes irreparable harm.

Engagement and Professional Development

Optimal learning through PD is a dynamic process that takes many factors into consideration, such as the level of resistance (natural by-product of forces for sameness and change), the way the information is presented, relevance or timeliness, and how much volition the educator has about this new material.

To maximize learning, educators also need to address the natural barriers that manifest over time, interfering with autonomy, creativity, and enjoyment of one's work. Forces for sameness and change are acting on people all the time, so we may confuse opposition or defiance with something more organic. If we treat reluctance as a threat, however, or fail to recognize the pull for familiarity, we may increase resistance.

Engagement as a by-product of intrinsic motivation or commitment to one's work is influenced on different planes of resistance. Personal, systemic, and societal influences must all be explored to appreciate why that educator may not seem cooperative. For the district leader who feels frustrated or discouraged by resistance, looking through these lenses may help. The same holds true for classroom leaders working with students.

The personal influences may be hidden, so we never want to assume we know what a person is going through. Taking an interest in people's experiences, even asking specifically about their personal and professional barriers to fully investing, would be novel. While some may treat this inquiry guardedly, sharing your intentions would likely encourage disclosure.

Systemic influences may also be barriers, such as the polarization between unions and school leadership. The sensitivity of these conflicts may not be addressed openly, causing mistrust and division. Even subgroups of support staff, aides or paras, and classroom teachers will harbor irritations that are seldom dealt with through group process and are instead left to fester.

Societal influences represent the third set of barriers, including county, state, and federal mandates. This plane also represents the support from businesses, parents, and the media. Some districts are fortunate to have a range of financial and political support while others have constant power struggles between the superintendent and the board. These issues trickle down to the frontline educator who is expected to implement policy, endure the pressure, or manage the environment that's already been established.

To help educators successfully navigate these planes of resistance, we want to embed this new lens into every aspect of mission and operations. When solving a problem or facing a challenge, appreciating the forces for sameness and change will improve empathy for those holding different viewpoints. This may be a parent who seems to be enabling his or her child or a teacher who seems reluctant to implement directives.

We can extend the same orientation for students who dilute contact. When such a student seems reticent to fully invest emotionally or academically, consider the forces for sameness taking the form of fear, despondency, or resentment. Consider how students feel inside their community and how they may be struggling to find their place.

If students are poorly motivated to attend school or turn in work, they may be misdiagnosed as lazy or apathetic.

If we consider motivation as a tool, we can better equip students with the skills to get their wants and needs met, feeling more hopeful and therefore more encouraged. Instead of responding to their indifference with encouragement or punishment, we can assess where the blocks are to their own self-propulsion and whether they lack the ability or conditions necessary to thrive. Conditions such as unrelenting stress from health concerns or family chaos can erode skills for meeting one's needs if they persist for long periods of time.

The same holds true for adults. Just as a student's engagement is impacted by stress, so, too, is an educator's investment. Our responsibility is to include these areas in professional learning so that teaching and learning pathways are optimized for low stress and high motivation.

The love of teaching versus the act of teaching is an important distinction to consider when appreciating ways to heighten engagement. The love of teaching is the intrinsic satisfaction educators gain from developing young minds. The act of teaching is the facilitation of learning activities through lesson plans and impromptu engagement measures.

Professional engagement, further broken down into awareness, enrichment, and experimentation, encompass a triad of investment pillars. Awareness is the ability to see oneself clearly in relation to others. Enrichment is the skills, theory, and practice that puts new ideas into place. Experimentation is the iterative process of examining what we have done and what we can do differently next time to achieve more desirable results.

Awareness is the foundation of engagement. If we don't know what our strengths and limitations are, how a child perceives us, or what our resistance is to change, we can't grow. Personal growth hinges on awareness derived from self-reflection and feedback. The Johari window provides a helpful illustration of this concept, showing how we use data from scanning within and input from others to grow. This paradigm helps us reduce our blind spots to better recognize how to make contact. If, for instance, we fail to identify a student seeming standoffish with us because they fear racial discrimination, we may invest less energy into them.

Enrichment is where most professional learning currently takes place, but it is seldom based on self-reflection, which would enhance the skill, theory, and practice being taught. Grounding new approaches in engagement theory might stimulate greater interest in experimentation.

Experimentation is the aspect of engagement that would make professional learning more sustainable. Rather than disseminating information and expecting educators to apply it in their work, have multiple sessions where designs were created and trials implemented. Too much learning from students or adults is not internalized because the proper application or extrapolation didn't occur, leaving the mind of the trainee soon after the training concluded.

The keys to all three aspects of engagement is determining an educator's level of readiness and resistance to new learning. We can't force people to be self-reflective; it happens when feeling safe and excited. While considering those elements, we will naturally look to the environment to determine whether any systemic or societal barriers need addressing.

If we look, however, to two large, recent studies done on PD, one by the Gates Foundation and the other by TNTP (previously known as The New Teacher Project), we find limitations in our current approaches. In the past decade, two federally funded experimental studies of sustained, content-focused, and job-embedded PD have found these interventions did not result in long-lasting, significant changes in teacher practice or student outcomes. Only 40 percent reported that most of their activities were a good use of their time (Jacob & McGovern, 2015; K–12 Education Team, 2015).

Furthermore, no set of specific development strategies resulted in widespread teacher improvement on its own. The studies did say, however, that there are still clear next steps that school systems can take to more effectively help their teachers. Much of this work involves creating the conditions that foster growth, not finding quick-fix PD solutions. This supports the premise that professional engagement may not be receiving the attention it deserves.

An important consideration being missed, likely responsible for the study results, is that for any professional engagement training to be effective, meaning impactful and sustainable, it needs to be based in part on the paradoxical theory of change. This is a psychological theory from Gestalt therapy that helps us appreciate a basic premise, that awareness of what is, is necessary before trying to make something different.

For example, if a student is misbehaving, our intervention may not lead to a desirable long-term result without knowing where the behavior emanates from. If a child isn't listening due to being upset about something going on at home and we simply employ a disciplinary tactic, we could see short-term change while exacerbating the problem.

Awareness is key for individuals but also for organizations. According to the Cleveland Institute of Gestalt Organizational Development, the most successful organizations are ones that can scan their environment, make meaning of data, and then successfully execute changes; in addition, they will look toward their employees as a consistent barometer for organizational health.

Schools as institutions lag behind for-profit companies when it comes to valuing their faculty, appreciating how their individual needs must be balanced against the organizational ones. Professional investment balanced with personal enrichment is the optimal integration of growth/development needed to keep systems running smoothly.

In the past this type of training related to individual health, relationships, and management was referred to as soft skills—perhaps because it's the lubricant for the main objective of academic learning. Moving forward, we want to remember engagement is not immediate and it doesn't fit into solution-focused models. Out of the box skills are attractive on many levels but seldom do they lead to deeper engagement.

Engagement and Social Emotional Learning

Engagement is the method by which we constructively differ or use conflict to explore differences while maintaining contact. Engagement measures the strength of our connection with others to navigate unlike opinions, ideas, beliefs, and feelings that vary according to familiarity or the degree of receptivity we help generate. Engagement is about the process, not the outcome of active exchange, from the earliest introduction through our efforts to sustain.

Through psychosocial emotional learning (PSEL), we appreciate that differences are a vehicle to deepening intimacy by learning more about ourselves. When we contrast our views, beliefs, values, or experiences, we become more thoughtful about the anchors that ground us. Why do we think or feel the way we do? Engagement is catalyzed by knowing ourselves so we can more intentionally deepen contact with others.

Engagement is helped by and helps with our self-awareness. The better we understand how others perceive us and the more we are cognizant of our own strengths and limitations, the more likely we will engage meaningfully with others. Bonding over similarities is most common; however, depth of contact occurs when we appreciate differences.

Pseudo-intimacy, or relatedness based on sameness, is short lived. It lacks the strength forged from knowing we can be at odds with somebody and still remain close. Through the course of a school year, we will have many disagreements with colleagues, but like a bone that heals stronger following a fracture, so, too, can conflict embolden relatedness.

A lack of social emotional skills will help us avoid conflict and stay on the surface with our relationships, making it difficult to invest ourselves fully in our work. Relationships give us fuel through support, sharing of resources, and catharsis. Relationships seem less fragile with the skills of empathy, differencing, and negotiation, balancing our needs with others.

The better we are able to identify, express, and negotiate our needs, the more likely we will have those needs met in a way that helps us more fully invest in others. An educator who is achieving higher-order needs, such as peace, fulfillment, and purpose, will be more creative and persistent in engaging with others, not discouraged by a lack of immediate reward.

Tim is a high school teacher feeling enervated early in his career, uninspired, and just "going through the motions." He was cordial with his coworkers and seldom the target of any quidnunc because he gave them little to inquire about. Arising from his personal growth work came a willingness to take risks, to disagree and firmly supplant himself in risky exchanges. As his skills for negotiating differences grew, so did the depth of relationships, growing enthusiasm clearly evident in his bounding energy with students.

Thus, the relationship between individual needs, SEL, and school climate ought to be clearer, as personal wellness promotes organizational health and vice versa. In schools where emotional safety and physical security is constant, members may look to grow their higher-order needs through social and emotional risk-taking. In school cultures lacking in physical security or emotional safety, such as the freedom to challenge authority, individuals will invest less in their community. Faculty will remain entrenched in self-protection and forgo risks needed to grow the spirit of the institution. This is the difference between surviving and thriving (see Figure 2.1).

With approximately 9 percent of teachers in the U.S. reporting they have been threatened with injury by a student and 5 percent reporting physical attack by a student, the absence of physical security is a real concern (de Brey, 2018). If faculty work under the constant threat of harm, self-protection trumps investing in their community.

Even without the threat of bullying, domestic violence, or gangs, the ever-present fear of catastrophic violence is on the minds of many. Since 2000, there have been more than 188 shootings at schools and universities, with more than two hundred students killed and at least two hundred more injured (de Brey, 2018). Unlike any other country, the U.S. has developed a contagion of dramatic violence, which has direct correlation with engagement and culture (Bump, 2018).

Violence, the manifestation of exclusive aggression, which is addressed in Chapter 15, is the complete breakdown of SEL. When children believe there is no hope of getting their needs met and lack the skills to do so, they may resort to destruction. Children who lack empathy believe that there is nothing to lose and nothing to gain, projecting blame onto the students who ostracized them and adults who failed to protect them.

Teacher engagement with all students is the best prevention method for school violence and requires no expensive program to purchase. Deep, meaningful contact with students is the bridge that quickly identifies at-risk kids and gives hope to those who feel alone. Engagement is the anchor spurring student effort even when hope is low or resources are limited; it is the model that helps kids aspire to get their wants and needs met.

Teachers have the potential to engage with students when they introduce new material, set realistic but challenging expectations,

Figure 2.1   Individual Portion of Flow Chart Only

What Makes Educators and Schools Successful

Surviving Mode

Chronic and acute stress feel overwhelming, diminishing resiliency.

Enervation and tension lead us to consider 'symptoms'.

Poor self-care such as unhealthy eating and reduced exercise.

Overthinking leads to fragmentation.

Treatment orientation leads to medical intervention.

Relating through thoughts, beliefs, and judgements.

Others withdraw, due to our lack of openness to intimacy.

Feel rejected and resentful, reinforcing world view as unfair.

We resort to coping such as alcohol, shopping, gambling.

Shame hastens our downward spiral.

Self-blame leads to self-harm and world blame leads to entitlement.

THRIVING MODE

Distress felt as a challenge to overcome, growing resiliency.

Driven by our wants and needs, balancing brain and body.

Messages from the body lead to intentional use of energy stores.

Activities that reinvest energy output, to recharge and revitalize.

Accepting our limitations and inequalities.

Sensations lead to exploration of unmet needs.

Relating through experiences and perceptions.

People are drawn to us because we are present, potent & peaceful.

Feel empowered as life's challenges provide learning.

We take risks, experimenting to find outlets for distress.

Curiosity promotes self-worth.

Giving back to our communities because we feel rewarded.

navigate conflicts among classmates, deal with parent complaints openly and honestly, and have even the briefest dialogue in the hallway.

When we are intentional in how we make contact with other human beings—aware of our own contributions and active in negotiating differences—we create an environment where people can be themselves, which is an important condition for students living in self-doubt. Such environments benefit all community members young and old, creating a sense of peace and reducing the insidious effects of stress.

Key Points

▶ Job satisfaction among teachers and principals was already low prior to the pandemic. This needs to be the focal point for all school improvement.

▶ Engagement is a process of developing depth of awareness in the service of self-sustained learning. The Gestalt contact is a well-researched construct to help us appreciate the steps of the process.

▶ Relational and academic engagement occur in stages that can be used to assess issues ranging from student behavior to teacher apathy.

▶ SEL can improve engagement, which then creates a more conducive learning environment: more physically secure and emotionally safer.

CHAPTER 3

The Psychology of Educator Stress

Overview of Educator Stress

Teacher stress began in 1635 in Dedham, Massachusetts, with the imminent threat of attack by displaced Native Americans. Acute stress has given way to chronic stress, which human beings were not designed to endure. Since the evolution from that one-room schoolhouse, to the industrialized institutions of contemporary education, both the source of stress has evolved as has its impact on education.

Until the pandemic, teacher stress was strikingly absent from prominent education debates, including international rankings, standardization, or segregation of public schools. While most can agree a new paradigm for progressing our stalled educational system is critical, preparing students for complex challenges of technology driven systems, attracting and retaining quality educators, and sustaining a hybrid model are not yet clear.

Growing deficits in social emotional maturity—such as the tolerance to sustain attention, the skills to negotiate, or the ability to work independently—impact academics and jeopardize mental health. To help these struggling students successfully prepare for both their personal and professional lives, our educators need to be better equipped to navigate their own stress first.

With high levels of daily stress, and a diminished joy for teaching, the omnipresent threat of burnout jeopardizes student preparation. Nearly 94 percent of educators surveyed agreed with the idea that burnout, a new classification in the *International Classification of Diseases* (11th revision; *ICD-11*), is a real risk in education (Scherz, 2019). Our country's most important natural resource often feels like factory workers without appreciation, autonomy, or the respect they once enjoyed.

Many educators struggle with some of the same issues as our students, including addictions to technology and low resiliency. In the same research, 33.5 percent agreed their own technology use has become problematic, reducing wellness. If educators are struggling themselves with technology and social media, consider the impact on their teaching, their ability to help assess student technology dependence, and the impact on all work relationships.

Expecting educators to engage students, keep up with technological innovation, and ensure that test scores are high does not feel fair or realistic to many teachers or administrators. Michael J. Hynes, Ed.D., superintendent of Port Washington School District in New York, cited the "de-professionalization of teaching" predicated upon our self-induced "data purgatory." Hynes believes this is a primary cause of elevated teacher stress since the inception of the No Child Left Behind Act (NCLB).

Identifying the causes of educator stress is the job of superintendents like Dr. Hynes but is also the responsibility of everybody within educational leadership. Understanding the role of educator well-being within the context of the larger educational ecosystem might be more attainable if we simplify the matter into three important questions: What are the greatest stressors for teachers? How does teacher stress impact student learning (learning environment)? Are we successfully addressing this issue?

In the U.S., consideration of teacher stress and wellness (the antidote for stress) is growing but still trailing other countries such as Australia and the U.K. The U.S. has considerable research on stress in the workplace and on school culture but not nearly enough on the interaction of the two. Part of the challenge is many competing definitions of school culture, difficult for those on the front line to assimilate.

Defining organizational health as the integration of three dimensions—adaptation, climate, and infrastructure—may help provide clarity. Climate is made up of the collective well-being of educators, which in turn lays the foundation for relationships, safety, and emotional investment in academics. Both individual and institutional stress influences the climate of the school.

The Source of Educator Stress

Appreciating the origin of educator stress helps us support educator well-being, illuminating individual and systemic factors. The ubiquitous expectation of sacrifice blends both those factors, reinforcing dynamics that aren't sustainable, such as time spent preparing for work while at home. If insufficient prep time is allocated, for instance, we may burden teachers who begin looking for shortcuts. But where are these expectations emanating from?

Through a multistate survey, the primary source of work-related stress for educators was found to be administration at 32.19 percent, closely followed by work-life balance at 28.77 percent, evidencing the need to integrate support for life inside and outside the classroom (Scherz, 2019). If educators are being on call, doing prep work, or giving up their own recreation time, they aren't likely refilling their energy stores to fuel them throughout the year.

Other notable results include stress from policy changes (11.11 percent) and lack of input into decisions (10.54 percent). From this list, it should be noted that in some districts student stress was rated even higher than work-life balance.

Surveyed teachers agreed at 97.3 percent with the notion that stress in one's home life impacts work in the classroom. This means that in addition to their stress over work-life balance, it may not be realistic to expect educators to leave their home life at the school door. Thus, it may not be effective for schools to only address workplace culture and expect these well-intended interventions to be sufficient for supporting their most important resource.

Our shift toward greater accountability has meant a heavier reliance on standardized curriculum and testing to measure outcomes. Teachers become stressed by the loss of autonomy or creativity and the pressure to prepare students for testing. Fedrick Cohens, executive director of curriculum for Georgetown County School District in South Carolina, sees this as a top concern for educators, which is why he de-emphasizes test scores, believing what's taught in the classroom will be naturally reflected in benchmarks regardless of test scores.

School leaders who recognize work-related sources of stress will likely identify several systemic factors that include the lack of administrative support, declining parental involvement, and the lack of input into decision-making. Student challenges—such as the lack of impulse control, a need for higher levels of stimulation to sustain student attention, and a lack of self-discipline or motivation—drain enjoyment.

Teachers will be less patient with students and possibly even less creative or invested when their own stress level is high. Overlooking students with behavioral or motivational challenges may also occur, which can increase the potential for self-harm and suicide, especially now that the environmental pressures have been raised with the pandemic.

Even if a teacher has the capacity to intervene, the growing influence of social media and technology play significant roles in the generation of stress. One teacher in a suburban New Jersey school district recently caught two students cheating using technology but then feared her instinct to address the issue may result in a legal violation of the student's privacy rights.

Legal and ethical questions around technology and communicating with students is a major concern we have yet to address. While virtual instruction has become an overnight necessity, we have yet to address the tsunami of boundary violations this quake will cause. We also want to consider the psychological impact of constant communication and accessibility. The stress of navigating expectations, boundaries, and compassion fatigue are all important considerations.

Educators are concurrently struggling with their own use of technology and isolation. Between the isolation, lack of movement, and use of technology for recreation, we may be adding to our cumulative stress levels.

The higher complexity of stressors and obstacles to peace means more innovative tools to restore wellness are needed. While we know that wellness is a crucial component to a strong school climate, we might estimate that stress will erode the very conditions needed to create a safe and supportive real or virtual environment for educators and learners.

Once this cycle builds momentum, the overall health of the organization begins to erode.

The Impact of Teacher Stress on Student Learning

When students come to school stressed, their learning is understandably impacted. When a teacher comes to school stressed, their teaching is impacted. Dawn Lazarus, with twenty-five years in education, currently the professional development (PD) specialist at Jumoke Academy, a charter school in Hartford, Connecticut, said, "We can't improve scholars if we aren't improving the staff... they are the delivery method. If they are not happy and healthy, neither will our children be."

Teaching requires a high level of vigilance sustained over a long period of time. Downtime for educators is brief and often without restoration, generally spent grading, supporting students, or prepping work; each of which still take a good deal of energy in the form of concentration and enthusiasm. When moderate to high levels of stress are applied to these complex tasks, we greatly jeopardize the quality of work.

Persistent stress, even lower levels, will lead to diminished returns for all activities, especially those requiring intellectual and emotional investment. Muscle weakness, reduced focus, and deteriorating mood resulting from stress can make even ordinary tasks burdensome. When we consider more complex tasks that educators face each day, the results are more critical.

As motivators, teachers need an abundance of energy to keep children interested over an extended period. Precipitous drops or even gradual declines in energy, eroded by personal and professional stress, will not be differentiated in their attribution to job satisfaction. A middle school teacher in Mount Laurel, New Jersey, shared her progressive decline in work investment over the years to "protect" herself from high levels of stress. What she realized, however, was being disengaged created a new type of stress—one that undermined her work ethic. She blamed the school for robbing her of her enthusiasm for teaching.

With over 84 percent of educators who were surveyed reporting moderate to very high levels of daily stress, this example may spiral our system out of control. With growing fears for psychological and physiological health, our workforce is in peril. For the one out of ten educators reporting very and extremely high daily stress levels, that's over three hundred thousand educators in the U.S. alone who are in danger of mental and physical health problems (Will, 2017).

With moderate to high levels of daily stress, extended over a period of weeks or months, we will likely see problems such as absenteeism, lateness in grading, less investment in addressing student behavioral issues, diminished effort around grading, a lack of creativity, and poor engagement with students. Schools with high levels of behavioral problems and poor grades always want to consider whether stress is resulting from or contributing to these issues.

Future Projection

The warning signs are flashing brightly, our awareness of the issue is growing, and the vocalization to improve is growing louder. In large and small districts, public and private, in all regions of the country, the consensus is that we need to do something and do it fast before we lose more qualified educators.

Efforts to address teacher stress are varied, with some addressing school culture, while others attend to the personal needs for educators outside of the classroom. Kathleen Taylor, Superintendent of Schools, Ocean City School District, sums this up in stating "While I always knew that a healthy faculty meant a greater investment in teaching, it's never been more apparent than it is now. Faculty need to feel safe, cared for, and valued, just as we ask them to do for their students. Their social and emotional well-being has to be a priority too."

Wellness, however, is not a simple fix. Stress relief to prevent burnout does not seem fully embraced by educators. According to our research sample of 350 educators, only 12 percent strongly agreed that stress relief training would be helpful, and 27 percent believed it would not be helpful (Scherz, 2019). For those who are not convinced of the value, we might question whether this is the quality of support or whether conditions seem beyond what can be repaired by improved coping. Additional research to determine if providing more in-depth stress support, including decreasing the source of the distress, recognizing how one perceives stress, or developing more constructive outlets to reduce stress, would be more valuable.

Stress relief requires creativity, occurring in unexpected ways. Opportunities to laugh will reduce tension levels. Even traditionally boring training, such as the mandatory bloodborne pathogens, can be an opportunity for stress relief. Providing educators more opportunities for collaboration is important to offset the inherently siloed nature of their work. When spending the day working with young people, stress relief from a simple adult conversation or even opportunities for deeper contact will become a natural and inexpensive antiseptic for stress.

Thus, the need to appreciate the perennial value of quality relationships, infusing greater fun in our work, and restoring the passion that brought educators to schools in the first place is paramount. This appreciation to slow down can be seen in new ways, such as the growing movement toward mindfulness in education, in service of our higher-order need for peace.

The term *mindfulness* represents a wide array of beliefs and strategies that vary by author or presenter, but the etiology is born from Zen Buddhism. Somewhat of a misnomer, mindfulness generally involves more balance between our overwrought brains and our neglected bodies. Mindfulness is growing in popularity in large part as a response to the increase in accountability efforts in the form of federal policy. When standardization increases, educators often lose real and perceived autonomy, leading to reduced feelings of power and control. When people feel a loss of power, their tension level rises until eventually feeling defeated. This is part of the burnout cycle that typifies high levels of chronic stress.

Mindfulness helps people feel more peaceful through paradigm and practice. Some districts have introduced wellness-related goals for faculty into their yearly plans, introducing activities such as yoga and nutrition. While educators often appreciate these opportunities, only a small percentage take advantage.

Supporting education is a matter of priority, according to Dr. Royce Avery, former superintendent of Manor ISD in Texas. Dr. Avery warns that without increased funding and higher pay for teachers, we will continue to struggle. Districts struggling to afford basics will have a difficult time considering higher-order needs.

To support the longevity of our educators and improve the health of our school learning environments, we can make one simple but powerful paradigm change. By introducing personal growth into PD, we will help our caretakers with their own improved self-care. A simple way to begin is by evaluating the wants and needs of your faculty. Simple polling can be done to determine how much and what types of stress exist among the faculty along with desired solutions. A warning, however, if you elect to assess results is to be prepared to act on them. We want to avoid the message that we know you are stressed but we aren't prepared to do anything about it.

Any creative method for supporting your most valuable human resource needs ongoing measurement; otherwise, time and energy spent devising and implementing strategy could produce diminishing returns. Rewards, for instance, require continuous adjustment as they lose value over time. And, most importantly, remember that teacher wellness and student outcomes are "inextricably linked. If we are taking care of ourselves and modeling healthy choices for students, such as pursuing our passions, self-care, connecting with others, negotiating to meet our basic needs, and moving toward greater self-actualization... our students will be more successful" (Heather McKinney, head of school at Fusion Academy Morristown).

Here are creative approaches to stress reduction from these school and district leaders:

▶ Dawn Lazarus (Jumoke Academy): More PD and team time embedded within schedule. Opportunities to work in groups, by department or grade level.

▶ Dr. Royce Avery (Manor ISD): Innovative schedule where faculty get a week off in October for rejuvenation.

▶ Michael Hynes (Port Washington School District): Yoga for teachers before and after school.

▶ Fedrick Cohens (Georgetown County School District): Teacher-led PD.

▶ Heather McKinney (Fusion Academy Morristown): Open microphone night for students and faculty to perform together; creating playlists to reflect mood, yoga, and meditation.

▶ Dr. Kathleen Taylor (Ocean City School District): With guidance and support of Dr. Jared Scherz, we made a commitment to social and emotional learning dedicating resources across our district, designating Wellness Rooms, and launching initiatives to eliminate stigma around mental health, because we know that both staff and students benefit from a culture that puts their well-being at the forefront.

▶ Shelby Iezzi (Pottstown School District): Fun and competitive activities for physical and nutritional activities.

Key Points

▶ Teacher stress is insidious in nature, impacting every aspect of the school environment. Social emotional learning (SEL) can be used to reduce stress and increase both peace and fulfillment.

▶ Burnout is a growing risk from stress and a new classification of disorder.

▶ Our increased reliance, dependence, and addiction to technology is a growing cause for educator stress.

▶ Educator stress is correlated with student outcomes as well as with physiological and psychological research.

Organizational Health and Educator Wellness

CHAPTER

4

"The reason one group or organization excels over another, given equitable resources, is the ability or competency of being able to scan one's internal and external environment, make meaning of the data collected and respond appropriately in ways that support reaching upon desired outcomes" (Gestalt Institute of Cleveland, 1988).

We don't typically think about schools in terms of organizational health, uncertain of how to measure this concept, how it differs from school culture, and what the contribution of individual wellness means for the collective whole of the school. Organizational health, a result of school culture, is the conceptual core for each learning institution. Through a thriving culture with a strong resiliency, relationships, and principles, the school will navigate obstacles while continuing to support its mission and vision, determining their overall health.

If we can abandon ambiguous terms, such as a *positive culture*, we can better appreciate the interconnections of these three dimensions and subcomponents. When people lazily apply the terms *positive* or *negative*, they are attempting to convey a complex set of characteristics with simplistic terminology. People need to feel satisfied with their work, but beyond that, ambiguity in defining culture makes the correlation less easily operationalized.

To provide some shared language, organizational health is the integration of three dimensions of culture: adaptation, climate, and infrastructure (see Table 4.1). Adaptation includes those tasks that allow

Table 4.1 Three Dimensions of School Culture

Adaptation	Climate	Infrastructure
Prof. Development	Morale	Leadership
Decision Making	Job Satisfaction	Supervision
Resiliency	Philosophical Accord	Policy/Procedures
Structure	Communication	Physical Environment
Learning	Autonomy/ Empowerment	Integrity/Values

the organization to adjust and grow. Climate refers to the experience of those within and the methods by which that experience is cultivated. Infrastructure includes the parameters that keep the organization operating smoothly.

Organizational Needs

We can predict the health of an organization much like we can a person, based on the extent to which needs are being met. Organizations or systemic organisms have needs that promote a balance between outcome and process. The original hierarchy of needs, described by Maslow, can also be applied to institutions of learning.

The needs of an organization can be assessed through simple surveys, to gain a sense of the collective health of the school. The needs are analogous to the engine of a car, driving the person or organization in pursuit of goals. There are eleven such needs to support the effort of organizational development, which are contrasted against our individual system of needs: (1) safety/security, (2) authority/agency, (3) efficiency/productivity, (4) enthusiasm/cohesion, (5) engagement/effort, (6) accountability/ownership, (7) flexibility/resilience, (8) innovation/creativity, (9) impact/efficacy, (10) integrity/ethics, and (11) mission/vision (see Table 4.2).

An individual without physical security and emotional safety will be hampered for meeting higher-order needs, which is similar to an organization. The foundational needs require processes making attainment

Table 4.2   Individual Versus Organizational Needs

Individual System of Needs	Organizational System of Needs
Purpose/Meaning	Actualized Mission/Vision
Peace/Harmony	Integrity/Ethics
Value/Importance	Impact/Efficacy
Love/Intimacy	Innovation/Creativity
Approval/Acceptance	Flexibility/Resilience
Affiliation/Belonging	Accountability/Ownership
Joy/Happiness	Engagement/Effort
Fun/Excitement	Enthusiasm/Cohesion
Freedom/Independence	Efficiency/Productivity
Power/Control	Authority/Agency
Safety/Security	Safety/Security

sustainable, affording the organization greater stability in the face of internal and external threats. Determining when an organizational need is met is more complex.

Unlike individuals who can use their sensations to identify unmet needs, leaders will use objective, subjective, and sensory data. Leaders can't easily determine how much *safety/security* is necessary, relying on objective data, self-reports (faculty and students), and their own perceptions to continuously calibrate. Leaders also need to examine how the needs are being met and whether there is a deficit or surplus. An excess of security, for instance, such as cameras and metal detectors, may stimulate mixed feelings of assurance and uneasiness. Therefore, we ought not to assume interventions to meet the needs of our faculty and students will serve the collective whole. Ongoing assessment allows for micro and macro adjustments in order to prevent reactivity and promote more proactive measures.

Authority/agency is next in importance. Strong leaders at the district, school, and classroom levels will help balance safety without sacrificing empowerment. An indicator of low authority/agency may be seen in behavioral problems during low structured time, such as in the cafeteria, playground, or hallway. Feeling unsafe or lacking volition may lead to defying authority.

Authority/agency represents each faculty and student's shared responsibility for leadership. Being an upstander, for instance, is an indicator that students aren't waiting for an adult to take charge, the goal for developing future leaders. The protection of morals and values is another example of agency, ensuring people follow rules from intrinsic beliefs as opposed to external rules. When each person feels imbued with healthy power, the need of agency is met.

Districts employing a shared decision-making or collaborative leadership model have the best chance for success in meeting this need. When the collective members are invested in balancing the agency and authority of a school, it generally means they trust the leadership, who, in turn, trusts the community.

Brian Brotchul, superintendent of the Delran School District in New Jersey, believes their community has endured the recent hardship of the pandemic through an innovative approach to leadership:

> [The district] has navigated the most pressing challenges together through defined collection and application of intra-organizational trust as it relates to wellness, organizational climate, organizational self-study, goal setting, all areas of teaching and learning, inclusive of drafting of curricula, development of professional improvement coursework and the selection of materials. The concept of developing and expanding upon the capacity of teachers, principals and supervisors has afforded the district to flourish in a culture that assumes the best intent from all parties with the overall goal of improving outcomes connected to teaching and learning.

This district leader's lack of ego and sincere desire to bolster a sense of ownership within his faculty has led to a simple but powerful rise in engagement, reflected in parallel growth in student achievement. Brian goes on to report that "our collaborative work affords every single member of the organization the ability to contribute to the extent desired be it as a member of a defined team or a contributor to our feedback loop process. Never has inclusivity of all stakeholders and embedded empowerment been more important to our work and our outcomes."

With balanced leadership and a collective sense of safety, an organization can attend to their product (learning) and service (teaching) by measuring the expended energy matching the desired results. Are teachers spending considerable time at the start of the school year doing remedial work, compensating for what the students didn't learn the year before? Efficiency and productivity can be applied to most any operations from teaching to administrating.

As with other needs, an organization can become too focused on *efficiency/productivity.* When we move toward the polarity of efficiency, we want to make certain we aren't sacrificing process. Having too many rules, expectations, or mechanized operations may diminish member creativity. Two little efficiency and districts will waste considerable time. One district in New York surveyed the secretaries and support staff to find at least 80 percent of their workday was spent fixing problems such as teachers filling out forms wrong or not following protocol.

A more intimate need for the organization is member *enthusiasm/cohesion.* This need represents the invisible energy producing morale, job satisfaction, and a sense of teamwork to grow school climate. When a high percentage of people are excited to do their jobs, especially in cooperation with others, the entire organization thrives.

Engagement/effort are good measures of both organizational health and individual wellness. Without either, low investment in their work can produce antipathy toward the organization and diminish both efficiency and productivity. This need is contingent on the others, especially the enthusiasm/cohesion of the community.

Accountability/ownership is the hallmark of an evolved community, where diversion and blame are seldom seen. This need represents the moral compass of the institution from the top down, helped by alignment with espoused values and daily operations. When superintendents are held accountable to the board and the board is responsible to the community, that mentality will flow downward. The absence of this need creates chaos and dissent.

Accountability is most effective when it flows in both directions. The students are accountable to the teachers, but it can also work in reverse. If teachers solicit input from how their class experiences them, teaching methods and modalities can be modified, the hallmark of an adaptive instructor. Too many educators get set in their ways and expect their students to mold around their proven methods; this is born out of complacency or arrogance.

In an era of continuous shifts in expectation from the federal government down to the state level, schools have a need for flexibility/resilience to withstand unanticipated hardship. In doing so, they can keep morale high and waste less time or energy struggling with resistance. This can be attitudinal as much as it is logistical, helped when leaders anticipate the response to change.

In organizations without research and development, the need for *innovation/creativity* may be higher. To prevent monotony or staleness, schools have a need to be generative or else risk stagnation. This need is most evident when schools lean toward one of the extremes—either introducing too much newness or overly relying on traditional practices. When schools have good balance in this area, students will be inspired toward their own creative thinking, inspired by faculty who are doing the same.

Among the higher-order needs for an organization are *impact/efficacy*. Schools that have a high percentage of students who graduate and move on to desirable careers will enhance local and regional communities to build this need. We also want to consider if these students are being prepared to become constructive members of society through the development of morals and psychological resiliency.

Schools that work within their communities will actualize this need more easily. Volunteering, community-driven work projects, and partnerships with local businesses will serve schools well, such as the Fontana School District in San Bernardino County, California. This district partnered with Tesla, Google, Microsoft, and others to bring opportunities for students, such as ensuring that all high school students have laptops for home use and being the first district in the country to provide free internet access citywide.

Assistant superintendent Joe Bremgartner says the following:

> We are trying to think about education differently. We want our students to be prepared for a world that we can only imagine and have formulated critical industry partnerships that will provide our students with unique and innovative opportunities. No matter a student's socioeconomic status, or background, we believe that all students deserve the best we have to offer. We truly believe that we can change the way we provide education to students, and our students will be future focused and ready for whatever lies ahead.

If the school is generating impact while producing other desired results, we might also consider if they are doing so adhering to the high standards and principles generated within the community. Schools that promote social consciousness, social justice, discernment, and moral development will more likely meet their need for *integrity/ethics*. Short-term goals can be attained when we take shortcuts, but sustainable growth is a result of people who believe in the school and the feeling that their school believes in them. Those organizations consistently meeting the previous ten needs and whose daily operations flow from the *mission/vision* are more likely to generate integrity. Many schools don't regard their mission/vision as a living document that requires ongoing consideration and amendment, or they don't include their faculty and students in the shaping of this need.

When schools become aware of these collective needs, they can take actions designed to achieve them and understand problems preventing them, similar to how we would help a student with unmet needs. This simplicity can be applied to organizations if we interpret problems through this lens. When schools are meeting their organizational needs, they are more likely to consider the individual needs of faculty, students, and parents.

The following represents some examples of healthy school dynamics we may find in schools where needs are being met:

- Risk-taking
- Allowance and celebration of mistakes as evidence of learning (accountability)
- Healthy conflict
- High expectations without a demand for perfection
- Ongoing and available support
- Attention on process and environment instead of output
- Aspirations over rules
- High investment by faculty
- Boundaries explored as points of contact
- Flexible and inclusive decision-making

Organizational health can be understood through the appreciation of its polarity—a less healthy organization where needs are not being met. Here are some examples of unhealthy school dynamics:

- A lack of measured risk (too much sameness)
- A culture of blame
- Avoidance or overpowering conflict
- Low or unclear expectations and burdensome expectations
- A lack of support promoting siloes and cliques
- Outcome over process
- Rules without aspirations
- Low faculty investment

 ❯ Boundaries defined as limits without exploration

 ❯ Rigidity and exclusive decision-making

The collective risk of burnout for educators, the ultimate barrier for organizational health, indicates how we are caring for our workforce. Burnout, resulting from risk factors outweighing prosocial factors, can be an effective measure of organizational health easily assessed with capturing time lapse data. This allows for more thorough exploration over reactivity.

When problems are noted, short-term strategies have the benefit of immediacy but limit full consideration. Long-term, data-driven processes that can be measured are burdensome and not easily agreed upon, but they generally yield better results. A starting point may be the exploration of why the problem exists. The paradoxical theory of change reminds us that something can't be different until we understand what it already is.

We can spend less time fixing a problem if we can appreciate what the problem tells us and the problematic conditions or dynamics requiring attention. The healthiest of organizations put effort into preventing problems before they occur. We can't prevent problems we aren't exploring and, even worse, generating through our own poorly reasoned decisions, which doesn't always mean data informed. Data driven can be just as problematic without considering what we are measuring and if we are using the right instruments. Decision-making is a process utilizing multiple streams of input. We also want to consider important data not easily measured, including phenomenological experience not easily quantifiable.

Some problems take many years and influences to form, such as soil erosion. Taking shortcuts, such as not replenishing nutrients into the soil or a lack of education, contribute to this depletion. Therefore, measuring a single solution is hazardous. Erosion of personhood or system is a complicated phenomenon, not altogether different from the erosion of our soil, putting our entire agricultural industry at risk. When we are unaware of the threat, such as to our food supply and the resulting health issues, the problem compounds, and layers of complexity make identification more challenging. Most of us just see dirt. If we notice a plant at all, we hardly consider the complex network of microbiomes, insects, minerals, rock, and other organic matter synthesized by air, water, and weather, over hundreds of years, to form the essential material needed for roots to grow. Without those roots, the seed wouldn't germinate and the plant won't grow, so we cannot blame the farmer.

For advanced farmers, the majority of their effort is spent balancing the soil through adding organic matter, ensuring sufficient water and drainage, and keeping the weeds out until just the right time to harvest. The real experts even know which plants to put near each other in the garden and how to discern between naturally occurring problems such as plant or animal infestation and a lack of early intervention.

If farmers were shortsighted about the soil, they would have difficulty sustaining their crops each season. The same holds true for educators and support personnel who are helping to raise strong children who can withstand the forces of nature. Raising resilient children who are healthy physically and psychologically also requires specific attention to the soil from which they develop: the school community.

When children are not in good health, such as the rise in anxiety, we create more harm by implementing solutions driven by symptom relief rather than underlying causes. It's often easier to find causes of physical health problems, such as doubling of childhood obesity since the late 1980s with changes in our diet. Growing our annual sugar consumption from 5 lb. to 170 lb. per year or increasing oils, fats, and meats in similar proportion is an easy correlation that we haven't been willing to change.

If technology dependency was undoubtedly correlated with the rise in childhood anxiety, we still may not be ready to adapt. If we haven't improved our diet, a known cause for obesity, what would motivate us to make a change with technology, something we are even more reliant upon? Human beings have a remarkable capacity to compromise in the short term, aligning our beliefs and our wants.

Aligning our beliefs and wants makes life simple. A person wronged us, but our discomfort with conflict makes it easier to dismiss the issue as not worthwhile, so we don't act. When our beliefs and wants don't match, we have more difficulty justifying our actions. A student wants to join an after-school club but believes it would be a better use of time to study instead.

Discrepancies between what we believe we should do and what we want or need may cause inner turmoil, which psychologists term *incongruence*. With enough incongruence occurring over time without a way to reconcile this conflict, we create stress. When our protective mechanisms are activated from the perceived threat, stress becomes amplified. We may try to solve this in a few ways. One method is by creating a "should" that justifies our want or need. "If I apologize to this man who wronged me, he might believe he can get one over on me again." We create justification with another should that aligns with what we want. In doing so, we alter our cognitions to suit our desire and then sometimes compromise our principles, beliefs, or health in the process. Young people with lesser developed sense of selves are more susceptible, also lacking the skill for anticipating the consequences of their actions.

Another way we reconcile our shoulds and wants is to accepts others' shoulds for validation. "I know it's going to hurt her feelings, but my best friend doesn't think I should go to the party, so I'm going to stay home." External reinforcement so we don't have to change our own belief system is common, especially with children who commonly defer to others, prioritizing a sense of belonging and affiliation.

Imagine sitting at a light waiting for the person ahead of you to turn, unaware the light had changed. When that person finally realizes it's clear to move, the light turns red and you have to wait. Then you hear the horn honking of the car behind you, expecting you to go through the light. Do you feel pressured to go, justified that you could have made it had the person ahead of you been alert?

This is the type of question that comes up during a school day; only the dilemma is fortified because it's the expectations of your colleagues, students, administrators, and even policies. When the organizational imperative doesn't match your want or need, what impact does this have on you? What choice do you make?

Reconciling our should and want is a more advanced version of balancing brain and body, navigating between the interplay of these two forces with our well-being at stake. The more closely aligned the values of the organization and individual with a process for negotiating these differences will increase the collective health of the school.

Organizational health is comprised, in large part, by the collective wellness of the community—both within and off campus. With our move toward virtual instruction, the definition of *campus* may be expanding, which invariably will also impact our idea of school culture.

When schools make decisions, reflecting the needs of the institution, but not the wants and needs of the faculty, friction may grow. Unresolved friction will compound to turmoil, fragmentation, and eventually polarization within the school. Subgrouping is common in schools because of the natural division between departments and grade levels, creating a fertile ground for weeds to grow. Weeds in a school suck the nutrients from the soil, taking over the root system. Weeds make the garden look ugly, draining community pride. Over time, faculty look for other more gratifying places to work or simply stay put with diminishing engagement. Weeds instigate the quick fix solution of chemical pesticides, which further deplete the soil and add another toxic element.

Teacher's Cafeteria Syndrome

There they are, all sitting in their clusters, complaining about administrators, parents, children, and even one another, although only if the person is out of earshot. If this were a group of thirteen- and fourteen-year-olds, we would call them cliques, but because they are adults, we don't give it a second thought. They are adults after all, and if they want to spend their time with people from their department or those they feel closest to, then why shouldn't they.

In school with poor cohesion, fragmentation, or ruthless competition, survival mode might be cited as the reason for subgrouping. The tendency, however, to affiliate with those most similar is common for educators. People gravitate toward safety, and those who share similar ideology, values, or approach provide respite for weary adults. If an educator's day is spent wrangling distractible and unmotivated students, perhaps associating with those who seem the easiest makes sense. While healthy conflict promotes depth and intimacy, it also takes work. If an educator expends more energy than generating, the likelihood of conserving effort outweighs the benefit, especially when return on investment seems low.

While teachers have a right to spend time with those they feel closest to opting for peace over depth, if this mindset becomes pervasive throughout branches of the school, the ripple effect influences the climate. Instead of exploring differences and valuing curiosity, we become stifled. The virus of protectionism spreads throughout the organization, fragmenting faculties. When students sense this climate, subgrouping may lead to more Darwinian attitudes. Survivalism creates student stratification, which leaders may respond to punitively with more rules, thereby intensifying the cycle.

Subgrouping brings out the best and worst in people, depending upon the intent of the members. When teachers group themselves in clusters that support each other complaining without action, not being direct around conflicts, spreading gossip or seek to gain power, they run the risk of undermining the very fabric of the institution, which students emulate. When children are not happy, they may disregard rules, undermine authority figures, or disrupt peers, which degrades the fabric of that community. For a classroom, this type of upheaval can jeopardize learning and diminish the health of that organization.

Organizational Health

Organizational health is the invisible energy that helps students and faculty feel safe, excited about learning, and engaged with their community. Health is the organization's ability to adapt to changes or threats, prevent problems, and intervene effectively through a shared vision guided by the mission and vision of the school.

Organizational health is supported through prevention such as school-based wellness and psychosocial emotional learning (PSEL). This proactive offering helps faculty and students feel valued, building the climate so long as these programs are well constructed. Skill building and singular offerings like an annual wellness fair demonstrate low commitment while year-round resources with depth and widespread buy-in are more likely to be valued by the community.

Individuals as well require daily prevention and not simply the occasional visit to the gym. With individual health, we require physical and psychological building blocks with regular maintenance to see if adjustments are needed. Doing the same exercises each visit produces diminishing returns, so variety is needed for maximum gain.

When our immune system falters, instead of rushing to eradicate the symptoms, we might try to understand how the disease originated. Symptoms, or messages from the body, tell us a great deal about where our fortification is needed. Most of the time, we can identify stress, sleep, diet, and activity as an area needing improvement.

If school leaders were immune to the influence of public perception, the organization could openly reflect on their own learning. Transparency could be held in high regard—eagerly soliciting input to reduce our blind spots—if self-protection was low. Faculty could discuss operations, policies, relationships, or decisions openly in shared owner-ship of improvement.

Organizational leaders may not explore culture because that inquiry could be scrutinized or create uncertainty around next steps in the same way a person may not investigate physical symptoms. This guarded approach to leadership is born of fear, and with playing defense, we remain in survival mode. Protection, which doesn't stimulate authentic-ity or cohesion among the faculty, will increase our blind spots, obscur-ing the full picture required for promoting growth.

Fear of exposure or further degradation should be taken more seri-ously in the midst of or following an acute or chronic trauma, such as the recovery from the pandemic. Predicting a healthy amount of time to remain in survival mode is easier once the aversive stimulus has been removed, which isn't the case when residual but realistic threats linger. Varying degrees of caution are related to personality and leadership styles, the pressure we face, and the ability to create and maintain safeguards.

When a person cycles back down to their basic need of safety/security, less time and energy will be spent on restoring coffers through attainment of higher-order needs. If well prepared with prevention (wellness and PSEL), or unless a person's trauma is ongoing or extreme, the memory of how to regenerate safety/security from within will allow a quicker shift toward the pursuit of higher-order needs.

Organizations, similar to people, can get stuck in survival mode. They may not realize they are in this mode because they (the leader-ship team) aren't scanning (or for an individual self-reflecting), become imbalanced between their personal brain and body, hyperfocusing on shoulds over wants or needs. The fear of making a critical error in judg-ment to worsen a situation can extend the time organizations remain conservative. The emphasis on basic needs for an organization in crisis is important so long as we don't remain in that mode when the threat no longer exists or the strategies are antiquated. Doing so may result in fragmentation of the system, interfering with their recalibrating toward greater whole school health.

Some school leaders may be in survival mode in their personal lives, obscuring their awareness for the organization's status. Once in survival mode, it can be difficult to work toward thriving, especially with large and complex systems lacking the support from their community or feel-ing political or community pressure.

Classroom teachers may find a similar set of dynamics in their smaller systems, as is the case with trauma. Both chronic and acute trauma impacting one child can infiltrate the entire classroom, erod-ing healthy protective factors that may not have fully taken root. And with two-thirds of all students experiencing some trauma by age sixteen, this is a more prevalent issue than we might imagine (National Child Traumatic Stress Initiative, 2020).

The following graphic (Figure 4.1) illustrates some of the hallmark indicators for organizations in surviving versus thriving mode:

Figure 4.1   Organization Portion of Flowchart Only

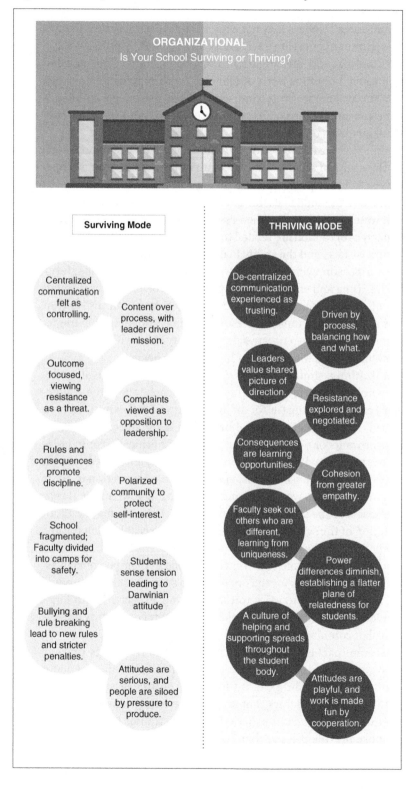

Key Points

▶ Organizations have needs the same way that humans have needs. There is a hierarchy that grows from basic to more advanced.

▶ Organizational health is the integration of three dimensions of culture: adaptation, climate, and infrastructure.

▶ School culture is not positive or negative; it is a complex set of dynamics that are influenced by and a result of organizational health.

▶ Surviving versus thriving is a key measure of organizational health.

PART II
PSYCHOSOCIAL EMOTIONAL LEARNING

Introduction to Psychosocial Emotional Learning

CHAPTER 5

Between 2010 and 2020, the number of new cancer cases in the United States is expected to grow 24 percent in men to more than one million cases per year and by about 21 percent in women to more than nine hundred thousand cases per year (American Cancer Society, 2020). In a country with the most advanced medical system in the world, this trend is unthinkable—even more so when we understand the causes.

There are over eighty-four thousand known toxins in our environment—some of which are consumed directly through our food supply. We eat genetically modified foods, some indirectly through animals feeding on pesticide-infused GMO corn and soy. This livestock is administered hormones to grow larger and injected with antibiotics to prevent infection. These injected medicines increase the resistance of bacteria leading to less curable illness (EcoWatch, 2015).

We eat less fermented foods due to refrigeration, lessening helpful intestinal bacteria and weakening our immunity. We eat fewer fruits and vegetables in favor of processed foods. The limited produce we do consume has diminished vitamins and minerals, grown from nutrient depleted soil. The overabundance of animal protein in our diet and reliance on cow's milk means casein exposure, which has been linked to cancer (Campbell, 2014).

Cancer is facilitated and even caused by our lifestyle. We invite this uncontrolled cell mutation by introducing harmful toxins into the environment, succumbing to marketing, and ignoring proven research, all in favor of convenience. We aren't completely ignorant to the facts, but we become more invested in solutions that allow us to maintain our creature comforts. Convenience and luxury are often more attractive than the risks—something large corporations count on for large profit.

The amount of money and time for cancer research and treatment is expected to exceed $100 billion in 2022, which far exceeds the money put into advocating lifestyle changes. With more teens dying from suicide than from cancer, heart disease, AIDS, birth defects, stroke, pneumonia, influenza, and chronic lung disease combined, we might question how long we will tolerate this spread (Centers for Disease Control and Prevention, 2015).

The importance of this health crisis should alarm us on multiple levels, beginning with our lack of prevention. With most issues, we wait until the crisis reaches epic proportions before we decide to throw resources at it, and when we do, the response is often poorly conceived. This certainly seemed to be the case with the COVID-19 spread, which scientists had been predicting years prior, or our ongoing ambivalence toward global warming and with it certainly the irreversible destruction of the world's oceans.

We maintain a reactive posture of quick fixes in education as well—exhausted administrators and frontline educators may agree that something needs to be fixed but lack time and energy to prioritize. Compassion fatigue is a serious problem, with well-intended educators unable to maintain much less add to what's expected of them. While burnout is now recognized by the World Health Organization as an actual pathology, few districts are prioritizing prevention.

Headline-grabbing issues, such as school violence, receive more attention; however, our prevention efforts don't reflect the complex etiology, implementing solutions that in many instances can exacerbate the problems. Effective prevention requires a comprehensive paradigm developed through a collaborative effort of the entire school community. To develop processes that reduce threats, we need to unburden schools, freeing teams to invest in whole school health. This begins with psychological, social, moral, and emotional learning, helping each member of the community explore their own personal growth.

To prevent intra- and interpersonal problems that endanger the welfare of students and faculty, we need a new paradigm—one that considers all aspects of the system. We need an approach that doesn't burden educators but supports the adults who have the responsibility to implement this paradigm, benefiting them beyond the obvious link to student success.

Psychosocial Emotional Learning and Needs

Psychosocial emotional learning (PSEL) is the method by which we navigate life, allowing vulnerability through risk-taking in the service of meeting our needs. The more accomplished we are in getting our needs met and tolerating when they aren't, the better we enjoy life.

People optimize success when we consistently meet our wants and needs—as long as we set the bar high enough and respond in a timely manner. Learned through emulating caregivers, children apply scripts and strategies, supplemented by experimentation and supported by other influential adults, such as teachers. The better the role models and more embodied the teachers are in their own personal growth, the more likely children will evolve their scripts and strategies, becoming more proficient in meeting their needs.

Needs are the driving forces that good health rewards and requires. A driving force is analogous to the engine of a car, powering the vehicle with gasoline as fuel. Humans are powered by their needs, using fuel in the form of energy. Needs are innately generated for each human being, although the degree of intensity results from how we live. If we experience consistent physical security and emotional safety, we will likely look for less of this need to be met externally. As we can internalize the need by having it satisfied early in our lives, we learn to generate it from within.

Satisfying these basic needs allows us to look higher up the diamond to more complex needs. We will revisit foundational needs depending upon how much chronic and acute stress we are subject to, becoming more proficient with experience. Efficiency in identifying, expressing, and negotiating our needs through supportive networks is critical for ongoing development.

As basic needs require replenishing, we cycle through the foundational PSELs, determining which strategy best fits the situation, over time becoming more sophisticated in how we operate. If, for instance, we have a need for increased belonging, identified through the sensation of emptiness and feeling of loneliness, we can reflexively implement the PSEL to meet this need. If we self-reflect and identify what frailty may be interfering with developing closeness, we can take immediate action to self-correct.

If we can't identify the unmet need; employ the wrong PSEL; or, worse, invoke self-protection to stave off the discomfort of having an unmet need, we stagnate our growth. Our goal is to reduce our protective mechanisms or at least grow more nuanced protections that interfere less with the satisfaction of our needs in order to be efficient in our need-meeting process.

If, for instance, we became withdrawn under duress as a child, perhaps a result of perceived rejection, we may need to learn how to stay present longer as an adult. Perhaps we grow another PSEL, tolerating distress, to help us verbalize our hurts quicker or even lessen our need for approval. Our PSEL improves our chances of getting needs met because we can self-reflect, gain a solid sense of self, and be open to intimacy.

We may not recognize the correlation between needs and stress because we don't listen to or understand our body's messages. When needs aren't met or are in danger of being diminished, we experience tension, a predecessor to stress. If we feel unsafe, alone, uncared for, bored, or any other number of feelings stemming from unmet needs, our alert system activates. If we don't rush to treat symptoms, we can act on the alarm before it intensifies.

Educators have varying degrees of experience with social emotional learning (SEL), but most seem to value the general premise. Research results revealed nearly 90 percent agreed with the following statement: "Social emotional learning for students is important to support learning and reduce teacher stress" (Scherz, 2019). Further research on including adult SEL is needed so educators can appreciate the inclusion of their own basic needs.

Basic needs, as first popularized by Maslow with new additions, represent a more contemporary human engine. This combined constellation of needs can be grouped into three categories: the self in relation to the self, the self in relation to others, and the self in relation to the world. The self in relation to the self includes safety/security, power/control, freedom/independence, fun/excitement, and joy/happiness. The self in relation to others includes love/intimacy, approval/acceptance, and affiliation/belonging. The self in relation to the world includes purpose/meaning, peace/harmony, and value/importance.

These needs are best imagined through a diamond, which demonstrates how the internalization of safety and security at the bottom will become less important over time, with greater reservations and less dependence upon our environment (see Figure 5.1).

For those young people who don't consistently get their needs met, lacking role models and strong environmental supports, the importance of PSEL from educators is critical. In school they can learn how to constructively meet their needs, improving academics and developing morality to address social injustice.

As we successfully meet our needs, we move closer to the ultimate goal of fulfillment. Feeling good about ourselves, our relationships, and our standing in society all provide this lofty but moving goalpost to inspire and motivate all of us to be better human beings.

If educator perception for existing psychosocial emotional skills is an indication of how well students are being prepared to meet their needs, we have considerable work to do. In the three-state research sample, 350 respondents found a minimum threshold (50 percent or higher) of deterioration over the past ten years in these important attributes (Scherz, 2019): independence: 62.96 percent; attention: 60.40 percent; social skills: 60 percent; impulse control: 51.57 percent; stress tolerance: 49.29 percent; maturity: 48.15 percent; and empathy: 39.89 percent. While this sample size is too small to be statistically significant or even able to be extrapolated across the entire country, it provides cause for further consideration.

If we agree that the importance of PSEL for both students and adults is of value for individual wellness and organizational health, we move into deeper consideration of how this will be accomplished. The following chapters explore the specific PSEL and the method by which it's taught and learned for people of all ages.

PSEL is divided into two parts: the specific psychological, social, or emotional competency and the method or process by which the learning takes place. Through education narratives, we explore how these fifteen PSELs are part of our personal and professional journeys.

Figure 5.1

Understanding Needs

The Key to Improving Student Engagement

UNMET NEEDS

Self in Relation to	Basic Need	Early Signs	Enduring Trait
Self	Safety/Security	Paranoid, suspicious	Victim
	Power/Control	Pleading, lacking initiative	Complacent
	Freedom/Independence	Edgy, sneaky	Conservative
	Fun/Excitement	Isolation, withdrawal	Bland
	Joy/Happiness	Melancholy, enervating	Dysphoric
Others	Love/Intimacy	Attention-seeking	Superfical
	Approval/Acceptance	Needy, obsequious	Dependent
	Affiliation/Belonging	Clingy, self-doubting	Detached
World	Purpose/Meaning	Topical, dispassionate	Despair
	Peace/Harmony	Uneasy, edgy	Anxious
	Value/Importance	Hesitant, subservient	Follower

Rethinking Maslow's Hierarchy

The ideal evolution of needs requires a nurturing environment allowing for the internalizing of safety/security

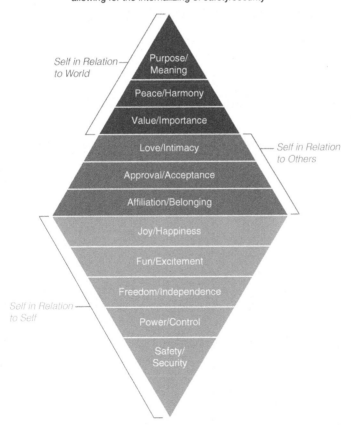

Key Points

- ▶ PSEL is the method by which we navigate life, allowing vulnerability through risk-taking in the service of meeting our needs.

- ▶ We may not recognize our needs because we are skewed toward our brain, away from our bodies.

- ▶ Basic needs are best represented through a diamond where we can learn to internalize our needs and be less dependent upon our environment.

- ▶ Educators perceive a sharp decline in key PSELs potentially disrupting how well young people get their needs met, making them susceptible to mental health problems.

Balancing Brain and Body

(Linda Y. is a former chemistry teacher and current human resources administrator in California.)

Pleasing people has always been a priority for me. The quickest way for me to do this was to follow the rules to which most people subscribed. Interestingly, if these rules conflicted with what that little voice in the back of my mind wanted, I just turned that volume down lower so I could ignore it. School has been my best haven because not only were you told the rules for each aspect but they were helpfully posted and published everywhere. There is no question of knowing how and what to teach in addition to how you should respond to others within that environment. One of the reasons I chose teaching was the control, because it was clear how all aspects of this job should be. I look back and laugh at this, because it wasn't until I began my journey to educate others that I learned sharing that control (or the illusion of control) makes your students your partners, which leads to greater fulfillment professionally and develops students who are better prepared to live their best lives.

The brain is responsible for self-protection, and the body is responsible for our needs. Through this lifetime push and pull, every aspect of our personhood influences this balancing act, shaping our emerging and unique identity. When brain and body are better balanced, working in concert, we feel harmonious with greater ease in decision-making. When imbalanced, we tend to become overly cautious or self-consumed.

We have all met people described as "heady" or "free spirits," which can be satisfying for the person even if they are not fully balanced. A skew in one direction doesn't doom us to a life of unhappiness; rather, it's about finding an intentional balance with known limitations we are accepting or working to improve.

We can live comfortably with our skew in one direction, right up until the point we have to relate with others. The more valuable the relationship, the more important these skews become in our ability to create depth and intimacy. As we will explore later, negotiating to get our needs met and engaging in constructive differencing requires an appreciation of our balance (or lack thereof) as we bump up against the imbalance of others.

Two STEM teachers may get along famously, as they stereotypically use logic and reason to navigate their overlapping work worlds. But when that STEM teacher meets a creative writing teacher—perhaps planning a school event—they may approach decision-making differently. With one using reason and other intuition, they may be challenged to negotiate differences if they are to work closely together. How will each of these teachers be influenced by the other, and how much do others shape our style if not our entire method for achieving homeostasis?

I started my job by listening to the (really) veteran teachers who knew how to teach. As a result, I had lesson plans for the entire year before the year started, eight sets of seating charts (rows, of course), three rules posters strategically placed where students in any row could view them, realia showing the steps for solving any type of problem, four copies of each test or quiz, and a sincere desire to have students come to love chemistry like I did. What I didn't have was any clue how to support and develop the emotional well-being of the 150+ different individuals I was to meet my first year. Nothing covered this in my teacher preparations, and if the veterans in my department knew, they weren't sharing. Obviously the social emotional well-being of my students couldn't matter nearly as much as the content associated with learning chemistry. I knew I must be an effective teacher that year because most of my students passed with reasonably good grades. Since I taught chemistry and everybody loves fires with explosions, I kidded myself into believing that by teaching the content students somehow translated this into becoming a better-developed person. Even though I covered the curriculum successfully—I had the evaluations to say so, after all—I didn't feel connected to my vocation or my students. I was bored with the mechanics of doing the job. I went on for a bit longer before the voice in my head couldn't be ignored. My head, heart, and body were all telling me that I was not doing the right thing with my life.

Sizable imbalances between brain and body make it difficult to engage fully with others, especially when we lean toward reason and out-comes. Those who emphasize brain over body will generally lean toward content versus process. Thinking orientations are likely to be content driven, using data to produce certain outcomes with less consideration for how people experience the task. Body-oriented individuals are going to use their experience, allowing for greater appreciation of how some-thing is being done and not just what they are achieving. Through pro-cess, we appreciate how we are enjoying reaching our destination while content generally helps with efficiency.

Is the drive to the new home we are considering purchasing scenic, or is it the quickest? Are we trying to grade the exams so we can get home, or do we bring the work home and do it leisurely alongside other activities? The way in which we go about tasks is directly related to our brain-body balance, which is also the case with the children we teach.

Appreciating the differences between our own lean and that of our students can be helpful. Efficiency may be your mode of operations, but what if your student is a meanderer, needing to socialize and entertain themselves to stay invested? From computational process to writing style, the children we teach are going to lie near us on the brain-body continuum or be some distance from our comfort zone. Appreciating those differences and how it influences our enjoyment and their engagement can be transformative in the personal growth of an educator.

I was getting ready to quit, to go work in a lab, when I met the student who was to change my perspective about teaching. M was truly gifted and one of my top students planning great things for her future, including the study of chemistry in college—until she stopped by my room one day after school to talk. In tears, she shared that her whole world had collapsed because instead of college she was going to be a mother. M looked me straight in the eye as she asked me for help—not with chemistry but with her next steps in life. I opened my mouth to say I didn't know but was glad that it was not about how she could finish my class at home. Of course, I wanted to do my best for her and give the right answer, so I discussed this with colleagues because they knew what should be done in situations like this. The answer I got was that I should not get involved with students in these kinds of situations and to let her family take care of it. I suppose if I had been happy just teaching chemistry I could have done that. But M really was asking for help meeting needs that had nothing to do with subject matter.

From the very beginning of our journey to recognize, express, and negotiate to get our needs met, the brain-body balance will help create a foundation for our success. If we are skewed too far toward our brain, reason drives us; if we are too far toward our body, emotion may guide us. The general principle of managing our shoulds with our wants or needs is a hidden formula most people never attend to, unaware of the hundreds of choice points influenced each day.

Our shoulds, have tos, oughts, or musts are a function of our brain's effort to steer us toward safety. Safety may be a function of our *superego*, which is a term in psychology to describe our internalized parental voice—the one that says don't do that or be careful. Collectively this is referred to as our should, representing what has to get done. For an educator, this may be supervising cafeteria duty or doing anything that distracts from academics.

We will examine the external application of shoulds and how the internalization of these messages is how we form our moral development, very closely tied to a future psychosocial emotional learning (PSEL) of ownership and accountability. For now, consider how shoulds are either internal or external, involving our own expectations or somebody else's rule, having little to do with our needs.

Wants are a mixture of brain and body (and also shoulds and needs), influenced by imagination, fantasy, and preferences. An example is wanting to join a club at school because we believe it will help with our social standing—wishing for a better chance at college entry—but also feeling instinctively drawn to the activity of the club. The most powerful want we appreciate more toward adulthood is determining the type of person we wish to be.

I chose to be different. If I was going to continue teaching, I had to connect with students in a meaningful way that went beyond content and meet them where they were as a whole person. Asking M what she needed and really focusing on hearing her responses began my journey to being that kind of teacher. It was a tough journey, though, because if I was going to support students in this way, I was going to have to change my life as well. Nothing fails the "sniff test" with teens quicker than a fraud.

Authenticity is not so much a need but a method by which we get many of our needs met. Our needs represent the engine that powers our human vehicle. Needs have traditionally been described in a hierarchy, with physical needs at the base and fulfillment at the point of the triangle. As we will explore through a future PSEL, the traditional triangle-shaped needs hierarchy may be antiquated. A diamond shape conveys the importance of internalizing needs as opposed to continuous dependency on our environment. Safety and security for instance don't become less important, they are simply manufactured from within, allowing us to move onto higher order needs.

I started listening to my long-ignored inner voice and began my efforts to connect with the person and not just the student. This started with deliberate efforts to learn who each student was and to really see him or her. I took the risk to be truly empathetic with students and care about them as individuals. It is scary because if you truly care about someone you make yourself vulnerable to being hurt. (I am sure it is no surprise to anyone that a hurting teen can be awful to the very ones who support them the most because they trust those people know this is an attempt to get help in a safe environment.) It was during this time that I began to allow myself the grace to make mistakes and view them not as a failure to meet someone else's expectations but as my opportunity for personal growth.

Most people in Western society become skewed toward their brain and away from their bodies, pursuing perfection as opposed to peace. We become so accustomed to listening to thoughts, which take over the mantle of decision-making, that we forget our bodies determine what makes us happy. By putting too much emphasis on our brain, we contribute to stress and burnout. A continuous flood of information to synthesize helps adults and children believe that thinking is the most important part of being a human.

In a small study of New Jersey teachers, the value placed on analyzing, computing, optimizing, innovating, and thinking all rated higher than feeling, sensing, experiencing, balancing, and engaging. All tasks related to cognition were higher than the highest of the tasks related to the body, reinforcing the commonly held belief of what we emphasize in school (see Figure 6.1).

Figure 6.1

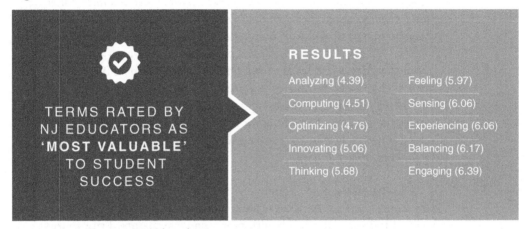

NOTE: Lower numbers represent higher value.

Schools are naturally skewed toward cognitive development, so it's less surprising that thinking rated higher than feeling. The extent to which we prioritize the soft skills is where we might further explore. If schools may fail to realize how psychological readiness may dilute a child's ability to perform brain activities, we may be less efficient and productive in teaching. The results may also mean that introducing wellness and social emotional learning (SEL) may evoke resistance from some who are fearful of diluting education. With the world-changing event of COVID-19, this may be less of a concern as we raise our collective awareness for the value of whole child education. With the stress and fear for the adults who have lived through a life-changing crisis, we may also see greater receptivity to whole school health.

My teaching philosophy was changing. I had been taught how to deliver the curriculum in such a manner that learning content was a destination and assessment was a referendum on student success. A student either made the grade or did not. Effort and growth did not factor into this nor did I use this as data to inform instruction the way I could have. As I got to know my students, this approach no longer made sense. I think about C and his inability to complete a homework assignment while managing to set the curve on every single exam. Don't misunderstand. C is brilliant, but that wasn't quite enough to produce these results. I asked him about it. His simple answer was to question me about why he should write it down again on paper to hand in when he worked the few problems he needed in his notes (he did keep a notebook) and then spent his time helping others. Before decreeing that he had to do homework because it was a percentage of his grade, I watched his interactions a little more closely for several weeks. Left on his own, C was not social and kept to himself. As others figured out how smart he was, they sought him out. While C was help- ing them with assignments, I saw him learning the communication skills he needed to grow as a person. For him, my letting go of how I thought a classroom should run had created an environment in which content mastery was increasing and a student who desperately needed to learn interpersonal skills had the confidence and safe environment to do so. No amount of writing out problems on a piece of paper was going to address his needs as effectively. His peer coaching became his homework grade. One of my greatest rewards as an educator is having the flexibility to extend learning beyond content. As a teacher, my journey involved challenging myself to help students find ways such as this to work on their needs that may or may not have anything to do with subject matter.

Through the global pandemic with people trapped in their homes, stretching us to the very limit of solitude, we may be valuing psycholog- ical fortitude and physical health more than ever before. Prior to this extended sensory deprivation experience, a sizable portion of educators recognized how their own health translated to improved productivity at work while a small group were still not convinced.

Nine out of ten educators surveyed agreed that "more diverse/ timely wellness should be offered by my district" (Scherz, 2019).

While a small percentage (6 percent) strongly disagreed, perhaps wanting greater separation between home and work, the vast majority of educators are in need of more support from their district.

Thus, brain-body balance, the very first PSEL, will influence our receptivity to whole school health. If we continue to emphasize out- comes with a greater need for tests and measurement, we may attract more educators who are skewed toward their brain. If we believe in expanding the role of the school to prepare children for life beyond pro- fessional success, we will embrace the integration of academic, psycho- logical, and moral learning in our schools.

C taught me that grades were not good enough to be finite labels for student performance. Instead data became my reflection of my own teaching. Blame and failure did not have a part in this. This is not to say that my students were not held to high standards. When the majority of students tanked on a test or missed a problem, for example, my thoughts changed from "Boy they blew that, time to move on or I won't be able to cover everything" to "How do I change what I do in my classroom to make this make sense?" Students were responsible during class discussions and tutoring sessions for identifying the missing pieces they needed to make sense of the concept. It was fascinating to watch their growth in efficacy as they determined what they knew and how to build on that to master concepts. In this way, I hoped I modeled true problem-solving and perseverance as life skills that went beyond chemistry.

Educators who are excited about whole child education will work to embody the very principles of PSEL as opposed to teaching them through a curriculum of skill building. PSEL as a way to grow our personhood may be a scary proposition for those districts struggling to implement expectations and exceed standards; however, brain-based learning may not be enough to traverse the complex challenges of recovering from this new and ongoing challenge.

If you really need it... The rule-following people pleaser in me had to have some structure just in case my principal or a parent questioned me. My guilty pleasure was assigning C some advanced problems tangentially related to the topic in class to provide him with a challenge. (I might have forgotten to tell him this.) In addition to this, C agreed that for any unit assessment he did not score at least 95 percent or higher he would go back to complete every assignment and retest (which never happened). Of course, other students squawked about C getting a special "deal," and I happily extended each their own opportunity as well. Most opted for the traditional structured experience after a few days. Teaching, for me, had become figuring out what the person who was my student needed to learn to move to their next step just as much as teaching content.

Perhaps the least traditional educational system when it comes to structure are the private Montessori schools. Their philosophy attended to the delicate balance to brain-body operations, helping students learn how to listen to other parts of themselves to become a more integrated organism. Autonomy and creativity were also espoused, generating more self-reflective students who are prepared to navigate the complexities of relationships.

Montessori appreciates the idea that children who learn how to listen and interpret messages from their bodies will more easily understand how to regulate emotions and inhibit impulses and also that children thrive in self-directed learning, taking pressure off the teacher to properly advise in every academic and emotional situation. Creating processes to guide students through conflict and problem-solving help create communities of shared responsibility.

Getting to know students and supporting their social emotional growth to the extent I did with both C and M is not sustainable with every student. While I knew this would be how I was going to approach teaching for the remainder of my career, connecting with students at this level can be as exhausting as it is rewarding. After nearly fifteen years, I needed a bit of a change that I hoped would impact more than the 150 plus students I worked with each year. Hopping out of my comfort zone, I involved myself with the teachers' union by becoming the president of one of the largest in my state. I wanted the opportunity to advocate for students at a different level and thought this would offer me that chance. Hindsight being what it is, I'm not sure I made it better for students as I hoped, but I did see many instances firsthand in which the failure to prioritize students' emotional well-being negatively impacted their success.

Our decision-making process through adulthood will be influenced by the early work of balancing brain and body, though we may never recognize these early influences. Nor do we appreciate how the PSELs, which are ordered sequentially, generally correspond to our developmental stages. The work of PSEL continues throughout our lifetime, revisited with each developmental stage, shaped by the conditions of our society. So while balancing brain and body is most notably an early-stage concentration, it will remain an important skill through middle school, high school, and college. Even as adults we will be working to find balance, especially when we are faced with new problems we have no history of overcoming.

As a union president, I spent my days problem-solving, which excited me, but it was working on the problems of adults engaged in the institution and not really about the students. On some levels, I knew bettering the conditions for teaching improved the conditions for learning, but I was no longer in a position to engage with students on the personal level necessary to effect change. Interestingly enough, I used my same philosophy with the adults I was supporting that I used with students. I cannot stress enough that patience and kindness while truly learning who the person is and what he or she needs is never the wrong approach. You can make no bigger misstep than by assuming the same circumstances with two different people will have the same outcomes. This, too, was a great job to learn the lesson that if all you do for someone wanting your help is to give them your answer instead of investing your time to help them to find their answer, you will forever be answering the same questions for the same person. These were interesting years—not to mention power can be kind of cool.

As the complexity of our problem-solving increases, the value of pulling from both our intellect and intuition grows. When working with large groups or systems as most educators do, we need to be aware of the processes that help and hinder personal growth. Tremendous responsibility lies with those who are leading others, and the ability to see oneself clearly in relation to that group will help determine our success. If we can appreciate our own sphere of influence and how we wield it to make decisions, we will have an easier time using another PSEL of self-reflection to improve our leadership.

At this point in time, chemistry teachers were becoming scarce and I was leaving a position in which I had quite a bit of "power," so I returned knowing that I was going to teach on my students' terms. This meant I committed to learning about and from students to figure out what to teach them. It was upon my return to the classroom that I realized a sense of urgency for the importance of our work as educators. Think about it: Each of us in our classrooms may be the one opportunity a student sees to change their lives or make different choices. My goal as an educator was to develop the whole student by using chemistry as my means to do so. For example, many of my students claimed to dislike or struggle with math word problems. My answer became to teach my students math disguised with chemistry problems. I even talked several math teachers with whom I shared students into using chemistry problems as examples with their classes. Many of my students were not native English speakers, so every day I had opportunities built in class to practice speaking in a safe environment. As confidence grew with the class, students opened up about their dreams and hopes for their futures as well as what they needed to reach them. I watched efficacy bloom both academically and socially.

Classroom, school, and district leaders who are well balanced in their own use of brain and body will be more confident, even more likely to create welcoming environments to a wide range of diverse learners requiring a safe space to move between reasoning and emotion.

I would like to say after learning about how to educate people from diverse perspectives for the past thirty years that I have all of life figured out. Ha! What I've actually learned is that as an educator if you accept people where they are (students or adults) and use education as a vehicle to support them along their journey, you can't go wrong. You can only do this with people and not for them. While pleasing people still remains a priority for me to this day, my journey has taught me to make the conscious decision not to exclude myself from those I seek to please.

Key Points

- ▶ The brain is responsible for self-protection, and the body is responsible for our needs.

- ▶ Emphasizing the brain (thinking) generally correlates with content while the body correlates with process.

- ▶ Appreciating our own lean toward brain-body helps improve student success.

- Our shoulds, have tos, oughts, or musts are a function of our brain's effort to steer us toward safety.

- Wants are a mixture of brain and body, influenced by imagination, fantasy, and preferences.

- Our needs represent the engine that powers our human vehicle.

- Technology is a new threat to brain-body balance in children, requiring educators to provide opportunities for daily calibration.

- Modeling is the most important tool for teaching brain-body balance.

Discussion Questions

Whether using the book for professional development (PD) or within a book group, please consider the following questions to stimulate your own ideas for exploration.

1. How do I recognize how imbalanced I may be?

2. How do I become imbalanced? Am I more like one parent in this regard?

3. What are the benefits and limitations of my imbalance?

4. Am I typically attracted to a romantic partner imbalanced toward one polarity?

5. Which students most or least appreciate my imbalance, and why?

Connecting Sensations With Feelings, Wants, and Needs

CHAPTER

7

(Jessica F. is a biology teacher in Pennsylvania.)

I have been teaching for seven years, and my career has been shaped by the two different schools in which I have worked. I began teaching in an inner-city school with angsty middle school students. As a naive, wide-eyed young teacher, I was responsible for teaching science to seventh- and eighth-grade students. If your first year of teaching isn't hard enough to figure out how to deliver new curriculum for the first time, I also had to manage all of the hormones and drama of middle school! In order to feel prepared for the next day, I would be up until at least midnight— usually closer to 2:00 a.m.—in order to get all of my materials prepped and feel ready to teach my lesson. When teaching middle school students, I quickly learned that if you're not prepared, the students would eat you alive! Now don't get me wrong—I loved my kids! I became so close with many of them that it broke my heart to see them leave middle school and transition to high school.

The physical toll of being a teacher isn't fully realized until somewhere through the first year of school. Even then, the depletion of managing young people, imbuing them with a daily dose of enthusiasm for learning, is only partially compensated with the intermittent elation of breaking through. More often than not, a teacher summons up any spare energy to tend to his or her family—only slightly mollifying the guilt of not having more to give. But you do it because educating students is the most important and sometimes rewarding job in the world.

Particularly in an inner city school, the bond you form with your kids is unique and special. They share their lives with you—and often tell you more than you ever want to know—but that also takes a toll. Now I was working myself into the ground and physically exhausted due to lack of sleep, but I was also mentally and emotionally exhausted from compassion and empathy fatigue. I was lucky to be surrounded with incredibly supportive colleagues who would allow me to vent.

The brain is responsible for protecting, planning, and deliberating while the body is responsible for our basic and higher-order needs. Teachers are often skewed toward their brains, spending their days thinking and anticipating how to keep their students safe and productive. With this skew, we risk not getting our needs as easily met. If we are less aware of our bodies, we may not listen to or accurately interpret the sensations or messages our bodies send to us, intended to clue us in to which needs are low, requiring replenishing.

If, for instance, a person notices an emptiness in her stomach but does not shift her focus toward her belly to fully appreciate this somatic message, there is risk. She may act on the sensation as though it were hunger, only partially aware of what is driving this experience of emptiness. If the message from her body is loneliness, which can feel similar to the void created by hunger, the wrong action may be taken. With chronic misinterpretation, a person could become susceptible to an eating disorder. With other conditions, such as new pressures and isolation, the risk factors multiply, distracting even further from deeper needs.

Thinking about colleagues . . . I certainly wouldn't have survived without my grade-level team! When you graduate from undergrad and take your first job, you're prepared for your job. You're not necessarily prepared for all the other curveballs life throws at you. That held particularly true for me! This was the first time I was living alone, and I was 4½ hours away from family. I'm from Pennsylvania, and it's extremely difficult to get a job right out of school with no experience, so I, like many of my classmates, moved to get a job to build up enough experience to eventually "move home." I had to buy a reliable, gas-efficient car and now worry about paying rent and utilities all before getting my first paycheck. (Due to the way finances were handled in my district, I didn't receive my first paycheck until OCTOBER.) After moving in August, my bank account was starting to get low. When I went for groceries, I couldn't necessarily afford fresh fruits or vegetables, and I opted for the $1.00 boxes of macaroni and cheese, microwavable meals, and anything else cheap I could find to try to stretch my dollar as far as I could. I would often take a bag of dry cereal for lunch because it was quick and cheap.

A person with poor self-care, who is not listening to their body, will find the intensity of the dis-ease growing. With our brain interpreting these indicators as warning signs, our programming directs us to see general physicians and specialists, where we undergo numerous tests to determine the cause of our "symptoms." As each test confirms idiopathic pathology, or a disease of unknown origin, our worry grows.

The simple intervention of placing a hyphen between *dis* and *ease*—*dis-ease*—may help us listen to our body where we become aware of tension—perhaps in the neck and shoulders triggering the headache. With additional work, we trace the source of this tension from our bodies to old wounds that have been reactivated by current stressors. We feel powerless again, just like we did when we were young, our parents arguing, fearing some loss. We then realize our marriage has been triggering similar feelings, compromising our wants and needs so that our partner won't leave. As we sacrifice our own wants and needs to prevent abandonment, messages are sent from the body that needs are going unmet, compounding to a dangerous level. Being treated for symptoms, enduring procedures, testing, and treatments, may cause new harm. In addition to the enormous amount of money spent in copays and by the insurance company, our worry amplifies with somber predictions. In actuality, however, we were simply missing the body's attempt to communicate with us about unmet needs for power and control.

When we fail to consider sensations—the only way our bodies can communicate with us—we miss important messages about unmet needs. As humans who don't want to feel pain or discomfort, our instinct is to remedy the problem as quickly as possible by whatever means necessary, which as we can see may compound the original problem. Without a support system, this may continue indefinitely.

My coworkers, unbeknownst to me, gathered and shared their concerns about my eating habits. They could see that I was starting to have bags under my eyes and looked pale. I was not as energetic as when they first met me. Then one day, the social studies teacher down the hall walked into my room with a bag of groceries, slyly convincing me that she simply "happened to buy extra that she couldn't use." I don't think I had ever had a turkey and cheese sandwich that tasted that good!

Without people who care for us, the lack of attention to our sensations, wants, and needs may mean increased reliance on our protective mechanisms—some of which lead to reliance on external sources, even creating addictions. Children and adults fall victim to alcohol and drug abuse through this very process, where we circumvent discomfort and other signals. Substances provide a chemical distraction from our bodies, similar to the effect of shopping, gambling, and having sex. Addictive behavior is an end run around our bodies.

Sensations include taste, smell, hearing, touch, and sight but also the kinesthetic experience in our body such as temperature, tension, and pressure. With the many technical distractions of modern society, we have even greater difficulty recognizing the deeper sensations beyond the ones we are biased toward. A bias is a preference or attention toward one sensation, such as taste, while discounting others. With this selective and diminished attention to our sensations, we miss out on the pleasure of arousal, living inside a cone of deprivation where our discomfort becomes more figural.

A few more weeks passed in my first year of teaching, and I made the drive back to Pennsylvania for Thanksgiving. When I got to my parents' house and slept in my childhood bed, I felt like I had died and gone to heaven. My parents were convinced that I wasn't waking up the next day because I slept until noon. However, instead of feeling well rested when I arose, I had a cough and my head was congested. This marked the first time my body slowed down since the school year started, and my immune system finally gave way. I was sick the entire vacation.

The same thing happened over Christmas vacation.

And spring break.

And the first week of summer vacation.

I wish I could share with you that I started to learn my lesson, but I thought to myself, "This is the expectation of your first year of teaching." After all, everyone says the first year is your hardest. Now that I had that under my belt, I figured the second year wouldn't be nearly as difficult so I could take on a new challenge: graduate school. I knew that to keep progressing in my career, I would need to get my master's degree, so I started taking online classes through Quinnipiac University in their teacher leadership program.

Extending our knowledge and proficiency helps combat stagnation, especially when learning helps create better balance. The reason why mindfulness has become so popular in schools and beyond is that it helps us slow down, shifting from our brains into our bodies. As we relax, breathe, and appreciate what is going on inside and around us, we become mindful. We move from our thoughts to our experiences, using our sensations as a guide to exploring our bodies.

From the moment we are born, we learn to use our senses, but very soon thereafter we are taught to inhibit this instinct. A young child is told not to touch or to take that out of their mouths. The child is asked to use their eyes to look but not touch for the purpose of self-restraint. While in many instances this is a safety issue, the lesson to use our eyes and, hence, our brain, over our bodies has a long-term impact.

The next year, instead of getting more sleep, I now shifted my schedule to be at school from 7:00 a.m. to 7:00 p.m. I then changed the scenery to shift to the local Starbucks, where I would work from 7:30 p.m. to 10:30 p.m. when they closed. I often packed both my lunch and dinner so I didn't lose any time there and could eat while I worked. I'm not sure if it was a good thing or bad thing, but the baristas at Starbucks started to get to know me and would make my drink for me as soon as they saw me come in the door without me even having to order. One sweet barista named Sam would even take pity on me and bring me over another drink on the house around 9:00 p.m. every once in a while. By the time I finished grad school two years later, I was up to drinking a dirty chai latte with three shots of espresso because that was the only drink that has enough caffeine to make a difference.

Just because we consume food and beverages doesn't mean we eat and drink. We can use food as a distraction, bypassing the purpose of these senses. Sight is the least valuable sense when it comes to connecting with the body because our eyes are most closely connected with our brain. When we see something, we instinctively categorize, judge, label, and analyze—all cognitively based activities. If we view something aesthetically beautiful, we may still be tempted to use thought, such as interpreting art or measuring some expanse of nature.

Sight also happens to be the medium most easily corrupted by technology. Our increased reliance, dependence, and addition to social media, cell phones, and computers means we are using our eyes as a medium for the brain. Sensory information is quickly transmuted into digital data that our brain synthesizes, rather than appreciating as an experience. In spite of being well connected to the internet, we become cut off from the world.

My friends saw me going down the path of becoming an old maid with lots of cats because all I did was work and never made time to have a personal life. My own mother was growing concerned and would send me cards and letters about how much our family means to her and that I shouldn't forget to make time to consider taking steps to build a family of my own. They finally sat me down and made me an online dating profile. When asked for two qualities to describe myself, all I could come up with was "tall and organized." How pathetic is that?! I had spent so much of my time immersed in school and in work that I didn't even know the best qualities about myself.

Intimacy or deep contact with another is not possible when we aren't in contact with ourselves. Learning how to listen and understand what our bodies are communicating requires attending to instincts, drives, feelings, sensations, wants, and needs. When listening to our bodies, we can determine what messages are the result of old programming versus current life circumstances. For instance, do we get tense around a different ethnic group because of our experiences growing up, or is it based on some more recent occurrence? Synthesizing data from our bodies becomes a mind-body cooperative effort.

Nevertheless, online dating didn't work out because I ended up falling in love with a friend from college. He was back in Pennsylvania and was the reason I moved back to the state to continue my teaching career. I made the jump from middle school general science to high school biology. I was finally teaching the content I loved (I was a biology major in undergrad), and I was closer to home. My master's degree was finished by the time I moved back, so I finally thought I would have time to relax and not stay up until the wee hours of the morning doing work.

Connecting sensations with feelings, wants, and needs is made possible by increasing our awareness, sometimes with intent and other times by chance opportunity. Noticing what our bodies are telling us begins with listening that is different from what we do with our ears. Noticing sensations allows us to identify feelings. If we notice butterflies in our stomach, we may feel fear. If we notice tension in our shoulders and neck, we may feel angry.

Recognizing feelings is how we identify needs that are unmet or seem threatened. If we are feeling fear, our need for safety/security may be compromised. If we feel angry, our need for affiliation/belonging may seem threatened, triggering our instinct to self-protect. Anger often represents a deeper feeling such as hurt or rejection, which can more easily alert us to unmet needs. The first challenge is lessening our protective mechanisms and reducing the outside distractions such as technology dependence, to free ourselves for this work.

Seven years later and I still find it difficult to pull myself away from my laptop and stop working. My honeymoon was the only vacation I have taken without bringing work along, but even then I felt guilty for not working. In my mind, there are always more lessons to improve, more data to analyze, and more differentiations to make to ensure every student can be successful. While I'm not having to start from scratch to prepare to teach a new curriculum every year, I'm endlessly making changes and taking on more responsibilities at my school. Even though my master's is done, I didn't want to stop learning and growing to have the greatest positive impact on students, so I'm now pursuing my doctorate at Penn State University.

The more we grow in this area, overcoming our early childhood lessons and injuries dissuading us from listening to our bodies, the more helpful we will be with modeling and encouraging the same for students. For educators working exclusively with children, we might always remember that all behavior reflects some need that a student is trying to meet or protecting from being taken away. If we can help children learn to trace needs back to feelings, through sensations, we are offering a process that has long-term benefits. Unlike punishing undesirable behavior or rewarding prosocial actions, we are teaching a process for understanding how and why we do things.

Keep in mind that for some children, distinguishing between wants and needs is more difficult. In addition to age and developmental levels, there are other factors to consider. It may feel like an enormous loss for children who have tantrums because they don't get to play with a toy. Perhaps their day was filled with disappointments or they are experiencing hardship, triggering a more pronounced response to the new disappointment. We may also be mindful of those children commonly visiting the nurse, reminded of the idea that acute stress and chronically unmet needs manifest in physical discomfort. If we can take notice and prevent them from entering the prescriptive world of medicine, we can literally save lives.

Throughout my seven-year career so far, I have had viruses that I haven't been able to shake for three months. I've experienced migraines that have resulted in me teaching my students in the dark and locking my door to sleep during my lunches because I'm in so much pain. I have even taught an entire day from a chair because I couldn't stand up while suffering from a UTI. The physical exhaustion after every week leaves me feeling like I just finished a triathlon every Friday night. I keep thinking the next year will be better because I will finally have my lessons to the point I'm happy with them, and I'll finally have enough differentiated activities and mini-lessons to meet the needs of all of my students. But I'm still waiting. . . .

For anybody who has used or heard the term *entitlement*, we imagine those self-righteous young people insatiable in their wants. The off-putting behavior we refer to may be a result of being told no when they are used to getting what they want, or they may have such extreme loss in their lives, the loss is heightened. Seemingly disproportionate reactions need to be explored so we know how best to intercede. Some level of entitlement can actually drive a person to expect more, to demand more out of their lives.

Young children lack the insight and communication skills to help us determine the cause of their behavior, whether that involves entitlement or defiance; thus, we begin with the expectation that help is needed around unmet needs. Determining which type of help, whether learning how to be at the periphery instead of the center of the universe, having their wants and needs met instantaneously, or recovering from trauma will be our north star.

However strong our instinct to change lives by serving as that twinkle of light for the many children living in darkness, we always want to remember to begin with self-care. If we are authentically guiding parallel to how we are living, our help will be that much more valuable.

My husband often tries to put things in perspective and tells me that if I burn myself out now trying to help a handful of kids, there are many more in the future that I will never reach because I gave too much of myself early on in my career. Although I know in my head that he's right, in my heart I can't let go of thinking there was something more I could have done to help a student now. I never feel like I'm doing enough, but my body screams at me to listen to my husband and slow down.

Key Points

▶ Helping children distinguish between wants and needs is important because a growing number of children are entitled, enabled, and corrupted by technology.

▶ The difference between wants and needs is important. Wants are influenced by preferences, situations, fears, and many other factors. We want chocolate, but we don't need it (debate is welcome).

▶ Needs are biopsychosocial (biological, psychological, social, and possibly spiritual).

▶ The quantity or intensity of these needs is different for each person, based on early life experience and current circumstances.

▶ A simple way to distinguish between a want and a need is through our sensations.

▶ The formula is as follows: Sensation > Feeling > Need; Belief > Thought > Value.

Discussion Questions

Whether using the book for professional development (PD) or within a book group, please consider the following questions to stimulate your own ideas for exploration.

1. Which sensations am I most aware of, and why?

2. Which sensations do I pay the least attention to, and why?

3. Which feelings am I most aware of, and why?

4. Which feelings do I pay the least attention to, and why?

5. Which needs am I most aware of, and why?

Differentiating Self-Regulation Versus Self-Control

CHAPTER

8

(Melissa W. is a fifth-grade special education teacher from Lumberton, New Jersey.)

Isn't it funny how so much of life is simply smoke and mirrors? I often wonder how many families omit details to protect their secrets and their image? How many families diligently obscure or embellish their truth to mislead those around them? This is what my own family has done, and I am complicit in the alternative narrative. In general, I present as someone who has my act together. Rather, the public presentation of my life is simply smoke and mirrors. Only those closest to me know the real story of my life's struggles, and even then, I doubt they really understand the full weight of the facts.

As we achieve balance between brain and body, learn to listen to messages sent by the body via sensations, and translate those sensations into feelings that convey needs, we are ready to act on this information. Identifying, expressing, and negotiating needs requires skills and, while we are waiting, the ability to contain all our urges.

With greater freedom to express thoughts and feelings, we can better meet our own needs, growing energy to give back through relationships and involvement with our community. Growing into a productive member of society requires becoming self-sufficient but accountable to the greater good. While navigating this tricky path, we learn to curtail thoughts, feelings, and actions to make space for others. This ongoing decision-making around when to act and when to hold back is a lifelong balancing act.

Children are not born with patience, which anybody with a one-year-old can attest to. Children don't instinctively wait for their turn, and they don't have inhibitions around taking what they want. While attempting to master their environment, aided by physical, psychological, and cognitive development, they exercise increasing amounts of self-control, helping build patience in meeting their own needs. This can be seen by a baby who wants to hold his or her own bottle, with growing patience and dexterity.

Successful development allows toddlers to relinquish control, helped by caregivers who reliably respond to the calls for hunger and discomfort. Dominant control where we demand and are satiated gives way to nondominant control, or a more reciprocal relationship with the environment that feels less demanding to caretakers.

For the better part of my life, I have carried my story around like invisible overpacked luggage, pretending that it's not too heavy for me to handle and that the dysfunction doesn't really affect me. Sometimes I even pretend that the luggage doesn't actually exist. One can only shove feelings aside for so long before they come spilling out in surprising ways.

Depending upon how fair life seems to a child, determined by the consistency of getting needs through the help of others, self-control will be impacted—either learning to control oneself or, less constructively, by trying to control what happens in the world. The toddler who knows that food will come with minimal crying can focus on something else instead of perseverating on the food.

In school, the children who don't learn to curb their instinct for control, continuing their dominant behavior, will have trouble keeping their hands to themselves, respecting the property of others, or learning how to work cooperatively. These same children are often the ones who don't discriminate well between thinking and doing. When a thought enters their mind, they say it or act on it—often described as being impulsive or having no filter.

Indulged children may present similarly, surprised when they don't get instant satisfaction. These children, however, will decrease their demand for attention as they recognize the preschool or kindergarten teacher won't tolerate their demands. Children with a deficit in needs being met may either be too fearful to constructively manipulate their environments or not be satisfied with quantity of attention available for them.

Educators may consider the influence of the physical environment the child grows up in and the internal environment where children wrestle with immediate gratification, emotional lability, and behavioral impulsivity. While we have little influence over a child's home life, we can help them to cope with the situations creating their inner conflicts.

The first time I recognized that pushing feelings aside had a negative effect on me was after what I like to call "one of the worst weeks of my life." The week in question was a hellish conglomeration of unrelated yet tragic incidences that included a bathroom destroyed by termites, a husband in isolation for meningitis, a mother who had a ministroke, a nephew who got sepsis from a bee sting, and a professor who wouldn't give me an extension on two papers that were due.

Kids who don't learn to modulate their feelings will have difficulty self-soothing, becoming overwhelmed by stress. They will fixate on emotional pain, become overly sensitive to the feelings of others, or become highly guarded because they get injured with the slightest inkling of hurt, rejection, or discomfort. These children may get labeled as drama queens or empaths.

Finding balance along the brain-body continuum, described earlier, will correlate with how over- or undercontrolled we are along the thinking/doing/feeling spectrums. Understanding in which direction we are skewed will help inform us personally and professionally whether help is needed removing the self-imposed restrictions, allowing for greater freedom of expression, or developing greater self-discipline.

But, the pièce de résistance for this incredible week was the phone call from my mom telling me that my brother was locked in his house with a gun and that he was threatening to kill himself. I grabbed my infant daughter and rushed to my brother's street, where I was met by a fleet of police cars and ambulances. I remember screaming to the police that my baby nephew was in the house and that they needed to get him to me immediately. The last thing I recall is my mother begging for someone, anyone to tell her if her son was still alive as I drove off with now two infants in my back seat.

When sensations are so intense that we have difficulty regulating them, an alarm goes off. This alarm triggers panic of an ensuring meltdown like the alarms at a nuclear power plant. These same alarms may be recognized by student behavior if we can make the connection to unmet needs. The better we do at recognizing these warning signs of a struggling child, the better we can intervene. If we treat problematic behaviors and seemingly disproportionate emotional displays like a detective solving a case, we can even reduce our own distress. If we use our observations to inform our interventions, we can build the psychosocial emotional learning (PSEL) like an insulating shield to promote greater resiliency.

A concerned teacher observing a young child who gives up space whenever a peer becomes dominant may intervene by helping to lift the restrictions of shyness. That same teacher may help the other student consider the feelings of their peer, so they don't become oppressive or bypass empathy.

Helping distinguish between emotional modulation and behavioral inhibition is key. Children need to understand how to self-sooth, temper the intensity of emotion, look beyond anger (three forms of modulation), and curb impulsivity (behavioral inhibition). To gain fortitude for holding feelings in abeyance and tolerating distress, soon to be explored, children need to learn restraint. While simpler, we can analogize this to slowing our breathing before learning to hold our breath underwater.

Thankfully, my brother survived his own mind that day, and I continued on in my life, stoically supporting those around me, offering a listening ear to my parents, making sure my brother's children had their needs met, and being the best wife and parent possible to my own husband and daughter. I not only felt but also appeared strong and relatively unaffected by what had transpired.

Without intervention, people cope in their own instinctive ways, often seeking immediate relief without consideration for long-term consequences. Through our distress we may learn patience, develop creativity, or find passion for helping others. Even if we don't work through all the unfinished business of our childhood, we may still become valued members of our community.

Those who are even more successful learn to recognize the correlation between what they experienced early in life and how they live and relate as adults. It begins with an appreciation for what our bodies are telling us, and then we use this data to regulate our feelings and control our actions—all in the service of meeting our needs, all made possible through listening to our guttural voice.

When children can attend to their bodies, understanding the relationship between sensations, feelings, and needs, they are better prepared with patience and creativity for the pursuit of more complex needs. As we age, most complex needs are not immediately satisfied, some requiring us to endure varying degrees of discomfort first. Consider the maturity of a middle schooler who can sense their teacher is frustrated with another student so decides to wait a few minutes before asking for help.

Self-soothing, or calming oneself down, is an important developmental task that young children generally show marked improvement in once they begin school. As young children see peers who aren't having tantrums, developing the ability to regroup after getting hurt, they feel healthy internal pressure to do the same.

Apparently, I was and am a master at delaying the overflow of emotion within me. Imagine my husband's confusion when I started sobbing in the car one regular Saturday seven months after this traumatic week. He turned his concerned face toward me, trying to make sense of why his wife fell apart so suddenly. When I could finally speak, I gasped, "That was the worst week of my life."

Some children become overly controlled, locking away emotions into a room where no key can be found. To survive, it becomes necessary to stop the constant surge of feelings that interfere with reason and decision-making. Too much self-protection and we lose sight of our own needs, sufficing with the gratification that comes with tending to others.

Some children develop more slowly, going well into their young adult years struggling to control impulses and/or regulate emotion. Teens who are self-injurious or harm others are likely struggling with either or both poor self-regulation and self-control.

That's how it started for me. The dysregulation would show up in the form of me crying a couple of times a year about how my dysfunctional family affects me. Then, as time ploughed on, I noticed that I used food as a way to self-soothe. A pattern evolved that I can now trace back to when I was a child. First, a dysfunctional family event would happen. Examples could include my niece showing up to Mother's Day covered in bruises from her father's beatings. Or my schizophrenic grandmother being committed to the psychiatric ward again for one of her many bizarre episodes. Or my mentally ill uncle's disability checks stolen again by the Hell's Angels. It doesn't matter the causal event because the effect is always the same: mindlessly reaching for food. Yet despite crying occasionally and eating too many sweets, I felt emotionally and mentally strong and was convinced that I was relatively unaffected by the dysfunction all around me.

Before we can self-regulate or self-control consistently or effectively, we have to become aware of our internal environment—the drives, impulses, feelings, needs, and urges that drive our actions. Balancing brain and body, the earliest PSEL is instrumental in allowing adequate attention to the source of these compulsions. Many children and even adults are lacking in this awareness or effort to scan their environments, making it difficult to assess the push from within.

Take a moment and pay attention to what is going on around you. How are you seated in your chair? Is there tension in your neck, shoulders, jaw? Is it noisy where you are? Do you feel rushed to finish this article and get on to your next task? Close your eyes for a moment and take a few deep breaths. What do you notice now? Did anything change in your posture? How about your heart rate? Maybe nothing is different. Notice that too, and notice how you feel about that.

The reflecting you just did was possible courtesy of your prefrontal cortex, the part of the brain that allows you to regulate your emotional responses and override any automatic behaviors or habits. It is central to self-regulation and empathy. This function fully develops in the mid to late twenties, and for others with challenging early life experiences, it takes a lifetime to recognize and improve upon.

My dysregulation evolved as my children grew older. I recall feeling alarmed and ashamed with myself one day when I lost my temper on my toddlers in a way that makes me feel uncomfortable to discuss. While I don't remember the details of what precipitated my outburst, I do shamefully remember the tone with which I was speaking and the curse words that I spoke. I even remember throwing a dish towel in the ultimate display of an adult temper tantrum. I wish I could say that this was an isolated incident. Regretfully, I noticed a new pattern emerging.

When we experience something threatening, the fight-or-flight response is immediately triggered, and the part of your brain that deals with emotions hijacks the thinking part of your brain. The prefrontal cortex, when activated, can serve as the "brakes" to this response, lowering the alert signals and allowing you to assess the situation with more reason.

Children, however, do not have a fully developed prefrontal cortex to help them easily regulate high emotions. What might not seem to the rational adult mind to be more than an annoyance is perceived in the child brain as a threat. Fear triggers the release of stress hormones, and if the child is unable to regulate the response, anxiety and then panic may set in. Over time, instincts turn into patterns that influence our character, even shaping or determining our personalities.

My naturally outgoing personality and cheerful demeanor have always dominated my daily interactions. However, the pressures of being a mom, a wife, and a teacher would compound with the dysfunction of my extended family. While I was simultaneously filling my children's days with fun adventures and joyful moments, I would subconsciously allow the stresses I was under to silently accumulate. One can only shove feelings aside for so long before they come spilling out in surprising ways. For me, the buildup of stress would explode out of me at seemingly random moments. Something that seemed benign the day before would suddenly become the trigger to provoke a gigantic adult temper tantrum typically aimed at the two sweetest humans I know. An untidy room that was simply an annoyance would soon become a sad symbol of every situation that I have zero control over. My lack of control over my extended family's pervasive issues made me act out of control toward my own innocent children.

As adults, we are continuously improving with self-control and self-regulation. Mastery of these skills doesn't end with the maturation from childhood, and for some of us, the work is greater if we didn't get consistent help early in our development or if we endured trauma that interfered with or prior to the opportunity to learn how to modulate our emotions.

A cup filled to the very brim with coffee needs to take on only a small drop to make it spill over. As people, we may become supersaturated with emotion, unable to regulate because we don't have enough internal space to hold back or enough processing speed to assimilate the stimuli. We become concerned about judgment about our uncontrollable crying spells or fits of anger—likely a mixture of difficulty with behavioral inhibition and emotional modulation.

Thankfully, these episodes don't happen very often because, after all, I am a master at delaying the overflow of emotion within me. However, they've happened often enough that I feel great shame for my inability to control myself when I am upset. I am ashamed as I remember my little daughters' faces staring up at me wondering why I'm yelling at them in such a scary way. I am ashamed as I recall my mind telling me that I need to stop myself from saying anything more and yet not being able to control myself enough to close my mouth. I am ashamed that I have to apologize profusely to these precious beings and try to explain to them that I am the one who is wrong and not them. I am ashamed that I have promised to try harder to control myself and yet have failed that promise more times than I can even count.

Even with improved awareness of how we are molded by life experiences, influencing how we get our needs met and allowing us to make changes, the residual impact is still felt. Guilt, shame, remorse, and other painful emotions may resurface, making it important to examine how early and current experiences shape our social emotional learning (SEL), allowing us to adjust the way we employ them. Self-awareness that hyperfixates us on our shortcomings may need softening. Self-control to the point of limited risk-taking had value at one point but now may be restricting our range of self-expression.

As we explore other PSELs, we may revisit our own differentiation between self-regulation and self-control. If, for instance, we have failed to develop a solid core sense of who we are (identity), how we are treated by others may have a greater impact on our actions. Each of the PSELs are influenced by the others, so making an adjustment in one means consideration of them all. This is hard work, but without it we risk passing along what we have learned and employed to our students—and especially our children.

This sense of failure feels like an ugly scar that both my daughters and I wear. This scar rips open each time I lack the ability to rein in my emotional outbursts. Recently, I have been trying very hard to practice the art of walking away. Separating myself from the kids gives me the time I need to settle myself down and come back to myself. Yes, this is an effective strategy when I'm feeling elevated. But it begs the bigger question: What else should I be doing to increase my self-control?

Self-control is not the same as *controlling*, a term used more often at the start of the year and with educators who are new to the profession. One does, however, influence the other, as a highly controlled educator may expect more discipline from his or her students. Sometimes, however, the opposite may hold true, with those who are overcontrolled expecting less from their students because we have done for them. Rules, organization, and even test preparation are all examples to help us consider this idea.

Imagine a novice teacher attempting to fit in with her new department. Differentiating between loneliness pervasive in her life and her instinct to please her peers to fit in will be an important differentiation to make. If the teacher doesn't consider emotion from action, she may find herself doing things outside her comfort zone. Being overly helpful, for instance, without getting anything back from colleagues may result in growing resentment that leads to a new, unproductive behavior.

I am reflective enough to know that my inability to self-regulate when I'm upset stems from the utter lack of control I have over various people or situations in my life. Over the years, I have identified that my body gives me little signs in the days that lead up to an outburst. For example, when the phone rings with more bad news, I might feel my chest constrict, and my breathing may become shallow. Another telltale sign is my blatant refusal to share the bad news with my husband or daughters. Talking about the dysfunction the first time is heavy enough that I do everything possible to avoid discussing it further. I am woefully consistent in ignoring these meaningful signs. What would be the result were I to address my feelings as they're happening?

The more intentional we are, made possible through our heightened self-awareness, the more likely we are to balance self-protection and PSEL skills. This means learning how to act in a manner congruent with our beliefs, values, and needs. Being intentional also serves to ensure we are recognizing sensations, feelings, and unmet needs that influence our desire to act and assessing how well this action served us. Looking inward to examine our emotions and behavior is the adult version of differentiating between self-regulation and self-control. Becoming nuanced in when to wait and consider—not giving up on our wants but becoming deliberate in how to get them met—is the hallmark of a mature adult.

When I am in the midst of a shameful adult temper tantrum, the sensations within my body change as well. My arms shake, my face burns red hot with anger, and words spill out of me with an utter lack of censorship. In my mind I will tell myself to stop, and yet, I continue yelling in an attempt to scratch a proverbial itch that can't be satisfied. Typically, as I'm coming down from an episode I start identifying what's really going on inside of me. The dialogue switches from me yelling about the house being a total mess to me sobbing that everything is out of control right now and that I need my home to bring me a sense of peace.

Our physical display of distress can be dramatic. We may exert considerable effort to hide this display from those in our home and work environment for fear of seeming judged or, worse, scorned. Without the freedom to be authentic in the moment, we lose the ability for catharsis: the honest expungement of energy buildup from painful emotion.

Our physical environments can influence how safe we feel being transparent with others to gain the support we need through caring or confrontation, to learn from our experience. Our environment impacts our patience or how well we wait before expressing feelings. In school environments conducive to safe exploration of feelings and support from leadership, we may have an easier time using external supports to help us stabilize. Conversely, schools in survival mode may instigate our instinct for self-protection, keeping feelings inside until they pressurize us to the point of erupting.

As adults working in a highly personal profession, we may consider how our home environment impacts our work experience. Educators are not machines who can leave their home life at the door of the school building. Teachers are cognizant of how stress in their home life impacts work in the classroom and even student learning, requiring our ability to measure how full our cup is upon the start of each day. In this helping profession, the absence of this monitoring can be harmful—even contributing to burnout.

I am naturally a people pleaser, a doer, a helper, and a fixer. Giving myself over to other people's problems comes naturally to me. I was raised in a family where unconditional love is the mantra no matter how horribly the other people behaved. I exist in a family where just two of us hold the distinguished role of "givers of all support" while the rest are content to be the recipients. These recipients are takers at their core—takers of time, money, and favors. Holding the esteemed role of chief support person in my family comes with a steep price. That price is my occasional inability to self-regulate while interacting with my own children. Boundaries are nearly impossible to put into place and uphold due to the complex nature of the larger family dynamics. I often wonder if boundaries would give me the space I need to process life's difficulties without losing my cool.

Boundaries are the points of contact between ourselves and others, allowing for data exchange and to define our sense of self. Without attention to boundaries, we may lose ourselves or at the very least lose sight of how to express or negotiate for meeting our needs. Paying attention to where I begin and where you end allows me to adjust how rigid or diffuse these boundaries are.

Professional development (PD) work seldom includes this type of deep dive into our personal growth, but that doesn't mean the classroom and school aren't perpetually influenced by these dynamics. While we are hearing more about the importance of SEL, we have a long way to go before understanding how vast this work will be.

With this growing awareness around the complexity of SEL, individual wellness, and organizational health, we will better meet the needs of our educators. The shift from viewing SEL as a purely student-driven task to a whole school approach will be slow but helped by the inclusion of the more intricate PSELs, such as differentiating self-regulation from self-control.

In my professional life as a teacher I am masterful in my patience and understanding of my students' social and emotional needs. My lifelong experiences of dealing with multiple mentally ill family members have given me a sixth sense in identifying students who are struggling. I have a rare level of compassion and empathy for the students who are hardest to reach. I know that my unconditional connection with them can foster their own resilience as they grow and navigate their own dysfunctional lives.

Educators are best equipped to support the psychological, social, emotional, and moral development of their students when they are engaged in parallel work. We already know that teachers have passion for academic instruction, preparing students to successfully pursue careers they enjoy. We also know that many educators enjoy getting through to those students who are harder to reach.

We will position our frontline teachers, aides, administrators, and support staff to make better contact with these hard-to-reach students—the ones struggling with family dynamics and circumstances often outside our purview—if we help them to understand the difference between self-regulation and self-control.

Teaching is inherently stressful, but it can be made incrementally more peaceful if we help our faculty through their own personal growth journey. While a certain level of responsibility falls on the teacher to engage their own personal growth work outside of school, it is incumbent on school leaders to integrate personal growth and PD in school. The interplay of personal and professional forces creating the stress that can lead to burnout is the shared responsibility of both parties.

My connections with my students give me a deep sense of purpose in my work as an educator, but it also brings additional stress that I allow to silently build up within me. I have a way of internalizing the problems I see within my students. During the day I will give every ounce of my patience and energy to the most difficult and oppositional students only to come home to my own children and feel annoyed at the slightest hint of back talk.

Teaching is one of the most personal of professions with our experiences from home influencing school and vice versa. As we sharpen our awareness to make meaning of the sensations and feelings elicited at home or work, the better we can determine if our disproportionate response means something unresolved from the previous setting. Then we can find interventions that match the dilemma.

I have a deep pocket of strategies that I use with my students that include deep breathing, listening to calming music, exercising, applying deep pressure on the arms, taking movement breaks, and meditating. I even have a strong awareness of what I need when dealing with a particularly challenging student or situation. Professionally, I know when to walk away and ask another adult to step in for me.

Unfortunately, it seems that my masterful implementation of these skills doesn't transfer well to my home life. Not only do I lack long-lasting patience with my own kids but I also struggle to consistently give them the same thoughtful approach when they're struggling with their own adolescent needs. One could say that I am the proverbial example of the this saying: "The cobbler's children have no shoes."

Educators have a remarkable capacity to generate boundless nurturing for their students. They require little in return to sustain this level of giving. They need to feel respected, valued, and reinforced to maintain a certain level of sacrifice. They need to know that their efforts are recognized and their intentions are good. They need to be treated like adults, given autonomy but also held accountable to standards mutually agreed upon by the teacher and administrator.

If we value these needs by including them in the school's mission and vision statement, we will inspire loyalty and industry. Educators know they are doing important work, but it doesn't mean the self-worth can overcome their own demons—not without the investment of the entire school community where individual and organizational health are made a priority.

Like most humans, I am my own worst critic. However, despite my self-criticism, what I know for certain is that I am an incredible mother even with all my faults and shortcomings. I provide my daughters with an insane amount of love and joy. I excel at living in the moment with a true carpe diem spirit, filling their days with happy laughter, exciting adventures, and frequent surprises. I hug and kiss them more often than they care to withstand.

I trust that I am a model of resilience for them, rising above life's challenges without complaint. I teach them about the acceptance of others and the gift of unconditional love. I show them that life's trials can shape and mold one's heart into a beautiful vehicle of empathy and compassion.

I am remarkably honest with my daughters about where I need to grow as a human and as a mother. I regularly ask for them to have patience with me as I continue to evolve, and thankfully, they not only extend me their patience but also their sweet grace. They understand that, like everyone on this beautiful earth, I am a work in progress. How lucky am I that I get to be the recipient of their own special brand of unconditional love?

Definitions

Self-regulation has to do with how a child modulates emotions. In simpler terms, it's how well children go from upset to okay, how extreme their emotions are, and how they monitor and make meaning of their internal data (how hungry they are, how aware they are of their needs).

Self-control has to do with how a child manages behavior. Are children impulsive? Do they lash out in anger? Are they disorganized in their speech or seem generally out of control?

Key Points

▶ How a child goes from upset to okay is termed *recovery*.

▶ Extreme emotions and actions reflect many elements, including home dynamics, community pressures, and school conditions.

▶ How a person monitors and makes meaning of internal data (sensations) helps inform what needs may be unmet or threatened.

▶ When we move from sensation to action without awareness, it precipitates problems with self-control.

▶ When a child gets into trouble or doesn't listen, it's time to consider the origin of the issue, whether that's emotional, behavioral, or a combination of the two.

▶ The key to helping children with emotional regulation and behavioral inhibition always begins with an adult's effort to understand intent.

▶ If a child acts in an undesirable way without regret, self-control is likely lacking.

▶ If a child feels entitled or justified, self-control may be your focus.

▶ If the child wasn't being impulsive but deliberate in one's actions, there may be a combination of self-regulation and self-control.

Discussion Questions

Whether using the book for PD or within a book group, please consider the following questions to stimulate your own ideas for exploration.

1. How easy or difficult is it for me in dealing with student behavioral or emotional issues?

2. Am I more likely to inhibit my behavior or feelings, and why?

3. What role have parents played in emotional and behavioral problems for students?

4. What are the most and least effective ways I've attempted to collaborate with a parent around his or her child's difficulty?

5. What impulses do I have the most difficult time containing?

Building Capacity to Hold Feelings in Abeyance

(Christy Lynn Anana is a school counselor
in Snohomish, Washington.)

*That Friday in late October started in a very ordinary way. I was
working in my role as an elementary school counselor, to start a new
curriculum of support for each classroom. The feedback was very positive
as everyone was ready to keep the project moving. I finished early that
day, trusting they would keep me apprised if anything more was needed.
Developing support for teachers and students was the most rewarding
part of my job.*

Thus far we have considered how our natural tendencies and environmental influences shape our thoughts, feelings, and behavior. We
appreciated the value of self-awareness to identify sensation as it relates
to feelings and needs. We considered how to create a natural and healthy
inhibition of impulses without endangering our attention to wants
and needs.

Along our developmental journey, our work evolves into a more
advanced objective to identify and manage our feelings, channeling
them into productive outlets. As we increase our awareness of feelings
and become more strategic around using that awareness to meet our
needs, we require time delays for deliberate action. This is an important
distinction between a toddler and an elementary school child, gaining
the ability to be purposeful. Without these delays to determine best
courses of action, we are prone to more impulsive behavior and may
even succumb to our most base drives and instincts.

*Then, a staff member pulled me into a room and told me a former
student from our school had shot someone at the feeder high school and
then shot himself. I wanted desperately to call this a rumor. It couldn't
be—especially not this student. He had recently visited our school, and
he embraced me on sight. I had been his elementary school counselor.
We had many of his cousins at our school. I felt close to his aunties
and extended family. Then, I felt a new shudder down my spine when
I heard about the victims of the shooting. Some were my former
students as well. Some had siblings attending. Families were coming*

to pick up their children, teary-eyed and full of shock. Some staff members at school had children at the high school who were witnesses to the event. Some staff were connected as family and embedded within the community.

Building time delays into our reaction process allows us to consider others' intentions, growing empathy to inhibit resentments from catapulting into aggression. With the ability to hold back, we will learn to navigate conflicts and deal with disappointments, rewarded by intimate relationships. In order to balance our needs with others, we have to further grow our patience, tempering both pleasant and unpleasant emotions.

After learning to identify our needs, we then build in more strategic planning to express and negotiate having those needs met. If we have determined we do in fact want or need something important and valuable to us, it doesn't mean the timing is right to take action. Sometimes we are better served by recognizing what we are feeling but doing nothing at that moment in time.

In this age of immediate gratification, driven by the constant actions of scrolls and clicks, we miss out on the value of nonaction. Learning how to be with ourselves and others, without taking action, simply noticing with curiosity our own and others' experiences can be a tremendous gift. Even when people seek comfort from us because they are suffering, it doesn't mean we have to rush to action. If we can curb our natural caring instinct to fix or help, we might find an even more valuable way of making contact.

Everyone was having an experience that in the moment could not be put into words. It was agonizing and sorrowful. There were things we could do. I spent time at the hospital with younger siblings, making them origami animals while they waited for their older sister to be taken off life support. Students made cards and letters for family members while golden retriever service dogs intuitively made their rounds to each child who was in need. I was entrusted to give the message at our morning assembly the next Monday after the shooting. The only words that I could muster that had any meaning at all came from Thich Nhat Hanh: "I am here for you." I told every child to look around and see all the adults that were saying that with their hearts.

The path toward integrating or disintegrating the fabric of our community begins early in life. Consider a young child at a birthday party who sees a friend opening a gift, which is a toy that the child had been wanting. The child gets excited to see the toy or is sad, wanting the toy, but what becomes important at that moment is not diminishing the joy of the friend. How does a young person learn to be happy for the friend while disappointed for themselves? For older students, this may be a friend who gets a better grade or an audition that results in somebody else getting the lead.

Acknowledging and expressing our complex and sometimes mixed feelings is imperative for healthy organismic functioning, allowing us to cleanse ourselves of pent up energy, or time for strategizing around getting our needs met. Having a safe space to express feelings without judgment or ridicule allows children to work through their own dis-ease to open themselves up for recognizing others. In this space, they grow their understanding for when to put feelings into motion and when to hold back. With age comes increasing complexity for this task, adding more people, more layers of intricacy, and the delicacy of situations to the equation.

People who learn to read the room, sensing when they have contributed too much or too little to a group exchange, will be more inclined to develop intimacy. We are drawn to those who sense when the dynamic of imbalance needs correcting. These same people who can read themselves in relation to others do well in leadership roles because they know how to balance giving and receiving.

Teachers who know when to draw out a student and when to elaborate further will excel in relationship building, because students implicitly trust this type of relationship attunement. This ability or skill can be subtle and difficult to identify because it manifests in different forms throughout our day.

We can appreciate this subtlety through the simple exercise of receiving appreciation or the deeper affirmation. If we can take in the other person for one's intention—meaning the good will attempting to be conveyed, valuing enjoyment for acknowledging our effort, and doing it without having to lessen the reward—we are evolving. Instead of "thank you, but it was no big deal," representing the action of relieving our discomfort at being valued, can we sit in the feeling while realizing what is being offered to us?

Holding space was not a new concept for me as a school counselor. However, the breadth of that work in this circumstance was immense. Over and over, I held space and offered, "I am here for you." Some staff members came to my room to find a safe place to cry. When we could connect and feel the depth of the loss, the floodgates were open. Sometimes there were words of disbelief, a striving for answers that would never come. Each person brought their own set of experiences to debrief. There was never a satisfying end to the conversation. It was daily heart-wrenching and soul-searching for a glimmer of hope to this despair. I felt so powerless. Persistently, I had the feeling that there was nothing I could do. There was no right word to say or gesture that would be a magic salve to ease the pain. It was like walking in wet concrete every day.

For those who can navigate this transformation from acting instinctively to meet a want or need with more deliberate planning, increased frustration tolerance and the ability to delay gratification are the rewards. Patience and peace are the by-products of maturing children who can now consider the wants and needs of others on par with themselves. But without this important element of maturation, the inability to express and curtail emotion will lessen their ability to tolerate distress.

The worst was the response from children who could not speak their emotions but rather displayed their pain. A third-grade relative to one of the victims soiled his pants in my office. It was close to the end of the day. After getting a change of clothes for him, I got his brother to escort him to his bus. I didn't want him to be alone. After he left, I sat in my office and cried.

As natural caregivers, it pains us to see children suffer. We want to infuse children with hope and happiness, enveloping them in a cloak of resiliency. We can't save every child from having the misfortunes of a troubled family or having their sense of safety stripped. Our instinct to love them and fill the voids left by the world cannot always be acted upon; otherwise, we might have to adopt half our class. This is what it means to hold feelings in abeyance.

The same dilemma occurs in our adult relationships. We may not always be able to give our coworkers, children, or intimate partners what they need. Sometimes as parents, mentors, and partners we have to allow others to learn difficult lessons, watching them struggle with their own pain. We can do this more easily when we develop confidence in our own understanding that feelings can occur without remedy.

Holding feelings in abeyance is the foundation for much of this work, forged from our earliest days with no memory of being soothed from crying, fed when hungry, and changed when wet. It also means being blanketed by the affirmation of smiles, laughter, and other soothing sensations that help us feel safe and loved. Young children who grow up with consistent nurturing will internalize the pleasant feeling, decreasing our reliance on external validation and giving us confidence that we can manufacture our own self-soothing. Sometimes, but less common, children who don't consistently get their needs met will also develop this ability.

The truth is that I was very good at the skill of abeyance since I was a child. Both of my parents were pretty self-centered. My needs were very unimportant. I became accustomed to not caring about my own needs since no one else did. I say this because sometimes a very normal skill acquisition can go awry. Most normal developing children entering school struggle with impulse control. It is taught with practices like waiting for everyone to be served before you eat your own cupcake. The social norms are strong. If you dip your finger into the frosting before the birthday song is finished, you may get a scolding from a self-righteous classmate.

Children on the other end of the continuum, who get everything they ask for, or perhaps material items in place of love, aren't likely to learn how to hold feelings in abeyance. These are children who expect to have their wants and needs met without having to endure discomfort or feel the reward of waiting patiently, maintaining a reliance or dependence on the outside world (through possessions) to help them feel happy. Without the opportunity to experience emotion without the urgency to act, without the models for containing excitement or the patience that comes through delaying reward, a child may become the disruptive outlier in your class.

Children build the capacity to hold their feelings in abeyance through practice. You have to wait your turn to speak for show-and-tell even though you are excited to show your special item. If you are someone who is good at listening, your friends may look to you for advice. It becomes very internally rewarding to be that good friend who everyone goes to for support.

If these children don't get what they want quickly or don't tolerate the discomfort of not getting what they want at all, they show us through behaviors we may find off putting. Our reactions to these behaviors are often obvious, helping to create a cycle of tumult. The child may eventually take on the role or identity of an unruly student, facilitated by the attitude of adults who haven't looked deeply into the unmet needs or inability to self-soothe.

As we explored with the previous psychosocial emotional learning (PSEL), when children have difficulty with self-regulation or self-control, they generally act before considering, speak before thinking, or feel without exploring. At the core of this trouble is emotional endurance—the fortitude to stay with a feeling without the need to act on it. This can simply be wanting to inject an idea into a conversation, being so excited that they can't wait their turn or appreciate the natural flow of energy in a dyad or group interaction. In extreme cases it can be the base for something much more serious.

This tragedy proved to be an unimaginable time of practicing this skill. As weeks passed, this work of healing did not subside. There was no goalpost to run toward. The holding of space was a forever marathon. We would hold space until waves of grief would continue to push us down to the point where it was difficult to even want to stand up again. Over time, the work was really hard.

The capacity to hold feelings in abeyance amounts to containing our desires to help and heal, our want for excitement and harnessing one's own enjoyable energy. The joyful exuberance that comes from hearing good news—looking forward to something enjoyable or being surprised—is at its height in our youth. As we age, we don't have to go run to find the gift that was hidden for us (well, I do) or give the present we bought for somebody else before their birthday.

Holding feelings in abeyance is important for enduring internal drives or impulses or acting on fantasies to experience pleasures in life. Our desire for fame and glory, financial freedom, and power to influence our world are perfectly normal to dream about, even motivating to work hard and earn our success. As molders of this nuanced PSEL, we want to be on the lookout for children who too easily give in to temptation and avoid pain at all costs. These children may grow into adults who don't lean into their own experiences or embrace the feelings of others.

There was a dark side to this work. Staff would compare their suffering and even ask out loud, "Why is she upset?" I couldn't judge why a person was impacted by this tragedy. It hits us in different places and brought up so much unresolved personal trauma. This was not the first death to hit this school. There was a string of student deaths from natural causes. Another child died after a stepfather accidentally shot the student while cleaning his gun. Some staff at school didn't survive this blow. It was too much. By the end of the year more than half transferred to another school or another district. This school had been identified by the state as "failing" and was finally starting to be able to make progress in student learning. When all of the students' safe people left, it was devasting to the school community and children. The ripple effect that this tragedy put in place was dizzying, and we had an opportunity to take care in each moment. That is all that we could do.

Whether we come together or get split apart during times of strife depends largely on our ability to hold feelings in abeyance. If we rush to the supermarket in our eagerness to safeguard our family, purchasing all the toilet paper on display, we begin to cut ourselves off from our own humanity.

Most notably, greed, gluttony, and power are generated from within, often conflicting with morality and/or our basic needs. When we don't easily tolerate the seduction these impulses summon, we may begin to lose sight of our values, altering our moral compass. If we feel excited at the prospect of giving into a drive, we need to hold on to that feeling long enough to examine the hubris driving us.

Holding feelings in abeyance can also be unpleasant feelings—the ones we typically label as negative in spite of their tremendous value. Our collective assignment of unpleasant emotion as bad makes them more difficult to explore and generates a reflex to find a quick remedy. Exploring sadness, disappointment, or embarrassment won't happen if the emotion needs to be fixed.

Holding feelings in abeyance will be incrementally easier if we remove these assigned labels and teach young people to embrace all feelings equally. All feelings are important because they offer a window into our needs, even though some are unpleasant. Our job as adults is to create safe spaces for ourselves and others so that permission to feel can help us cope.

I came to realize that my job with children was simply to help them know that they were safe. They build capacity to heal themselves by feeling safety within. I offered space to feel. We slowed the pace of the day. We gave opportunities to find gratitude for each other in welcoming rituals. The class meetings that I had taught were a blessing. We greeted each other with handshakes, high fives, or hugs. There were lots of hugs.

The task of appreciating the value of all emotions, pleasant and unpleasant, is made especially difficult in a society that values quick fixes. As educators and human beings, we are attracted to anything that simplifies our lives, removing the work associated with deeper rewards.

The remediation of unpleasantness creates thriving business in first world countries, with a plethora of products and services aimed at reliving your "suffering" or promoting greater pleasure. Businesses capitalize on our need for instant gratification, helping us achieve more with less time, highly appealing to most people with poor work-life balance. Thus, we are highly susceptible to the incessant marketing campaigns, wanting to believe these products and services are necessary for thriving.

Dunkin' Donuts tells us that "America Runs on Dunkin'." AT&T uses the tagline "Your World. Delivered." Some companies don't require marketing or a tagline because their name is synonymous with instant gratification, such as Google. Children and adults are influenced to believe that our lives are better when we use a product or a service, but better generally means faster. How are we supposed to be in the moment, to find peace, to practice good self-care when our lives are dictated by quick fixes.

There was no guidebook to this work. I had no answers to give. My job was to be present, to breathe, to be with the person who needed me. Then, my job was to explore my own self-care. One day, I realized I had eaten only two Oreos for dinner. I knew if I continued this way not attending to my own well-being, I would surely get sick. I went to acupuncture weekly, got more exercise, and eventually made my way to therapy myself. There is no shame to healing emotional wounds so that I am empowered to continue to do this work.

We have become a society of instant gratification in large part due to the immediacy of technology. Whether that means expecting an immediate response to a text message or looking information up online, we don't do well waiting. We haven't begun to appreciate the impact this is having on our children, who see their cell phones as an extension of their body, or perhaps more important than the arm that carriers it. We certainly fall short when it comes to teaching children how to appreciate the process and not simply the outcome.

The visual that we shared with students was a winding road going up a mountain. We called it the "Path to Feeling Better." When you think about driving in the mountains, the road doesn't go straight up. There are S-shaped curves that almost seem like you are going backward, but if you stay on the road you end up finding your way to the summit of the mountain. So it goes with healing. There are days that make you feel like it will never end. As long as you stick to the path, you'll be okay.

Its estimated that twenty-one million or half of all teens are addicted to their cell phones. It's not just children and teens, however, who are impacted by technology. A decade after the emergence of smartphones, Facebook, and Twitter, more than four out of five adults in the U.S. (86 percent) report they constantly or often check their email, texts, and social media accounts. The American Psychological Association's (2017) report on "Stress in America" suggests the results of the study are correlated with confirmed elevations in stress for the constant checkers.

We had students brainstorm things that can help you stay on the "path to feeling better." They had lots of great ideas: getting hugs, watching sunsets, eating sandwiches, breathing, going swimming, playing with friends, talking about the hurt, looking at pictures of your loved ones, staying grounded with your cultural and spiritual practices, and crying.

Engagement has become a popular marketing catchphrase for ed tech companies hoping to increase the number of sustained users. As our reliance, dependence, and addiction to technology grows, so does their profit. We don't yet seem concerned with how we are using technology in education, ensuring it's a catalyst and not a replacement for actual engagement.

The responsible use of technology will be revisited, allowing us to further consider the impact of social media, cell phones, and other devices on the development of PSEL. For now it's enough to appreciate that holding feelings in abeyance may be compromised by our inundation with technology and our strong appetite for all things faster.

Our increasing reliance, dependence, and addiction to technology makes it more difficult for educators to provide stimulating academic work in the classroom, always searching for how to compete with the seduction of constant action. If we want to learn how to hold feelings in abeyance and improve our capacity for distress, we have to make it a priority. If we don't, the frequency of trauma will grow because our threshold for enduring feelings will continue to decline.

I don't recommend this pathway to develop your abilities to hold space. If I had a magic wand, I would wish that no one had to experience pain like this ever again. Unfortunately, I know that many people are reading this and knowing this suffering. It is a club that you would never want to join. There are opportunities daily to be present with another and to deeply feel what they are striving to express. To put your needs and feelings on pause in lieu of offering time for someone to be heard is a true honor. It could be the greatest gift you give to someone else. It is the deepest act of service that you can provide.

Holding feelings in abeyance and the emotional catharsis that comes with learning patience to delay action is instrumental in all facets of life. Our relationships will be deeper; our peace will be more easily accessible; and our ability to endure discomfort—the counterpart to this PSEL—will be enhanced.

Key Points

▶ In a world of immediacy, where information is available on demand, it is increasingly important for children to learn how to wait.

▶ We have "googleized" our children, lacking the skills for discernment.

▶ Learning how to delay gratification is accomplished through containing one's feelings without immediate resolution.

▶ When children have difficulty with self-regulation or self-control, they generally act before considering, speak before thinking, or feel without exploring.

▶ At the core of this trouble to self-regulate or control our behavior is emotional endurance.

▶ Fortitude to stay with a feeling without acting on our impulse to remediate is important.

▶ Waiting one's turn in a conversation is an example of how children learn this social emotional learning (SEL).

▶ The capacity to hold feelings in abeyance amounts to containing excitement and harnessing one's own enjoyable energy.

▶ Remember that we never label feelings as positive and negative (good or bad) because they are all natural and have value. Labeling makes exploration more difficult.

Discussion Questions

Whether using the book for professional development (PD) or within a book group, please consider the following questions to stimulate your own ideas for exploration.

1. What surprised me most when reading through the chapter?

2. What was a time I was excited and had difficulty keeping the feeling contained?

3. What was a time I felt concerned and wanted to rescue a student?

4. What are the limitations of rescuing a student from experiencing emotional distress?

5. Who is a student you suspect had difficulty holding feelings in abeyance, and why?

Improving Tolerance for Distress

CHAPTER
10

(Melissa P. is a high school English teacher from New Jersey.)

A teacher with even just a year of experience will easily recognize the following scenario. It's a typical interaction that may have occurred between one of my seniors and me early in my career teaching high school English.

Student A: Why is this assignment so much work? This isn't fair, and it's stupid.

This out-of-the blue comment appears to be a direct attack from one of my seniors. My body tingles. My face gets hot. My stomach feels tight. I know this means danger. I must defend myself.

Me: This is a college-level class. Do you plan to go to college next year?

Student A: Yeah.

Me: Well, then, this is good practice at time management. If you can't handle this, you're going to struggle when you have to do three papers a week next year. The reason why this is fair is because I'm preparing you for your future. As far as the assignment being "stupid," if you're having trouble with it, that doesn't mean it's stupid. The assignment is asking you to—

Student A looks mollified and settles in to do his work.

Student B: Well, I'm going to be an electrician, so why do I have to do this?

Me: Because you took a college-level class.

At first glance, this interaction doesn't seem so bad. It didn't end in a detention or a discipline referral, and I got the students to stop complaining and do their work. But when I look back at it now, I see some sorely missed opportunities that would have not only deepened their understanding but deepened our human connection.

When I started teaching high school English twenty-eight years ago, I was twenty-two years old. I went into my profession with a love of kids and a passion for the literature that had ushered me into a world that matched the complexities and sensitivities of my own inner dialogue. I wanted to share it with kids. I wanted to inspire them about literature and about life. I had a lot of shiny new pedagogical skills and the wisdom gained by some tough life experiences, but what I did not yet have were the insights that time and a lot of learning about my deeper emotional landscape would bring. My success in the classroom could never have happened without this exploration.

Because I grew up with a bipolar and borderline mother, I learned at an early age to pack away my gut instinct and my emotional needs and to tune in acutely to the moods and needs of others. Already a highly sensitive child, my senses were further fine-tuned to heed basic survival instincts: How safe was my environment? This was a moment-by-moment necessity, and I learned to detect my mother's mood by the way she closed a door. Her erratic swings would bring our household to a halt, and someone was always to blame.

One of my earliest memories is resting my forehead on the doorknob of her bedroom door—about eye level at my age—and building up my courage to open the door and to stand looking at her grim, impassive face on the pillow while I apologized for whatever I did that time to make her stop being my mom. I still remember the fear I felt: my pounding heart, my shaking hands. Pushing past those sensations would have far-reaching effects—both good and bad. My dad, powerless and ineffectual, had told me I must make this apology. I had been the reason for her "mom strike" this time, and to get things in the house back to status quo, I was today's sacrificial lamb.

For some children growing up, opportunities are plentiful, rich with luxuries of wealth or comfort. There is nothing to want for; every want and need is provided whether earned through hard work or not. Then there are those for whom extreme deprivation or overstimulation is a constant. Lacking a stable source of food or safety, for instance, can reduce expectations of getting those and other needs met. With lesser expectations we default to protection mode, possibly viewing the world as unfair or as a threat to protect against.

While it may not be immediately apparent, neither group is well prepared for life. When we lack struggle or drown in it, our brains and bodies are out of balance, and we lean away from listening to sensations and feelings, which amplify our displeasure. Our threshold for pain is compromised because we haven't learned to regulate emotion, finding it easier to turn off the emotional spigot as opposed to making gradual adjustments.

Even when the unescapable torment of our childhood moves past and we gain greater volition over our lives, the challenges don't end. Past reminders keep us stuck in antiquated coping mechanisms on top of the daily stressors ubiquitous to adulthood. With setbacks waiting for us each day, authenticity, hope, and accessibility are perennially threatened, and if not for some degree of psychological fortitude required to evolve from surviving to thriving, we may live within the shadow of our past, obscuring the rays of hope for a better today.

Paradoxically, being the lamb always felt like the easiest role for me to play; watching other people in that position felt unbearable to me. This, too, has had lasting and life-altering implications, also good and bad. As a result of the combination of my sensitivity and my intolerance for seeing others suffer unjustly, I felt deeply compelled that my very purpose in this world was to protect others from any kind of emotional pain. It's become a great cipher to understanding my future emotional troubles that at such a tender age I thought I had that much power in the world. When you've been made to believe that you can bring the world of grown-ups to a halt by not cleaning up your blocks, it's easy to inherit a false sense of your own place in the balance and order of the universe.

The building blocks for this work begins early. When we learn to balance our brains and bodies, allowing us to link sensations with feelings and needs, our foundation for all the other need-satisfying tasks is established. Nearly parallel to this process is the ability to endure the tension arising from pleasant and unpleasant experiences or not having our needs met.

Holding feelings in abeyance is a prelude for tolerating distress. Less about when to express a feeling, tolerating distress is about our threshold to experience emotions like shame, hurt, and sadness as well as sensations that create emotional pain, without implosion or explosion. This maturation is paramount in facing both acute and chronic adversity in life without physical or psychological deterioration.

As children learn to delay gratification based on age-expected norms, waiting to express feelings to meet needs, they will also grow their potential for tolerating discomfort. Discomfort is a universal and regular experience for human beings, where gratification is less likely, and we anticipate not having our wants and needs met. In families where extremes of acute or chronic trauma become familiar, adaptation to turmoil takes a different form.

Things only worsened in my house as I got older. My mother's episodes became more frequent and more dramatic. There were episodes such as sleeping pills being wrestled out of her hands and her threatening my father with a knife. My mother said terribly abusive things to me, among them that no one would ever love me—a common insult that sometimes felt more like a prophecy to my young ears. In the meantime, it was my teachers who gave me my reason to live—the teachers who saw me and took the time to make connections. From an early age, I knew this is what I would do. I would be a teacher.

For the fortunate ones—those with sufficient tenacity to overcome the unfairness of life or the wherewithal to maintain hope when none is offered—the developmental process and corresponding skill building will continue. Many, however, are not so lucky, succumbing to the misfortune with harmful coping outlets like substance abuse, mental health problems, and debilitating self-doubt. These are the people who just couldn't endure what life presented, or the glimmer of hope was too faded to guide their decisions.

When I was eighteen years old, my dad died just two and a half months after being diagnosed with a cancerous brain tumor. Two weeks later, my mother disowned me, going so far as to make me remove from the house every personal item of mine, every photo album, every trinket I had ever given her—every trace of my existence. She said she wished I were never born. This wasn't the first time she had told me this—just the first time she tried to annihilate me from her physical environment as well as her emotional one.

Although the grief of the loss of my father to cancer and my mother to mental illness washed over me in intense waves throughout this time, being on my own was the best thing that had ever happened to me. Being out of that toxic environment and finding a good therapist to help me to begin working through years of emotional abuse brought the worst of my anxiety and panic attacks to a halt. I began to thrive.

I graduated college with honors twenty-eight years ago, married my high school sweetheart two days later, started my job teaching high school English that fall, and went on to have two kids. The toughest moments of my childhood had given me some self-confidence. Looking back on what I had come out of, I could clearly recognize my own innate optimism and resiliency to survive as a person with good motives, strong values, a heightened sense of empathy, and a pathological desire to keep others from suffering. I had pluck, grit, and resolve. What I didn't have was a full understanding of the more subtle psychological processes at work.

The benefits to enduring higher levels of emotional pain are largely unknown to people yet correspond to every aspect of our lives. If we can endure pain, we can prevent ordinary relationship problems from devolving into disrepair. We can put up with disparities at work, preventing us from irrevocable missteps. We can remain grounded when catastrophe envelops us or the continuous strangeness of the world puts our stability at risk. And for the everyday residual strain of our personal and professional lives, the ability to tolerate higher levels of distress allow us to remain intentional about our actions, making constructive choices instead of reacting instinctively out of fear.

While my intentions were always pure, my dysfunctional upbringing left me with an emotional myopia. I thought I had stepped carefully

*into a marriage that would be a move away from the emotional pat-
terns of my parents, only to find out that it mirrored it in ways I never
could have foreseen. Ten years ago, after eighteen years of trying to
save my husband by sacrificing myself the way I had learned to do as a
"good daughter," I let go of him and our highly dysfunctional marriage
and began to do the hardest work of my life.*

*I've come to know that a healthy brain is one in which—
figuratively speaking—all the doors are open, and the rooms are well
informed of each other. Emotional wholeness can't happen without
that. I've also come to know that it's possible to think they're all
open—to be sure of it—only to realize that all along there are doors
that remain tightly closed. It's finding the closed doors and working
to understand what's behind them that the work of social emotional
learning (SEL) begins.*

Life can seem unbearable at times, and when we can't link the pain
with anything immediate it's even more disconcerting. If our reactions
are disproportionate or our reflex to self-protect seems premature in
retrospect, we may be dangerously close to one of those locked doors
that we believe are keeping us safe.

Whether that perceived threat is a circumstance outside of our
control or curbing our own internal drives and impulses, differentiating between what is real and what is imagined takes constant attention
and the help of trusted supports who can help us gauge our filter. If we
can identify what triggers are touching off unresolved feelings, we have
hope to reign in our protective response and be more deliberate about
our actions.

This is one of the jolting realities for people who are decades
removed from early life experiences. Even when our hard work leads to
success, managing to break free of the roles which confined us, our work
is still incomplete. People can be remarkably resilient, but this doesn't
mean we will thrive if at the core is a bruised and battered person who
isn't prepared for yet another emotional injury.

*The therapy I found early in life was triage. It helped me to stop the
bleeding of my most obvious and immediate wounds inflicted from
growing up under the emotional trauma that comes from having a
bipolar, borderline mother and a passive, ineffectual father. Twenty-
eight years ago when I became a teacher, I thought that my early work
in therapy had given me the insights I had needed to go forward on
a path away from the generations-old cycle of dysfunction that had
followed my parents to the place where they had raised me. Life taught
me otherwise. The therapy I found later in life was more like the science of archaeology. My therapist and I became a team, surveying,
excavating, and analyzing the data we discovered in the rubble hidden
behind those closed doors. Our tools were time, a swivel chair, a couch,
and boxes and boxes of tissues.*

This emotional integration has increased my ability to be an impactful and effective educator in ways that are incalculable. Over the past twenty-eight years, I have worked with over 3,500 adolescents, all with their own struggles, their own closed doors, and all during a time in their development where their depth of understanding and their impulse control is limited by their still-developing brains.

I've come to understand the level of influence that kindness, patience, and a complex emotional understanding has on kids. For some of them, it's oxygen. I know this because I was one of the kids who needed that from my teachers. I know this, too, because of the many students who have kept in touch with me over the years to tell me that during that time in their lives they needed emotional understanding even more than comma skills or an understanding of Romeo and Juliet.

Skilled educators will have a range of approaches to employ when student challenges confront them. Self-reflective educators are the ones who can look deep inside themselves to recognize what is being stirred up through student interactions, allowing them to better intuit what those children are needing.

We can estimate that 95 percent of what a person is going through cannot be seen through their actions alone. People are too complex, even young people who have personality factors, temporal conditions, early life experiences, and a constellation of intra- and interpersonal dynamics that influence any given event. Also invisible to us adults are the internal struggles to modulate pain, filter data, or inhibit our impulse to self-protect.

Similar to a thermostat that turns on the air-conditioning to a certain temperature, our own internal regulatory system will kick in when our tension level rises to an intolerable level. As an evolving adult, improvement in this area means not rushing to the fire extinguishers when we see glowing embers—or more aptly, the case for many adults is not resorting to behaviors that distract us away from the embers. Gaining mastery of this process is a lifetime of work but is crucial if we are going to be healthy enough to model and support the SEL of students.

Right from the outset of my career—before my most intense work in therapy—it was clear that the pain I had endured in childhood would help me connect to my students in a way that other teachers—ones with enviable childhoods—couldn't. This has held true throughout my career. I know that a child may have way more going on behind the scenes than anyone could ever guess. Because of my practice in detecting even the slightest energy shifts, I can tell when students may be going through something they're not talking about. I can detect their pain and speak to it so well that I've taken many kids by surprise.

But these by-products of my experience are double-edged swords. My overly sensitive nature means that I can detect others' hurt, but it also means that my feelings are easily hurt. Because I was held to impossible standards, I could always easily forgive others' mistakes; however, until therapy, I didn't feel worthy enough to be forgiven for mine. Subconsciously I was driven to extreme perfectionism and an overly sweet disposition formed to prevent conflict and feelings of shame or unworthiness of any kind. As a child, someone's displeasure with me for the slightest reason meant total abandonment and a direct threat to my survival. I still fight those feelings now, but what I've come to understand is that I am worthy of making mistakes, of being human. I'm worthy of asserting my own feelings of displeasure, and that conflict is a necessary and healthy part of every relationship. It is where true connection is born. It's taken a lot of personal anguish to get to this point of understanding.

As humans who live our lives in figurative houses where some rooms are frequently used and others become dusty with the residue of old hurts, we instinctively choose early on what areas of our home we will inhabit and which we will avoid. When we close doors to insulate us from pain, we are acting instinctively, unaware of what limitations these healthy reflexes may produce down the road. What has helped us survive early in our lives will invariably be the barriers to wholeness in our adulthood.

This cordoning off of our suspected acceptable and unacceptable "parts" leaves us fragmented, showing the world only those aspects of ourselves we are comfortable with, burying the others under piles of clutter. Whether we are too afraid or lack sufficient confidence to form a solid sense of self, we are limited in how well we can respond to the pain of others when cut off from our own.

The first step on my journey to getting healthy was to identify my own deeply submerged feelings and opinions. Since my goal had been to make no waves, these were things I hadn't even needed to consider. My opinions had been everyone else's. However, now that I was getting healthy, I needed to know where I started and ended and where others began. When I didn't have boundaries, I could be an easy target for others, and sometimes it led to being taken advantage of. As I started to find my voice, I made a lot of mistakes working through how to be assertive without being aggressive. I had opened up a floodgate— feelings that I hadn't even known were trapped behind those closed doors. Once I did, I didn't know how to share my feelings and my experience of others in a constructive way.

Some colleagues who had known me for many years began to wonder what had happened to me and, rather than confronting me, began to shut me out and talk about me. These teachers, altruistic and well-intentioned at heart, have also formed their personalities and interpersonal habits around their own closed doors and their instincts toward reducing stress in whatever way possible. Teaching is a rewarding profession, but even in the best of school environments, it can be incredibly enervating and stressful. People need a release and a way to feel connected to each other. Sadly, gossip fits those needs, and it's an ugly reality in the workplace.

Each school has its own culture and corresponding degree of organizational health. What may seem healthy to one, however, may not be to others. If a person grows up in a divided family where it's expected to take sides between parents during conflicts, a school environment with solid cliques may seem perfectly appropriate, especially if this subgrouping leaves a safe and stable feeling. To another, this organizational fragmentation may stir up the very insecurity that comes from a chaotic home, too threatening to ever feel safe no matter what group they belong to.

In an organization where self-reflection isn't encouraged, the boundaries, roles, communication patterns, decision-making processes, and every other facet of the working environment will be affected. As human beings with basic needs, including a sense of belonging, we will create milieus reflected of the level of evolvement we have achieved as individuals. This cumulative effect will set the tone for the entire building climate. This is the intersection of individual wellness and organizational health with strong influence over how we experience our jobs, invest in our work, and give back to our students.

No matter how skilled we are at stimulating learning, how knowledgeable we are about our field of study, or how much passion we bring to the classroom, no individual can optimally engage in their work when they are protecting themselves from other adults whom they work closely with. Our capacity for distress can only endure for so long before an erosion of happiness and confidence inundates us.

It was easy to know that I was the subject of gossip. When I walked into the teacher's room, the conversation would stop. When there was conversation, it wasn't with me; it was in whispers to each other. At work, my fight-or-flight response was always fully activated. I didn't feel safe, and this left me feeling utterly devastated.

My husband (I remarried seven years ago) offered all the support he could, but he was confused about why what seemed to him like petty gossip would have me this emotionally shattered after all that I had survived in my life. I searched for a way to explain my feelings to him and realized that being the target of gossip felt more than emotionally unsafe; it felt dangerous on a primal level. As I heard myself say it aloud, I thought it sounded melodramatic, but it ended up being a key realization and the beginning of enormous personal growth.

In therapy I talked about how somewhere just under the surface I felt that I deserved this treatment and that my mother's predictions had come true: No one could love me. This workplace gossip was not only personal rejection and isolation from social connection but a mirroring of my childhood abandonment. It felt like a threat to my survival.

To add to that, I discovered that while I was feeling deep down that I wasn't worthy of love, I had also created a concurrent and contradictory narrative that I was an undeserving victim of cruelty and that these women were villains. This uncovered another huge portion of the rubble from behind those closed doors. In my childhood, my bipolar mother had created a world of perfect heroes and unworthy villains. With my baby food I had absorbed the notion that even just one mistake made me a villain. The story I was telling myself now fit right into this antiquated paradigm, and I came to understand that not only did I expect perfection from myself but I expected it from others. The minute I could see this clearly, a veil began to be lifted from my eyes. I had made mistakes from my limitations, and however horribly mean the gossip seemed, these women had made mistakes from theirs.

Psychosocial emotional development is a complex lifelong task that often requires help from others. The Johari window helps us to appreciate that we are limited in how much we can know about ourselves without feedback from others. In the Johari window, we have four quadrants representing what is known to ourselves and others, with the goal of greater transparency and self-awareness.

And when our batteries are running low, a jump start from a caring other can provide the lift we need to continue progressing. The mental churn and emotional energy to keep ourselves looking inward, attending to our protective mechanisms so they don't automatically kick in when we are trying to be accessible, can fatigue us.

Changing old scripts and building new paradigms requires additional tolerance for distress because we are leaning outside our comfort zone. No matter how much pain and "stuckedness" our current belief system provides, the familiarity of what we have always known and done may trump the unknown. For this reason, it's vital to have a support system to engage in midair refueling for the long journey. With borrowed energy, greater insight, and new skills to practice, we can engage in important experiments to try out new, more productive ways of getting our needs met.

It was time to try to mend things, and I felt ready to do it. So many months of being socially isolated by a peer group at work had functioned as immersion therapy. I had been tasked to endure my biggest unconscious fear: social abandonment. At first it had felt like nearly unbearable agony, but I eventually got to a place beyond the mere intellectual concept of being worthy. For the first time I started to really believe it—even in the face of group rejection. As I made plans to have individual conversations with the women at work, I knew I needed to divorce myself from any outcome of my attempts at making peace. It was the attempt itself that was important for my own growth. I went into each conversation with purity of intention, and I took responsibility for my role in the dynamic that had played out. I had a different experience with each woman I talked to, but what remained the same was the melting of the ice between us. For some women, it was a slow thaw over time. For most of them, it was immediate.

Therapy has taught me that the tools of survival I used as a child are now antiquated. They have become impediments to wholeness and true connection. Instead of using them, I have new tools in my inventory:

▶ *While I'm still hard on myself, I now focus on wholeness, not perfection.*

▶ *Listening to my body is essential. It has a way of telling me when a need is being submerged, and instead of ignoring these sensations as I had been conditioned to do, I take the information and use it to negotiate my needs with others.*

▶ *My body also has a way of telling me when old stuff is being triggered. I've learned that it's imperative to distinguish between old and new emotional pain. When my hurt feelings trigger a wound from childhood, I work to identify it as such and to avoid being swept up in the pain of the past so that I can put it into a realistic perspective.*

▶ *My pathological urge to save everyone has evolved into a compassionate empathy and moved away from self-sacrifice.*

▶ *My people pleasing and overexplaining is a protective mechanism to stave off rejection and is not a way of making meaningful contact with others. Even if people don't like me, I am still safe and worthy. I am now free to be myself.*

▶ *Anger has high tides and low tides. I need to allow the high tide but wait for the low tide to begin a constructive conversation.*

▶ *Others' moods and reactions aren't always about me. I don't have the power my parents led me to believe I had. When someone is moody or upset, it's not my fault, and although I can offer concern and goodwill, it's not my job to make them happy.*

▶ *Sometimes conflict in a relationship is coming from my own emotional triggers, and sometimes it's coming from the other person's emotional triggers. A safe conversation allows for exploration of what part of a conflict is mine to own and what part is theirs.*

Working on improving our tolerance for distress is a complex task for even the most self-aware individuals. The intricacy and nuance of strengthening this invisible psychological musculature is often helped through professional guidance, and even then it seems there are few clinicians who can effectively identify the importance of this work.

This should lead us to question how to best help students to be successful in navigating this difficult evolution of psychosocial emotional learning (PSEL) and what educators need in order to equip themselves with the best tools for the job. Like everything else, the better we know ourselves and are actively engaged in this work, the more easily we will develop sensitivities for what students may also value.

If we begin with a general appreciation for young people for whom resiliency is not yet ideal, we can better appreciate what former or current forces are responsible. Using their behavior as a window into their soul, we can begin this speculation. When a child's tolerance for distress is low, the likelihood is greater to act impulsively, turn to exclusive aggression (a future PSEL), or regress under pressure through less age-expected responses. Children who don't endure discomfort well may overreact to adults and peers, misinterpret situations, give up too easily, make excuses, and diminish others for personal gain.

As educators it's critical to remember that we aren't tending just to the child but to the environment this child is raised in. As does the mindful gardener, we want to treat the class like a garden, constantly assessing the density of nutrients in the soil.

The skills I've learned have made me effective in the classroom in ways that extend far past the subject that I teach. My students have told me that they feel safe in my classroom. I believe this is partly due to the way that I resolve conflict when it presents itself, even in the smallest ways. Asking a student to put away a cell phone can escalate into a discipline referral, or it can become an opportunity to build trust and respect.

Instead of getting into a power struggle with students, I'm able to focus on what's driving their behavior. I know that if a student is acting out, there's always something going on emotionally.

Student:	Why is this assignment so much work? This isn't fair, and it's stupid.
	This appears to be a direct attack from one of my seniors. My body tingles. My face gets hot. My stomach feels tight. I recognize these sensations. They're alerting me to old wounds. I realize that deep down I fear that he may be right. Maybe I have no idea what I'm doing. What if I really messed up here? An old reaction would be to dig in and launch a polite defense, going into a long, careful explanation of all my reasoning behind assigning it. Instead, I acknowledge the trigger of my old fears and move past them. I do know what I'm doing. I have twenty-nine years of experience, and I was thoughtful and intentional in designing this

assignment. This attention to my bodily sensations, my initial impulses, and the sorting out of old and new helps me to know that I should be confident yet remain open to feedback, curious about what's driving him, and compassionate, not defensive, in addressing him.

Me: I hear that you're upset about this. I'd like to talk just the two of us for a minute.

I motion to the classroom door.

He huffs, rolls his eyes, and stomps over to meet me outside the door.

Me: I'm concerned and curious about why you're so angry. I'm open to hearing what you have to say, but I need you to say it in a way that helps me to stay with you in this conversation.

His face softens, but he's still cautious.

Student: This is just a lot. That's all. And I really don't see the point in it. I graduate in two months, and this has nothing to do with what my major will be. And I have work every night this week and don't even get home until 10:00.

Me: I'm glad you shared that with me. I hear you. That sounds overwhelming. First, please know that if you need an extension because you have so much other stuff going on, you can always come to me and we can discuss it. I care that you're going through that. The value of this assignment is another conversation altogether, which I'm glad to discuss.

Conversations like this don't just impact that particular student. The success of the interaction extends to the other kids' sensing their own emotional safety in my classroom. Students learn that their needs and feelings matter and that if they stumble in their outlet of these emotions, I will help them. Because I feel innately worthy, I can humble myself, I can be authentic, I can remain curious and compassionate rather than defensive. This is what kids need in order to be authentic as well. When kids feel that their feelings are valued and that they are safe from shame, something like magic happens in the classroom. Students not only become open to learning; they are willing to take emotional and educational risks.

Being curious and compassionate are two of the most important elements of a successful teacher-student relationship. To remain open, when faced with resistance (the forces for change and sameness), opposition, or subversion, it takes an adult with a high capacity for discomfort and a recognition that we can't personalize. In the most personal of professions, where our success is directly correlated with our personal and professional worth, this is no small task.

An improved tolerance for distress is potentially the most important of all the PSELs because, in part, it's the least understood or addressed. A low tolerance for distress may be the single most important determinant of health, happiness, and peace. Conversely, our susceptibility for psychological dis-ease is also linked to our low tolerance, similar to a poor immune system and the onset of illness.

Even in therapy, where the focus is on personal growth, people seldom identify a "higher tolerance for distress" as their intended goal. However, it is the foundational work for every person—whether they recognized it or not—and hinges on their success. How else will people learn to lean into discomfort, take important risks, or explore their pain if they won't experience their discomfort. Unfortunately, only a small percentage of people doing personal growth work have this PSEL in their awareness—largely because helping professionals aren't aware themselves.

From the influence of managed care and pharmaceutical companies who promote a more prescriptive method of *treatment*, to the graduate schools producing solution-oriented approaches for their students, clients and patients in therapy are less likely to explore etiology or the source of their struggles through professional personal growth work.

This also means that school guidance counselor and child study teams are also at a disadvantage; whether it's their own evaluative process or reliance on community providers for intervention, the likelihood of getting to this core PSEL as part of growth is unlikely. And if we aren't addressing resilience through intervention, we are even less likely to address it through prevention.

There is another important reason for improving our tolerance for distress, having to do with the increasing complexity of life's opportunities. Similar to the board game Monopoly, if we want to stay in the game longer, we need to spend money on properties. In life, we have to spend emotional capital through time and energy, to build up our reserves.

If we want to build a loving relationship, we need to risk through trust, such as sharing our inequities and frailties, explored in a later chapter. These types of risk often go unrewarded, or worse, they result in more pain. At these moments we are faced with a choice: to never love again or to wait until we heal to try again.

A person's natural risk-taking, to achieve higher-order needs, is a direct result of how much distress we can tolerate. If a child or adult can't or doesn't believe they can tolerate distress, they are less likely to take risks needed for achieving fulfillment, peace, and meaning.

There is tremendous value in raising our capacity for discomfort. When we can endure higher thresholds for emotional pain, we can be more intentional, finding constructive choices for action, which is the basis for living a well-purposed life. An educator who can endure the misbehavior of a child or the inconsistency of a school leader without reacting can be experimental in creating best practices.

Emotional safety opens for students a limitless space of creativity, imagination, and insight. This is the kind of fertile learning environment that produces true scholars, and it's only possible when their teacher has the social and emotional tools to navigate the tough situations that arise in every classroom. For me, those tools were numerous, but none were more important than a greater capacity to endure emotional distress.

As we grow our self-awareness—becoming more accepting of our inequities and frailties—we will inherit self-confidence, building our identity as adaptable. Such flexibility serves us personally and professionally with our students, modeling for them greater accountability and the resulting depth of relatedness. Distress is a crucial ingredient helping us feel proud of what we have overcome to reach this state of openness.

For those who have taken yoga, you may be familiar with the expression "set your intention." This refers to the idea that we make bodily awareness figural, sensing where we are tight or how deeply we are breathing. The result of such awareness is nearly always beneficial, finding relief or obstacles needing to be navigated.

Eating is the most global example we can all relate to, because it's the most shared experience of attempting to satisfy a need contingent on our self-awareness. A young woman who eats to satisfy a sense of emptiness in her stomach helps us to appreciate just how easy it is to misinterpret our body and increase our internal tension. As the young woman becomes purposeful, or mindful about her eating, she may realize that her sense of emptiness is loneliness and not hunger. If she can resist eating to distract from the loneliness, tolerating the distress, she may discover what actions would better satisfy her unmet need.

Recall that it all begins with brain-body balance, growing our ability to scan our own body to gain information about sensations that inform our needs. Putting that information to use requires discernment of thoughts versus feelings and holding back to deliberate our best course of action. The more opportunities children have to develop these skills and capacities, the better they will overcome early life experiences that taught them the world may be unjust.

Key Points

▶ Whether it's expecting an immediate response to a text message or looking information up online, we don't do well waiting—and we are getting worse.

▶ When a child's tolerance for distress is low, the likelihood is greater to act impulsively, turn to aggression (the bad kind to be explained later), or regress under pressure.

▶ An improved tolerance for distress is at the core for all the other PSELs.

▶ A person's natural risk-taking (to achieve greater levels of happiness and fulfillment) is a direct result of how much distress they can tolerate.

▶ If children or adults can't or doesn't believe they can tolerate distress, they are less likely to take the important risks for growth.

▶ People seldom learn how to raise their threshold for discomfort, but doing so can reduce anxiety, depression, addictions, and nearly every other stress-induced pathology.

Discussion Questions

Whether using the book for professional development (PD) or within a book group, please consider the following questions to stimulate your own ideas for exploration.

1. How naturally good am I with tolerating emotional discomfort?

2. Would I rather experience physical or emotional pain, and why?

3. What was a time my capacity for distress was low, and why was that?

4. How have I increased my tolerance for distress over the years?

5. Who in my life do I look up to with having a high threshold for psychological pain?

CHAPTER 11

Stimulating Self-Reflective Practices

(Jacob Barry is an educator working in Elkhorn, Nebraska.)

I went into teaching for the same reason as many others: to make a difference. Exactly what this looked like, I did not know; however, I knew from my own experience as a student that things could be done more effectively, purposefully, and meaningfully. During my culminating undergraduate project, I researched and presented on the idea of what could be called a transcendental constructivist reform of education— an educational reform that was innovative and empowering, one that encompassed research-based practices, high expectations, and applicable learning experiences for all students. Along with that, an overall societal respect of teachers would undoubtedly ensue. My research did not prepare me for the truth I would learn once I became less naive about the realities of the teaching profession.

Awareness is the key to intentionality. Awareness plays a role in calibrating where we are along the brain-body continuum— appreciating how sensations are connected with feelings and needs— recognizing the difference between curbing impulses and modulating emotion, and assessing our tolerance for discomfort or distress. Through every facet of our introspection and self-exploration, we can be measured in how we adapt to the world, becoming more successful in meeting our wants and needs while learning from disappointment.

We begin with consideration for how to increase our awareness to become more intentional, which for some may be instinctive but for most is a learned experience, sharpened with practice. The responsibility is shared between child and adult, only successful with active work on the part of the individual with modeling and guidance from parents and educators.

Success in using self-reflection means greater ease in building a solid but flexible sense of self, growing self-worth for important risk-taking. As we grow through each psychosexual, intellectual, and moral stage of development, our psychosocial emotional learning (PSEL) creates an iterative process that recycles with regular opportunities for improvement at each juncture.

I took my first job. I did this as all early career educators do: setting out with an unrealistic optimism to change the world one student at a time. I would be the teacher to reach through to all my students. I even had what I felt was an amazing opportunity at the time to semi-skip student teaching and simply jump right into the profession. To me, this was a sign of the success sure to come. I would soon find out just how wrong I was.

Distinguishing the real from the ideal relies upon our brain-body balance where energy is divided between what is believed and what is experienced. An unhealthy progression with poor balance may lead us away from our bodies overcontrolling situations with excessive worry to prevent perceived harm. The risk for those who look outward versus inward, meaning less self-reflection, is covert manipulation to meet our wants and needs rather than sensing and expressing with greater transparency.

Struggling to stay afront and transcend a steep learning curve, the challenges of the classroom mounted and morale waned. Just like so many young educators, I found myself spending countless hours focused on my classroom, my students, and the extra duties with which I was expected to assist. Regardless of the amount of time I spent preparing for lessons and grading papers, I began to feel more and more ineffective. Like many young educators, the errant desire for perfection engulfed me. In my mind, without perfection, my competency would be questioned. As the hours accumulated, my family (at the time, a wife and two sons) became further and further secondary priorities. The pressure mounted to succeed. I was burning the candle at both ends. I was losing motivation. I was running on fumes. I was alone.

With a dwindling flame, I finished the school year, planning to return to the classroom trenches in a new district. Over the summer, the fire was rekindled, and I, again, found a hope to change the lives of the students I had the opportunity to work with. However, my wick was already spent. As the year progressed, I finally lost the flame completely, pining for the grass on the other side of the fence that appeared greener. At the end of my second year of teaching, I became part of the growing statistic of burnt-out early career educators to leave the profession.

With any meaningful evolution through these developmental stages allowing us to take on complex life decisions, we require a heightened level of insight and awareness. Our awareness begins with listening to our bodies to appreciate the meaning of sensations, growing to a recognition of when we are meeting wants or needs. With awareness we can learn to regulate our emotions and delay before taking action in order to be deliberate. Through insight we can make meaning of our emerging awareness.

Self-awareness is equally valuable for improving relationships; for children this may be peers and family, and for adults we include coworkers, supervisors, and parents. Self-reflection allows us to know ourselves more completely and as we age to sense how others view us. When we can see ourselves clearly in relation to others, we can understand our motives, their motives, and the protective mechanisms we both employ to keep ourselves safe.

Outside the classroom, I pursued many interests to earn an income: financial planning, umpiring, and copyediting, to name a few. At the end of August, I took a job that I would work for the next year at a communications company as a technical support specialist. To put it in blatant terms, I was the guy people called when their phone, Internet, or cable was not in working order. My job was to work with the customer to troubleshoot and fix the problem.

Throughout my time in technical support, I found myself excited about learning again. Technology has always piqued my interest, and now I had the opportunity to immerse myself and learn from so many others that knew much more than I did. Formally, I was trained to understand the different codes and systems for the company and how to best troubleshoot malfunctioning equipment. During this process, I kept taking mental notes about worthwhile learning opportunities for the different projects and activities we participated in during the training process. It was at that point that I knew I belonged back in the classroom. I had unfinished business as an educator.

As an educator, we can thrive off of the energetic exchanges with students, made easier when we appreciate how they perceive us, what projections they are making, and what biases they may be placing upon us. To see ourselves clearly in relation to others, we first have to look inward to appreciate how we are perceiving the other. What unconscious motives of race, gender, ethnicity, and sexual orientation do we carry? What behaviors are most off putting to us, and why? Who does the person remind us of, and what instinct do we sense in how we may protect ourselves from them? A simple exercise is to think of the student we most would like and least would like in our class and then recognize the characteristics we are drawn to and repelled from and why.

Once we appreciate our own projections, we can imagine the same for the other. How are they experiencing us in all of the same ways? We may speculate about these questions or gather the data more directly through dialogue. With educators, we aren't used to looking through the eyes of children to see ourselves, but doing so is an extremely valuable tool for understanding their attitudes and behaviors, especially toward us.

Everything a student does, every attitude they exude, every characteristic they display is all going to impress upon us in some way. Consider how much time we spend in reflection upon how those qualities influence how we, in turn, feel toward the child. If the student elicits some strong reaction within us, how will we use that information to support the child's growth, which is far more useful than judging if we can endure our own displeasure.

Since no schools were hiring in August, I put my name in as a substitute. I worked the second shift—3:30 p.m. to 12:00 a.m.—so I could substitute by day and work technical support by night. As I learned the ins and outs of being a technical support representative, I realized I had forgotten the most important piece of being a teacher: I was still a learner. It was okay to make mistakes. It was okay not to know everything. The hardest pill for me to swallow was that I had to be willing to admit when I was wrong.

Beyond that, I awoke to the fact that learning was about the experience, not just the content. I had to create a better experience in my classroom for my students and for myself—one that constantly reinvigorated me as a teacher and inspired my fellow learners. I had found a new lens that showed possibilities, as opposed to the lens of perfectionism through which I could only see impending failure. I stepped back into the classroom as a substitute, willing to attack any problems openly and with unparalleled optimism. Each day was a chance for a new learning experience—for me and for my students. We were now all on this learning journey together. I had finally boarded the train.

On this train, I worked double-duty days, substituting and working full-time. I was physically exhausted, but I was more alive than I had ever been. My excitement boiled over as I thought more divergently and openly about the challenges inside my classroom that I would have the opportunity to tackle alongside my students. We could work together as a team. We could learn content but through more natural methods of learning. Learning, after all, is a marathon, not a sprint. It takes time, and there are often growing pains, but I realized that within the pain could also be time to enjoy the roses and all the other flowers—to simply have fun and relish the journey. Not every day had to be a race day—a day to put our noses to the grindstone. We would need to find a balance. Otherwise, burnout was sure to find all of us learners and extinguish the flames of enthusiasm, squashing our hopes, ambitions, and optimism for the future.

Self-reflective practitioners are successful instructors, supervisors, and counselors, forging intimate relationships with peers and adults. Instead of reacting, self-reflective practitioners are proactive, anticipating our own instincts before acting. We exhibit self-control based on our growing awareness of how to better get our needs met rather than self-protecting to prevent the possibility a need won't be met.

Like the phoenix, I found a new fire amidst my own ashes, and a spark of passion was renewed for education. I always knew students mattered and were the focal point of education, but now, through my own struggles, I also understood that teachers needed more support too. My goal was to come back to the classroom with my new experience within the business sector and help transform the lives of my students and my fellow educators. I would not allow my colleagues to find the same shortcomings as I had. The system needed to change. Supports needed to be put in place to lessen the burnout rate that seemed to be ever increasing.

Taking this knowledge and this frustration—this burning ball of energy yet to have a place to be harbored or harnessed—I was lucky enough to be offered the chance to return to the classroom. I did, and I vowed I would not leave. Challenges were sure to come, but I had a new mindset—a healthier, more resilient mindset. I would overcome those challenges and help resolve some of the difficulties faced by educators. With that, I stepped into my comeback campaign tour as a teacher.

When educators use self-reflective practices to growth their confidence and strengthen resiliency, they are better positioned to help this growth for their students. One specific way this happens is by being less reactive to the traps set up by students who test us. Let's use a seventh-grade boy to illustrate this dynamic. Joe (age twelve) is resentful toward his mother for leaving the family but not fully aware of his feelings. If he were aware, he might be able to access the hurt that underlies his protective anger. In class, he antagonizes his teacher, not realizing he is testing to see if she will abandon him as well. If the teacher is set off by his antagonizing, she might well fall into the unconscious trap he has set.

Students anticipate similar hurt from educators as they have experienced from their caregivers. The transactional games we play for protection are often hidden to us, especially as children, requiring us as adults to attend to their experience and our own. The reactions we have to the real or perceived games of students will become opportunities for contact when we are better able to appreciate our own reactions and the possible agenda for the students.

Self-reflective practitioners and parents are the key to modeling prosocial behavior for children. For many, this is an unfamiliar practice. Our eyes look outward, tapping into our brains over our bodies, analyzing behaviors instead of sensing motivations with our bodies.

Attributional biases distort our perceptions of self and others. If we become aware of these biases, we will lessen their influence over the way we treat children, which, in turn, alters their behavior. Understanding how we use these biases will model the same for children.

Self-serving bias is the tendency to view our own actions in the most favorable light, to bolster our self-esteem. The *actor-observer bias* refers to a tendency to attribute one's own actions to external causes while attributing other people's behaviors to internal causes. An example would be blaming the weather if we perform poorly in a sporting event but judging another to be less proficient under the same conditions.

Learning from self-reflection is limitless, beginning with the clarity gained of broader perspectives. Eliminating or at least reducing the tint in our lens helps bring our attitude into focus. From there we can begin to identify our other layers of distortion such as our values, interest, needs, agendas, and preferences.

From there, I found my stride and began the marathon that is the profession of education. Never had I felt so comfortable inside the classroom. I knew this was where I belonged. To solidify my choice, I was placed on a new team of teachers that pushed one another to continue to grow in best practices and truly do what was right for students. More than that, we built a community of educators that supported each other in the tough times and cheered alongside each other in the good times. I realized this was what I was missing in my first two years: community. Before I had isolated myself when, in reality, the problems I faced needed to be attacked using multiple minds with multiple perspectives, not just my own. This made teaching exciting, enjoyable, and invigorating. To this day, I still work with this amazing team of professional educators.

Exploring our strengths and limitations through multiple perspectives helps us to build coalitions to bolster our personal growth. With support, we can more easily examine challenging problems, such as why engagement is more difficult with certain students. We can explore why some students draw us in while others repel us. We can anticipate our own biases projected outward to students. Through small-group work we can excitedly overcome impediments to peaceful teaching and extend our longevity in education, even illuminating new paths.

Without education there are many routes we may take in addition to or even beyond classroom instruction. We may discover hidden passions or talents that lead us into other aspects of education. Through our reflection we generate opportunities for experimentation, sometimes in ways we never contemplated when going into education.

Upon this revelation in the second semester of my comeback tour, I found myself at the annual statewide meeting for the Nebraska State Education Association (NSEA). There, a proposal for a new group to be formed to support early career educators—NGEN (New Generation of Educators in Nebraska)—was to be voted into existence. Knowing the importance of this type of support community firsthand, I not only voted in favor of this group but I stood up and spoke to the entire assembly about the significance of an opportunity like this for new educators, sharing my story of birth, burnout, and rebirth as an educator.

As is usually the case in education, when you speak up, you are volunteered to assist. This is how I became an active member in the early stages of NGEN, of which I am now the state cochair.

There was, and still is, a lot of work to be done, but I now had a platform to channel my built-up energy and work with other passionate educators to change the landscape of schools, especially for new teachers. On top of that, I had yet another community of tremendous educators to help shape my skills and knowledge as an educator and to support me within my challenging days.

This group has been nothing short of astounding. Slowly but surely, we are working to change the landscape of education via this community. It is through connections in this community that I developed my graduate research project: setting up a successful conglomerate of educators around purposeful professional development (PD). It just so happened that the NSEA would be hosting a webinar series with this PD already created. From this, my research project was born: creating a group of educators to attend these webinars, meeting once a month to discuss strategies used, successes, and failures in the classroom. My intention was to heighten the level of self-efficacy, especially in early career educators, and to simply provide support, motivation, and a community to help better equip all educators to handle the ever-changing challenges of the classroom.

PD is inclusive of personal growth and encourages us to look inward; it is especially helpful for new teachers, who learn to appreciate sensitive buttons pushed by intuitive students. Through self-reflection and the appreciation for polarities, we might see how our extreme patience may be paired with a reticence to act. A student who is pushing limits may get too far because of our inaction, which we have labeled as kind to justify our passivity. We will use our improved understanding of self to better appreciate our feeling toward students, such as the one who gives up too quickly or the one who eagerly jumps in making careless errors.

Appreciating how every aspect of who we are—whether we are proud of it or displeased by it—comes in polarities and takes pressure off the educator. If we are organized, for instance, we may lack in spontaneity. There is not a strength without a limitation; they always come in pairs, which is a primary reason why judging, especially character traits, lacks value.

Self-reflective practices help us to appreciate our motivation and our resistance. What drives us to act and what holds us back are both important pieces of information that all people in social services can benefit from. If we are going to motivate children to look inward, we must be doing our own introspection to understand how it works and model best practices.

The basis for all learning—academic, social emotional, or moral—requires constant examination of our blind spots. Learning is about expanding our perspective, seeing the world more clearly though the tint of our own subjective lens while on the lookout for unconscious bias. Self-reflection becomes the most important element for any effective prevention strategy, growing a cohesive school community and reducing tension from discord and inequity that previously followed us home.

Currently, my family community consists of my wife, four sons, and one daughter. I am involved in a number of projects and committees at school and through the NSEA. This May, I graduated with my master's degree in curriculum and instruction with an emphasis on instructional leadership. On top of the degree, I earned an endorsement in information technology, deepening my skills in the technology I found such a passion for during my hiatus from teaching. I am busier than ever before, but I am also more energized than ever before.

Energy is heightened for problem-solving and decision-making when self-reflection leads to important breakthroughs. Major epiphanies and even daily realizations benefit those with access to a handy mirror. Math teachers may try to understand a student's thought process to appreciate how they inaccurately solved an equation. A social studies teacher may explore a student's rationale for a hypothesis for why a war had started. A science teacher will use reverse engineering to help determine why a student miscalculated a formula. Similar understanding is valuable for teaching PSEL, appreciating what the current approach is and how it may have been learned. As the paradoxical theory of change teaches us, nothing can be different until we first understand what it already is.

Consider a school with racial tension stemming in part from the disparity of minority students without diversity represented in the faculty. If a Hispanic student in this school believes that all Caucasian teachers are similarly intentioned, this myopia will be helped through adults appreciative of the student's experience. To help them grow, they must be willing to look inward, be receptive to expanding their perspective, and even be excited by the opportunities for building depth through differences; so, too, must the teachers be willing to do the same.

For those first two years of teaching, I failed to see what I truly needed as an educator. I needed a community to lean on when times were tough, to celebrate with when successes were found, and to hone new ideas with. I failed to create that community; thus, I failed to find resolve and satisfaction in my work, no matter how hard I worked. I felt isolated and did not use one of the most coveted tools in education—collaboration.

Self-reflection is important when it comes to contrasting beliefs, not possible without colleagues to collaborate with. School is a place of debate, deliberation, and discussion, exploring what is hidden to us and what those differences elicit, made more enriching and enjoyable as part of a team. If we are isolated, we may feel more unsure, treating feedback with suspicion. In this new model a supportive team treats agreeing or disagreeing as an early stage tool to begin our discovery of self within the team. The choice often comes down to the perceived safety of being isolated versus the risk of constructive differencing to grow our intimacy and drive our passion.

I failed to stimulate my passions. All I knew was school, school, school. Of course, I love school and I love teaching, but that is only one part of what makes me who I am. I failed to invigorate the other areas of my life. I failed to use outside experiences to help guide the learning experiences I was attempting to create inside my classroom.

In addition to the personal benefits of self-reflection, this PSEL will be instrumental in helping students become valued members of the workforce, a parallel process to our own professional journey. From selecting the best-fitting jobs to enhancing more symbiotic work environments, job satisfaction and success are enhanced through self-reflection. To check this hypothesis, do an informal poll of your faculty to see if the highly self-reflective teachers are the ones with tools in place to overcome obstacles and endure disruptions.

I now have habits and systems in place that help me succeed and help me refocus when necessary. When I become frustrated or overwhelmed, I no longer simply hunker down in my classroom alone. I step back and take some time to reflect. I read, write, exercise, and try new activities or recipes. I talk and deliberate tough questions with friends, family, and other people in my communities whether it is colleagues from my school, educators across the state or nation via webinars or virtual meetings, or acquaintances from other professions and industries. I look for inspiration in all my surroundings. I look for it in conversations, games, and activities with my own family at home. I look for it in webinars and podcasts, TV shows, and the news. I look for it in myself within my writing and in my past failures and successes. I look for it in magazines, journals, and books—both nonfiction and fiction; I have learned just as much from characters like Atticus Finch and Albus Dumbledore as I have from any book or article on best practices for teaching and education. I look for it in anything and everything, because I know the world will speak to me and help me if I only listen.

Adults on the lookout for growth treat each day as a new opportunity. These adults pass along their enthusiasm for soaking up the rays of knowledge to their students who learn to do the same. These students become the successful workforce of tomorrow, who come to value information that others hold for us, like a Celestine prophecy.

These same students can effectively work on teams and problem-solve in groups, which employers report as in demand. Without being overly consumed with self, students who can focus on their own task while working effectively within a group are learning a valued but lacking skill.

Facilitating teams is a significant part of an educator's day. To properly motivate students, balancing caring with authority means knowing when we are leaning too far in either direction. Other polarities including structure and freedom, external versus internal motivation, and fun versus serious are all part of an educators' repertoire, involving their ability to sense the needs of others. The constant micro adjustments teachers make during the day grow a nimble classroom, able to pivot with new information. Through a collection of highly self-reflective educators, these nimble classrooms create an agile school, adapting to any threat or opportunity encountered. Self-reflective educators understand that we are always in a state of becoming, even the organization, so we can tolerate when something is not ideal so long as we are actively working to improve. It is a valuable lesson for both teachers and students.

I no longer feel like the pressure of success falls on just me. It is me plus all my "teammates" and conspirators. Perfection has ceased to be the end goal. Learning is messy; perfection is unrealistic. To succeed, I simply have to do what I ask of my students all the time: Make connections to my surroundings and apply them to the challenges inside the classroom. I have to look at my talents and passions and listen to what the world around me is saying to ignite my own flames and the flames of my students. Experiences stemming from these reflections are those that will truly make the difference I strive for in my classroom.

Key Points

▶ Self-reflection continues the development of all the other PSELs, generating awareness for deeper insight.

▶ The more aware we are of why we feel, think, or do, the more intentional we can become about our choices.

▶ To see ourselves clearly in relation to others and to grow our social emotional skills requires understanding our motives and protective mechanisms.

▶ Self-reflective practitioners and parents are the key to modeling this for children.

▶ Looking inward to assess strengths and limitations helps us provide balanced feedback.

▶ It can be helpful to appreciate that every aspect of who we are—whether we are proud of it or displeased by it—comes in polarities.

▶ There isn't any such thing as a strength without a limitation.

    a. If we are organized, we may lack in spontaneity.

    b. If we are spontaneous, we may lack planning.

    c. We should never judge traits or characteristics.

Discussion Questions

Whether using the book for PD or within a book group, please consider the following questions to stimulate your own ideas for exploration.

1. Do males or females tend to self-reflect more, and why?

2. How much do I value introspection?

3. How often (how much time) do I practice self-reflection? Why?

4. How difficult is it in a school with all the commotion to self-reflect?

5. What have I learned about myself over the past year from self-reflection?

Helping Integrate Inequities and Frailties

(Chandra Joseph-Lacet is a new teacher developer at Boston Public Schools.)

I was eleven. She was thirty-seven. It was a night I would never forget. My mother had a stroke right in front of me. That moment and the subsequent flurry of ambulances, hospitals, and rehab centers forever changed my life and my perspective. Growing up, I was always told that because I was a Black girl, I had two strikes against me: I was Black, and I was female. My mother's illness added a third strike: poverty. I grew up in a single-parent home, with just one income and one source of strength. Now, all of that was gone. Over the course of a year and a half, I was hustled from relative to relative as my mother was transferred from one facility to another. In light of my newfound circumstance, it was clear that I needed to be twice as good and twice as strong.

Thankfully, I had always considered myself to be strong, self-assured, self-confident, and knowledgeable. My mom made sure of that. She knew what was waiting for me as a Black woman out in the world. She knew that the world could be a cruel and difficult place fraught with inequities, overt racism, sexism, and a playing field that would never be level. She taught me that the frail would be eaten alive. "Never let them see you sweat. You show up and show out. You work hard, and always, always put your best foot forward," she would say. She made it clear that my roots needed to be strong and firmly planted and my foundation secure. In life, I needed to be well grounded in who I was and what I wanted to do.

Who we become is shaped by our life experiences—some of which we recognize and consider and others we hardly give a second thought to. Perhaps they are too painful and seem safer locked away in the recesses of our mind. Suggesting we peer inside these dark spaces is not well received, especially when our life is already filled with pressure. But when we actively decide the value in transparency, both within ourselves and outwardly to the world, is valuable, we now find there are more rooms in this house to explore and expand to.

The primary value for becoming self-reflective is to appreciate how continuums of different traits and characteristics shape identity and influence self-esteem. By removing the subjective bias of good or bad, right or wrong, we can examine our strengths and limitations with greater receptivity, learning how we might use this awareness for personal growth. If we are lacking in a particular area such as self-care, we may recognize how this limitation also yields a particular strength, such as generosity. For the really adventurous soul, we tie in where we are along these continuums to the scripts we live by, written early in our lives using pens passed down from earlier generations.

My mother's counsel served me well as I navigated the world. The confidence that she instilled in me propelled my journey through elementary school, high school, college, and graduate school. I graduated summa cum laude from eighth grade. I went to and graduated from one of the top specialized exam schools in the nation. I went to college and graduate school and obtained a bachelor's degree and two master's degrees. I was taught that education was my key to success, so I amassed academic achievements, awards, honors, scholarships, and accolades despite—and perhaps because of—my circumstances. I worked hard and put my best foot forward at all times. I had to. I needed to. And I was too afraid to fail. So when I began my career in education, I was prepared, determined, and knew that I would succeed. After all, failure was not an option.

Abandoning judgment to explore polarities is more difficult when we are outcome focused or fearful of failure. While being driven to succeed is a noble pursuit and can help us overcome tremendous obstacles, it can also place additional pressure, causing us to lose enjoyment of our work. In education this burden is scaffolded by the push to be more outcome focused. Focusing on outcomes may help with accountability; however, the polarity is a lack of creativity and autonomy, both helpful in self-reflection. Grades for students, ratings for teachers, and rankings for schools fail to capture the true value of self-reflective processes and the open window this provides for developing identities.

Consider a teacher who is highly structured and always prepared, viewing organization as a key strategy for keeping students on target. If we polled the classroom parents, half will applaud this teacher who keeps everybody prepared, knowing just what to expect. This same group will feel safe and comforted with predictability. There will, however, be the other half who experience this type of efficiency as controlling, lacking in spontaneity, and even boring.

A pessimistic view might assess this conundrum as having no way to win, leaving the person feeling discouraged. A more hopeful view will find relief in knowing universal acceptance isn't ideal because it leaves us without growth opportunities, nor is it possible using the lens of polarities. There isn't such a thing as perfect, and pursuit of such an ideal creates despair. We will feel perpetually disappointed by the results and depleted by our effort of trying to please everybody. By recognizing where we fall along continuums, deciding if we want to accept or evolve, we free ourselves of this burden.

I began my education career in higher education. I worked as a student activities associate, residence director, and director of student activities. In each of these positions, I worked with students who felt academically unprepared for college. In many cases, their sentiments proved correct as they struggled to complete basic coursework. I often found myself tutoring students or editing papers for them, having book discussions, and annotating texts with them. Something was ignited in me during those years. The struggles of these students ignited a passion in me to teach.

When I stepped into the classroom for the first time as an elementary school teacher, I was ready. I had the education. I had the commitment. I had the drive. And I had the passion and desire to change the world, one class at a time. Yes, I was ready—or so I thought. I had no idea how much teaching would rock my self-confidence and expose so many of my latent personal and human frailties. I had no idea that I would be forced to question my self-worth and everything that I truly believed about myself. I had no idea that working twice as hard would not be enough to save me from the emotional trappings of teaching.

Our best instincts and intentions can unknowingly land us in positions where our dark side haunts us. Until we realize or recognize from the help of others that we are fighting an internal battle—more than an external one—we suffer in confusion. A student who uses self-reflection to appreciate how competitiveness in sports brings individual success but poor team relationships can decide if greater balance is needed. A teacher who realizes strictness is limiting trust in student relationships can decide if rigidity can be tempered. Through self-reflection we can be purposeful about where we fall on these continuums and, with work, move ourselves toward a more desirable place.

Using self-reflection to explore our inequities is most critical for appreciating our protective mechanisms—the ones that insulate us from fear of rejection, shame, hurt, and other unpleasantness. Protective mechanisms require a fair amount of energy to deploy and insulate us from getting our needs met, which we will explore more fully. Relief from the energy expenditure of self-protection can only be found in learning to make our inequities and frailties transparent, lessening our effort to hide parts of ourselves from the world.

During my first year, I, like many first-year teachers, experienced challenging days and endless nights of tears and frustration. I came to work early; I left late. I worked on lesson plans well into the night. I worked twice as hard on Sunday to make each week better than the week before for my students. I was tired. I was exhausted. I literally remember crying every night for at least the first few months that fall. I was giving teaching my absolute all, and I had nothing left. I felt awful for myself and my students. I felt like a complete failure. How much longer could I go on like this?

I vividly remember rolling up my class meeting rug one Friday afternoon, leaving for the weekend, and telling my principal that I wouldn't be returning on Monday. I had enough. I was clearly not cut out for this. I felt awful, inept, incompetent, and had NEVER EVER felt like this before. After all, I was an achiever, and I was strong. This is who I was. But there were things about teaching that absolutely broke me. And it hurt. My first year was not the last time that these feelings would come over me.

There would be several bouts of self-doubt, defeat, and feelings of incompetence over the years. And it would hurt each time. As I grew in my role, I got better at teaching and handling my professional responsibilities and varied tasks. I remained exhausted over the course of the school year, but I learned better coping strategies so that I had more balance. I was no longer staying up all night nor was I crying every day. But there were other challenges. There were challenges presented in the emotional and academic needs of my students. There were the challenges of working in underresourced schools and communities. There was the constant challenge of grappling with an educational pendulum that never rested on one curriculum for long. There was always some new protocol to follow just when you had settled into the last one. And then, there were my own life changes.

We can't rely on education to prioritize the health and wellness of educators any more than we can expect school districts to embrace organizational health overnight. The working environments for many social service institutions are client centered, and the resulting struggle for worker well-being leaves many feeling guarded, sometimes moving to survival mode. This may not be as necessary as we imagine it to be.

Imagine approaching our workplace with self-protection seeming less necessary, not acting on the instinct to insulate ourselves from harm. Consider how free we might feel if don't have to keep others at bay or maintain an illusory image that shows only what we believe others will accept. Hiding generates stress, and transparency creates peace. Once we develop the tolerance for distress that comes with the fear of judgment and the esteem not to care, we will use this peace to grow fuller integration in the service of becoming more whole.

It seems that society, school districts, and schools often forget that teachers are people too. We often talk about the "whole child," but rarely do we talk about the "whole teacher." We've moved past asking students to leave who they are and what they experience outside of the classroom door; however, teachers are not afforded the same latitude. We are expected to be on and at our best at all times, no matter what.

And sometimes, that is extremely hard. Life happens. Life happens to teachers as well, and somehow we are expected not to skip a beat. In fact, we are expected very often to leave the very essence of ourselves outside of the school and remember that we have a role to play. After all, the show must go on. Sometimes, though, teachers get sick, experience loss, or have their own personal struggles. What then? I often found myself asking this question when life happened to me.

While self-actualization may seem an unreachable ideal in the midst of turmoil, we simply need to remember to keep momentum, no matter how slow. The pinnacle of Maslow's hierarchy is a place we move toward instead of achieving. We want to embrace this idea for ourselves and for the young people we are helping to evolve in the face of disproportionate adversity. Whether students live in poverty or wealth, despair or hope, they are all facing the universally difficult life task of looking inward to discover aspects of who they are, which they consider unfavorable. Looking inward to explore those undesirable parts, believing others will not accept or even ridicule us for them, is the biggest (perceived) threat to self-worth.

With psychological, moral, and cognitive development allowing for abstract reasoning and subsequent self-reflection, preteens and teens become available to the liberating concept that frailties are assets. Appreciating frailties openly means there is nothing to protect ourselves from opening the door to greater authenticity and peace.

This may be a foreign or frightening notion for the teacher who would not dare leave her home without makeup. Imagine, however, confidently strolling about your school wearing socks with sandals, accepting your lack of fashion sense. Or imagine experiencing the excitement that comes after others know of a secret you have been carrying, unburdened from your cocoon. In most instances our liberation also comes from hearing other people share their inequities and feeling closer to you for paving the way.

To reach this point of vulnerability or perhaps better reframed as accessibility, we must be ready for the unleashing of pain we may have kept buried because it was too much to face at the time it was going on. Growing our tolerance for distress precedes this evolution of psychosocial emotional learning (PSEL) because recovering from trauma and other life pain is some of the hardest work we may ever do in our lives.

During my teaching career, I experienced the loss of a child, the loss of a parent, a sick child, an ailing parent, and many other life events. Each event took an emotional toll. Each event came with the cards and calls of condolences and care from colleagues and school leaders. Each event also came with the calls to return to school: "We need you." Each event came with the guilt of not being in my classroom, not being my best self. I distinctly remember a phone conversation with my principal within weeks of my son's death, in the midst of my mourning, being asked when I felt I would be ready to return to work. I will never forget that. I remember asking myself, "Was I not dedicated enough? Why wasn't I just pressing on?" I remember saying to myself that I needed to be strong. The guilt was almost unbearable. And the fact that I was experiencing guilt at all, given the circumstances, was unbelievable.

Initially we may lack appreciation for how frailties can help us grow. We frown at the idea of these hidden aspects of ourselves, wishing to keep them submerged where nobody can gain access to hold them against us, but once we stop running from our dark side or burying these parts so far below the surface, we reduce stress and invite peace. Owning our inequities and frailties may be less appreciated than any other PSEL, seeming antithetical to a lifetime of self-protection.

I had many bouts of guilt over the years as I felt the need to choose between teaching and my life—one or the other. There rarely seemed to be a balance or integration of the two. My whole self was never an option, and this emotional tug-of-war has left definite imprints over the years. I have spent years facing the demons of despair, incompetence, and sometimes depression—carrying my own emotional weight, the emotional weight of the students and families I serve, and the weight of a society that devalues teachers and the teaching profession. That realization hurts, and that hurt never goes away.

Pigs Eat Wolves is a book written by former author and therapist Charles Bates (2002). In his use of the fairy tale, the author describes three houses made of sticks, stones, and bricks, which are symbolic of the protective mechanisms of each pig's protection from the wolf. We eventually learn that the wolf is merely a projection onto the world of all our fears and fantasies, requiring us to ingest these barriers to peace.

Without a wolf to hide from, people are capable of the most incredible risks, bringing about happiness without requiring extraordinary accomplishments. While Olympic athletes, world leaders, and Nobel Prize winners can attest to the joy that comes from mastery of task, everyday people have just as much power to face our fears directly and announce to the world we will not hide. Not only is this idea freeing but it leads to all types of new revelations such as depth of contact. It is our dark side after all that makes us interesting, allowing others to shed their armor and engage in more authentic relatedness.

I look back over my teaching career and think about how I had to grapple with and fight against the tide of failure often. The feeling of failure associated with not being enough and not doing enough is real. There are still days that I want to throw in the towel. And yet, I am still here standing strong, twenty years later, because that's who I am. It's always who I've been. But I am also a teacher-human who falls, fails, and grieves; I can also become overwhelmed and overwrought.

I am all of these things. This is my whole self. It is my whole self that has allowed me to not only survive but thrive as a teacher.

Today, we are in the midst of a global pandemic, and in the blink of an eye, teachers have been catapulted into a brave new world. We have been asked to create virtual classrooms overnight. We are expected to still complete X amount of professional development (PD) hours, attend grade-level team meetings and schoolwide committee meetings, keep attendance, maintain contact with all students and families, and be highly engaging. We are expected to do all of this while homeschooling our own children; caring for our aging parents; and dealing with COVID-19 exposure and deaths of family, friends, colleagues, and coworkers from this awful virus. Teachers are once again being asked to put themselves aside, to carry on. I lost an aunt and an uncle to COVID-19 in the span of one week. I attended their virtual funerals in between Zoom sessions for work.

There was something very wrong about that. But I felt the pull to leave part of me outside and press on. The tug-of-war never totally goes away. But I am aware of the tug now and pull back when I need to. And I hope that I am teaching the teachers that I work with to do the same.

As we become more aware of our dark side through self-reflective practices, where we exist along continuums and what polarity we may lean toward, the more we can work toward balancing or accepting these characteristics. Balancing means finding ourselves too near a polarity and the limitations that come from this extremity. If I am a math teacher promoting logic as the key to problem-solving but lack empathy for others' feelings, I can make subtle adjustments without abdicating my beliefs.

Another unrecognized value in this personal growth work for educators is the ease in which our relationships with students will grow. Educators are already challenged to engage students who seek high levels of stimulation to sustain their attention—some of whom are actively engaged in self-protection so their dark side is not exposed. If we can reduce resistance toward self-examination through modeling this PSEL, we will stimulate curiosity and perhaps inspire growth. Sharing our intimate personal growth work toward making adjustments based on our own identified limitations may be the most precious gift you can offer a child or even a colleague.

As a new teacher developer, I see myself in the early career teachers that I work with. I often share my very personal story with them. I share my entire journey—the good, the bad, and the ugly. I share it all so they know that I understand; that I get it; and most importantly, so that they'll understand that teaching is a journey toward becoming your whole self. For me, feelings of doubt, despair, and incompetence still rear their ugly heads from time to time. The difference now is that I'm not afraid to acknowledge them. I embrace them, alongside the confidence and drive that my mother instilled in me early on, as part of who I am as a human being and as a teacher. I'm not afraid to show some of my weaknesses and be vulnerable because I've learned that it is in these vulnerable places that true strength, endurance, and fortitude can be found.

I know that it will never be enough that I, nor any single teacher, comes through our journeys worn but strong. The weariness of the journey is too high a price to pay.

We lose far too many teachers because of it. Schools and districts need to do much more to support the social emotional health of teachers, especially in those early years, when they are first adjusting to the role. We must work hard to support and develop our teachers with the whole teacher in mind. We must create spaces where teachers are allowed to be their complete selves, show their vulnerabilities, and work through them.

We must acknowledge the pains and aches of this profession and provide people, resources, and systems that are dedicated to building up teachers holistically. Initiatives that introduce mindfulness, encourage teachers to find and incorporate their passions and interests, and allow sabbaticals for teachers to explore those parts of themselves and the world that refuel and energize them hold promise. These are beginning steps—giving teachers time and space to learn who they are as people, provide strategies and systems of support through the struggles, and allow them to develop fully as teachers and, yes, as human beings. This benefits teachers and the students that they serve. I am committed to this journey of supporting teachers in this way. I have begun the conversation here and in my own work. I have begun building sacred spaces where teachers feel they have the opportunity to pause, breathe, speak freely, develop, and grow completely. I am determined to continue to create, hold, and expand these spaces across schools, districts, and our virtual world. No teacher should ever have to leave who they are outside of the classroom door. I'm determined for this to no longer happen. Who will join me?

For children and adults, confidence and ultimately our sense of self is derived from lessening our protective mechanisms to accept and embrace ourselves more fully. Accepting our less desirables is key to emerging self-worth, which we will explore in the next PSEL. Integrating our inequities and frailties is also key to taking ownership and being accountable: the final PSEL.

Key Points

▶ Human beings of all ages use defense mechanisms or protective strategies to insulate themselves from fear of rejection, shame, hurt, and other unpleasantness.

▶ As we learn to own all aspects of ourselves, including our less favorable, we don't need to hide.

▶ As we become more aware through self-reflective practices— where we exist along continuums and what polarity we may lean toward—the more we can work toward balancing or accepting.

▶ Balancing means recalibrating when we find ourselves too far toward an extreme and the limitations are too great (i.e., we are so logical that we lack empathy for others' feelings).

▶ Confidence means lessening protective mechanisms to accept and embrace oneself more fully.

▶ Accepting our less desirable traits, characteristics, and tendencies is key.

▶ If we can help others be less guarded, they don't need to create strong defense or protective mechanisms that insulate them from deeper contact with others.

▶ Being less guarded means fewer excuses and encourages ownership of responsibility.

Discussion Questions

Whether using the book for PD or within a book group, please consider the following questions to stimulate your own ideas for exploration.

1. Do males or females in my grade tend to identify and integrate inequities, and why?

2. What aspects of myself am I most reluctant to share with the world?

3. What protective mechanisms do I use to hide my inequities?

4. How did I learn these particular protective mechanisms, and what is it like to employ them?

5. What protective mechanisms do I most dislike in students?

CHAPTER 13

Evolving Identity Formation

(Shondra M. is an educator in New York.)

The shaping of one's identity can have a long-standing impact on the ability to develop a healthy self-image, self-esteem, and relational intelligence. In my experience, the early onset of trauma brought about several undesirable detours on the path to self-love and appreciation. Although I believe courage was in my heart at a young age, I did not redeem it until much later.

The most significant goal for all children is a stable sense of self, culminating through celebration of uniqueness. Disruptions to this important work can have long-standing implications throughout lives. As we work to overcome and integrate hardships, embrace our individuality with an increasingly stable core, we can balance wants and needs, use sound judgment, resist being misled, consider long-term goals, and build interdependence with intimacy.

As we better understand what matters to us, we can relate as separate entities instead of following, pleasing, or dominating. Rather than proving our worth through thoughts or deeds designed to impress others, children and adults will see themselves more clearly in relation to others, creating fertile ground to negotiate needs. Instead of trying to fit in through conformity or dominance, we learn to build reciprocity in our relationships.

Balanced relationships are based on knowing where I start and you begin. Learning to assess when I am becoming depleted through giving or selfish through taking allows us to make our micro adjustments. Growing recognition when the motives of others are pure, when negotiation provides a realistic chance of equity, and even when to walk away are vital to our sense of self.

We explore our identity through others because we exist in the context of "I-other" relatedness. If I see myself as happy, it is because I contrast myself with others who seem similar or different. If I cannot see myself distinctly from another, I have no way to decide where changes are needed. I may also measure myself as a result of the quality or quantity of friend, work, and family relationships. Quality is the key determinant, evolving from how many likes or followers we have. I grow from "I need you" (for approval and acceptance) to I want to be with you because I may offer and receive value from you. The most poignant relationships are ones where you help me grow as a person rather than allowing me to simmer in sameness.

Our evolving identity, occurring most dramatically over the first eighteen years of life, is increasingly derived from interdependence. From the infant who is fully dependent on a caretaker to the young child who is learning to tie their shoes, the process of individuation-separation determines our self-reliance. We become unique individuals who can exist on our own but are more fulfilled when we can live together. With well-intended parents or a relatively stable caregiver, we develop ego strength to grow our personhood, walking carefully through the hidden land mines of pain on the path to interdependence.

During my formative years, I lived in a home with two genuinely loving, physically present parents, though my father was emotionally depleted and my mother at times too. I had been privy to their arguments over stressful financial situations, and I was already becoming "bad" and "mischievous." I was carrying a burden: I had buried the secret of sexual abuse deep inside. That period cemented feelings of fear, guilt, and shame, as too did my bad behaviors, the consequential chastisement, and the dark cloud that seemed to follow me. As hard as I tried, I failed at being consistent—consistently honest, smart, clean, prompt, and pleasing. When I courageously told my parents that someone had "touched me" years prior, I saw rage and helplessness in my father's eyes. Somehow, they wished to have known sooner but recalled the signs that were there. By the early teenage years, what I knew about God settled deep in my bones, and I prayed to be a better girl—for everyone's sake. It only made my struggles that much more offensive. As I walked through a minefield, avoiding explosions as best I could, whoever I was becoming was albeit without trust and boundaries—two of life's dire essentials.

Early in life we wear our pain like an emblematic letter, unable to conceal our shame. With age we work to adorn this badge of valor as a reminder of what we overcome. Who we are is not simply a culmination of our experiences but how we choose to integrate them. A stable sense of self does not mean that our identity is fixed; in fact, the continuous change process is a sign of good health. Thus, without altering our identity with every external influence, we do seek to adapt, evolving when frailties undermine our well-being. Self-improvement means growing our strengths and either accepting or developing our limitations, helped through ongoing self-reflection.

Traditionally, most of us recognize our sense of self as determined by our roles (e.g., my job) and our relationships (e.g., father, husband). We see ourselves in relation to others, using that contrast to decide with whom we are alike and who we are dissimilar to. Contrasting allows us to categorize ourselves and establish affiliations that define us.

This is most common early in our lives when our need for affiliation and belonging is highest.

By the time I graduated high school, I learned to try on motivation and consistency like new shoes. I graduated in the top half of my class, and my love for computers helped me focus. The brief stint at a SUNY college had lasted only the summer following my high school graduation. Time was up, tuition was due, and neither my parents nor I knew the realities of funding higher education. I recall one afternoon, as I sat in the corner of the summer dorm room, I screamed in a vocal relay with my parents to match the emotional exhaustion we all breathed. It was my brain's signal to my body to finish the summer orientation, pack up, and leave the campus in August never to return. Following that episode, I decided to find work, enroll myself in the local community college, and pay my own tuition. I chose to major in communications, though my father begged me to study law. I knew my father was thinking about my financial security—how much I would not likely make in a communications career. He would soon learn that I would be happy and financially stable even as a young adult.

Children lack defined roles and relationships to aid in the identity building, so they go to school to find an area of study as a prelude for locating a profession. We then position ourselves according to these roles, which informs our fit within the community. A physician's job is to treat illness, a plumber to build our infrastructure, and a teacher to educate. Before we can head down this path, however, we still seek out some way of establishing who we are. Without defined roles, children and teens join peer groups, using affiliation to establish identity.

Young people often attribute their worth to a sense of belonging that conveys value or purpose. I am a cheerleader; therefore, my value comes from inspiring school spirit. I get good grades, so my value is in my identity as a hard worker. A young person would have a difficult time without associating with a hobby, interest, or social group, even though paradoxically the ultimate reward young adults prize is being self-reliant. Young people use their interests and aptitudes to guide them in decision-making, often rushing this process because of the urgency to provide self-reliance and cement their role within society.

During the day, it was invigorating to witness just how digital archiving systems had become vital to the current generation. As new technologies were unveiled and I gained more responsibilities, the thousands of pages I scanned for Condé Nast and other major publications became quite intriguing and inspiring. The World Wide Web and other media were on the brink of taking over our lives. I wondered about the business world and travel in addition to developing my niche. Ironically, it was the second time I found myself working for a smart, no-nonsense woman. The first had been a director of a telemarketing firm for which I worked part-time in high school. Other mentors invested in me along the way and became constant spiritual and professional thinking partners. Shortly thereafter, I transferred into RIT and completed an undergrad degree in technical communications. I was already working in another web development and branding start-up. I observed life closely both on and off the job. When I received other lucrative offers with the added bonus of relocating, I remained loyal to my employer and hometown.

In those days, I attended my first professional development (PD) seminar: The Poised and Polished Professional. At the time, I did not know everyone needed continuous development even after obtaining degrees. I thought I was working on myself, asserting my communication, but I ended up blending into the plush life of people pleasing. It was not easy to remain steadfast on the path to self-love. I shape-shifted, code-switched and attempted to avoid dissension at all costs.

During our pursuit of interests, we sometimes find models to emulate helping us examine our own strengths and limitations. People pleaser, problem solver, and easygoing are self-identifiers we take on during our experimental phase, much the same way students use labels such as nerds, jocks, and preps that help distinguish us. The price for gaining admission to some peer groups, similar to our self-identifiers, is the ironic loss of individuality. Through labels we limit our range of choice, and through groups we give up certain freedoms for the commitment to the whole. From after-school clubs to gangs, our identity diffusion serves as a pledge of allegiance.

This group is so important to me that I will proudly wear the uniform, colors, or brands that symbolize my participation, often to the exclusion for my own preferences. Perhaps this is a welcome sacrifice or it may carry the penalty of harmful exclusivity. If I am willing to give up uniqueness to feel a part of a group, especially a group unaccepting of all people, am I considering what other consequence this may bring? Not only is this a dilemma for students but this choice to affiliate continues into our adulthood, most notably for teachers through unions.

Collective bargaining is a practical application of professional grouping. While recent laws provide greater freedom to those opting away from unions, the benefit of many voices is in greater power and influence. Being part of the union is less about belonging and more about volition, which is a similar theme for children who feel alone.

For some children, the group represents the only stable source of identity with the loss of individuality a way of proving loyalty. The lack of effort or knowledge in developing an identity outside this peer group puts kids at risk of losing their unique voice or for appreciating how their inequities are potential learning opportunities. Morals, values, and ethics may also be deferred to the collective voice of the group, further shaping one's sense of self.

We know historically how groupthink can be catastrophic; however, many students are ignorant to how the simple act of sharing one voice can devolve to such a dangerous level. Children who feel lost are not fully considering the long-term implications of yielding their voice because the immediacy of affiliation surpasses any unique but partially formed ethos. Becoming found in our early adult years is ironically accomplished when we stop looking outwardly or quickly for the answer to who we are.

My emotions were developing simultaneously; they developed in light of love and despite dysfunction. I accepted that everyone else was engaged in the evolving identity process at the same time. I had not considered the journey in that way until I began to experience significant changes in my life—major events that made me pause. They were not only events of shame, regret, misunderstanding and confusion; soon enough I could celebrate change, progress, accolades, and awards, becoming a wife and a mother. That is what we must come to: a sheer admiration of the fact that we as humans can evolve in our thinking and in the shaping of our identity to see our truest character and potential.

John Dewey once said, "Education is life itself." That admission is full of reason and purpose. Knowledge helps us view identity with a viable lens. I knew this, even as I left the branding and technology industry to apply for a master's in education and change professions to the high calling of teaching. According to the old proverb "To whom much is given, much is required" and by my third decade of life, I had become aware of our ability to reinvent ourselves as humans. I was requiring more of myself as an integral part of the community, and teaching was key to a redemptive plan.

Who we are meant to be is a combination of intrinsic drives and life experiences. We find passion through helping, creating, selling, or doing any number of different vehicles to optimize our skills and interests. The greater the value we feel in our work, the more worth we develop. It doesn't have to be an identity displayed to the world but a reason for being. If we are industrious or creative, playful or persistent, we can find ourselves through the values and beliefs we hold to be important. At this intersection of I want, I need, and I believe, we can make difficult decisions sometimes abandoning what is safe or familiar.

By the time I stepped into the first year of teaching, my marriage began to crumble. Prior to that, my life politely aligned to a theocracy in which I was rooted on all sides. Stark realities and inconsistencies upended my truth, and I simply felt alienated—a stranger in a peculiar land. I struggled to see myself physically, emotionally, and spiritually. I needed a complete overhaul to reevaluate how things should be in the world. Spiritually, my fears seemed insurmountable. I knew that divorcing meant that I had failed to see marriage through to the end. I was confused and resorted to uncharted minefields. I was already forging a new identity. Who was I at that point? My comfort zone had meant operating in the context of my marriage, my home, and my church and my being a wife, mother, daughter, sister, niece, and friend. I had placed my self-image in a box and stacked what others thought of me above my own perception. I was slightly self-loathing, allowing prior decisions in which I relinquished control to beat drums through my mind as I considered all the what-ifs. I could not recognize a framework for some of the choices, and I grasped for explanation.

The whirlwind became so strong that I could not face it. Alternatively, I rebelled. I rebelled against religion. I quietly rebelled against anything—ant invasions, the thought of too much ice cream, the heads of wilted lettuce, oppressive systems—of any kind. I allowed myself to question. I trusted a subtle underdog theology. Alas, when I came through, I realized that I had had truth all along—that I had the strength to make new choices and changes and to take charge of my evolving identity. I needed to return to the four-year-old self and ask her why she never had the chance to learn about trust and setting boundaries. I processed growing up as an only child (my brother lived with his mother), never acquiring the joy and skill of negotiating with any siblings in my formative years. There was so much to revisit, but I exercised gentleness and patience with myself for once.

In the midst of painful self-exploration, we begin a consolidation of who we have been, including our choices and preferences, and through this metanalysis begin to picture how we will reemerge, happier and healthier. We can do this alone, however having a network of believers who want more for us than we might have imagined will hasten our repurposing.

A strong peer group affiliation protects the individual from repeating old patterns, making similar choices that may not have worked before, feeling alone through our difficult choices, or the imago of being unlikable, not accepted by others. This is a powerful force for a young person who has yet to develop adequate self-worth to embrace their individuality as it is for a well-established adult. Personal growth with outside guidance helps us see what is hidden but mostly makes the journey more enjoyable.

Adults use affiliations—whether we call them cohorts or cliques—to guard against the real and perceived threats of society. As we use self-reflection, esteem, and integration of our frailties and inequities to shape our identity development, we now see ourselves more clearly in relation to society. We may realize more fully how the world views us and what the new barriers are and whether we want to hurdle them. We may once again lean toward the comfort of similarity, as we did on the playground when we were seven or with greater intentionality when we enrolled in the LBGTQ club our freshman year. We may instead decide to lean into discomfort, deciding our authenticity requires standing up to the injustices of the world.

As a new teacher, I used education, aptitude, and relational qualities to shine that first year, obtaining a First Year New Teacher Award. I continued developing other aspects of life, as my personal vision for success compelled me. It included a sincere love for children (my own and others) and my family as well as a vision for togetherness, for benevolent communities that would not judge people by the color of their skin. Indeed, adding to the shattering divorce was the dissolution of my family—a Black family, to be exact. I had wrestled with my place in the world, grappling with it in high school and college. However, long before and whilst on road trips to Georgia with my family, I learned I was a "little Black girl" living in an America that would not always value me. I knew the best way to teach was to model, and I had wanted desperately to be that solid family foundation. I picked up shame once again. In my mind, I carried the weight and responsibility for dispelling all the myths about Black people being uneducated, incapable of maintaining careers, families, homes and general happiness. As I engaged in teaching, I had moments I did not feel valued. I looked closely at the brown faces of the children in front of me, and I knew, theoretically, that I should matter, but sometimes inconsequently I did not. Those few instances affected me—affected how I saw myself and how I saw the group to which I belonged racially and culturally.

So there I was teaching children but realizing that I was still developing—my brain still malleable. New revelations were both terrifying and beautiful, hurtful and helpful, eager and slow. That is when I realized the humility teaching requires. With its myriad eye-opening moments, transformation began, and not just in my classroom. Being a mother empowered me to become self-aware and reflective. It took years to discover my lack of trust and boundaries, and as I reintroduced myself to me, I decided to love me (and thus God and baby girl) even more strongly.

The responsibilities of adulthood can easily outweigh our ideological framework for improving the world. Familiarity, comfort, and routine are all motivating factors for a busy adult. Add in the fear of consequences from losing affiliation with one's peer group—or even just the hint of tension from doing something outside the norm—and we can appreciate why young people in particular will revert to what is familiar. Conformity via traditions, beliefs, and etiquette maintain cliques, making it likely that commonalities will be the glue that holds peer groups together at any age.

Unless we have the external support and the internal drive to break free of the fear maintaining our sameness, we will continue our affiliation until we are freed of being the first to rebel. The fear of rejection, abandonment, and ostracism are some of the most powerful forces exerted on a human being, not easily overcome by child or adult, but the very same ones that make school culture difficult to evolve.

The evolving identity is a commitment to reinventing oneself and to embracing change—not just for the sake of change but for the deepening of the soul. As I studied Baldwin, Hansberry and Shakespeare with students, I realized each of us is a complexity and that we might relentlessly pursue ourselves as a rhetorical question. For we all are better off learning to question, to relate and communicate, to listen fully, and to set good parameters for respectful argument. If we could only learn how to fail, how to try again, then we could build stamina that undergirds the lifelong learning process.

    The very first time I heard the International Baccalaureate philosophy that referred to a teacher as "no longer the sage on the stage but the guide on the side" it was a welcomed relief. Before, the pressure was on. Teachers were afraid to make mistakes (any mistakes), to show less than favorable test scores, and bear the societal blame, scapegoating and shaming—the perpetual cycle. Somehow, we have made education about competition, and we are afraid to take risks, because we fear failure. Society inequitably divides tools amongst children, giving some all the tools they need, others some of the tools they need, and many as unworthy of holding or seeing any tools at all. Unfortunately, this has been the less desirable part of the self-preserving nature of humanity.

When a stronger force than fear is summoned, we can search for elements of a personal identity outside our role and relationships. That force may be a desire for freedom, propelled by excitement for higher-order needs to be met. Beginning with Maslow's original hierarchy of needs, the potential for love and fulfillment are at the top of the pyramid. If we add meaning, peace, and value into the equation, we can break free of conventional motivation.

In summoning the motivation to pursue these higher-order needs, we may begin to recognize that identity, at the core, is more about who we are as people than which group we are affiliated with or what role we assume. This is especially promising for kids who don't have well-established roles and haven't found a group to belong to.

Education has to be about standing against that nature and about valuing a person because they are here, in the world. That is the first part of a healthy identity: feeling safe and loved and having a sense of belonging. We must meet crucial, fundamental needs for the journey to begin. I had to understand that powerful message—that I am what is right in the world. That I could safely trust the process. That I have a unique purpose to use my voice and my platform. I used to tell my students, "You're stuck with me. You know, I wanted to be a singer—on a stage in front of millions, and so you are here with me now. You are my millions; you are my million-dollar audience—you are everything

*to me. This is my stage, so let me show up and show out for you:
I want to teach you what you need to learn, I want you to interact and
engage with me, and I want us to have the time of our lives, learning
and growing together." They would look at me and finally burst into
hilarity. They knew it was true though.*

For children or adults experiencing identity confusion or crisis,
perpetuated by sexual orientation, job dissatisfaction, or relationship
disruption, the freedom to maintain one's identity even with the
potential loss of acceptance will help us strengthen our individual core.

The important questions can now shift from what we do and who we
know to what is our persona? What do we stand for, and what purpose
drives our being? Deeper and more sustainable elements of identity are
based on these questions and can be used to help children develop more
fluidly without getting stuck in unmet needs.

*As I woke up every day to get my beautiful daughter prepared and
go out into the world, I knew I had the tools to shape and carve out
my identity. The classroom lessons really gave me hope. From* The
Outsiders *to* Macbeth *to* Their Eyes Were Watching God *and more,
I delved with students into a world of hubris, rejection, rebellion, love,
and courage—collecting each golden nugget like a precious stone.
I recall two young boys almost having a fight in my classroom; later,
when I was alone, I cried. All I could think about was how imperative
education is for urban, underprivileged children especially—the
ones who do not get sixteen chances and for whom there is no trust
fund. Granted, not every American experiences that either, but the
disparities in education are evident. I had to confront my biases by
reaffirming my identity and reinforcing new ideas about America's
own conflicting identity and narrative. Given that legacy, I have no
choice but to embrace a transformative life and be an agent for change.*

As children learn to balance their brains and bodies, self-reflect, and
accept their frailties, they are halfway toward securing a core sense of
self, based on these more complex qualities. From this base, a child or
adult can further grow their self-worth, which will continue expanding
one's opportunity for identity development. The more stable but flexible
our sense of self, the less we have to guard against the imagined threats
of difference; in fact, we even learn to appreciate how differences form
the basis for deeper intimacy.

*That is the thrill of embracing an evolving identity—you know there
will be peaks and valleys, you know there will be highs and lows, and
you know this because people have told you so, and because life begins
to show up in that way. In a scapegoating society, we look to assign
the blame; perhaps we think tools of reflection and accountability are*

beneath us or belong to another. Unequivocally, the evolving soul looks within first. That is the point at which an individual becomes metacognitive and understands what is actually happening. Many times in life, we ask ourselves, "How did I get here? What happened here?" We summon me, myself, and I into a room for question and listen to their stories to try to find clarity. Since we lend that process and framework as educators, it is necessary that we continue growing and finding ourselves—trying on new lenses to see the world from others' eyes. Furthermore, with our global access and reach, and as Chimamanda Ngozi Adichie implores, we can avoid the "danger of a single story"(TED, 2009). We do not have to limit ourselves to one perspective, one story. Another thing is the story need not end prematurely. We are still writing—all complex works in progress. We must work to enhance our identities, speak truth to power, and assign ourselves new visions and hopes, learning to value and see change optimistically. When I think of being hardwired to think on the bright side, as Tali Sharot (2011) posits in The Optimism Bias, *I think of how paramount it is to develop a relational intelligence for living and thriving as a global community. We must be able to talk to and reach each other. Teaching and learning gave me a new language that communicates, "I believe in you, you believe in me, and we will not hold each other hostage if one of us is wrong about something." Imagine the possibilities if we opened up to a world of forgiveness education. Tutu's philosophy certainly escorted freedom and forgiveness into my heart, home, and classroom. Understanding the process, we must help all generations authentically see, love, learn, forgive, and reinvent themselves.*

Our individual and collective risk for not evolving our identity is that we first stagnate and then begin to regress. We can easily devolve into fragmentation when believing we have to "take care of our own" or become dichotomous in our thinking. There are very few rights and wrongs in the world, but believing so will put you on a side, seeing half the world as adversaries or just as deleterious, remaining internally conflicted. Identity is about a cohesive whole, integrating all our parts, not simply the ones we are most comfortable with.

In retrospect, I was hard on myself. Somewhere along the way, I had learned to be. To me, teaching (learning) is about finding balance— helping people find a balance in this life, because we will not be without challenges. We have the tools: our brains, able to think through problems, as well as our relationships, which provide us love and comfort as we evolve. Today, over a decade later, I am an intentional, soulful teacher that promotes educational equity and justice and that also works at the helm to directly facilitate inquiry into new narratives, attitudes, and belief systems of students—and colleagues for that matter.

Key Points

▶ Who we are is fluid, which allows us to evolve.

▶ Early in life we are more susceptible to the influence of peer groups, prioritizing affiliation over our unique identity.

▶ Polarization in the U.S. is a direct result of people staying stuck in one set of beliefs without effort to evolve.

▶ Without a solid core, we will be more easily influenced by others, the cause of everything from groupthink to larger catastrophes.

▶ Preferences, beliefs, opinions, and attitudes expand with new experiences.

▶ A deeper and more sustainable way of developing our identity is through nonaffiliative associations, such as our sense of purpose.

Discussion Questions

Whether using the book for PD or within a book group, please consider the following questions to stimulate your own ideas for exploration.

1. Do males or females in my grade tend to evolve their identity quicker, and why?

2. How has my identity changed since I was young?

3. What life experiences have shaped who I am—for better and worse?

4. How stable is my identity now?

5. What are the components—and percentages of those components—that make up my identity?

Growing Self-Worth

(Meredith McCullough is a secondary teacher in Soldotna, Alaska.)

One of my favorite lines from Le Petit Prince by Antoine de Saint-Exupéry is "Les grandes personnes aiment les chiffres." Grown-ups like numbers. The fact is, adults do like numbers and hard facts. We like to create labels and organizational strategies to categorize our world. Sharing these labels is a mark of pride when we meet other adults, and it becomes the sole definition of who we are and what our value is to those around us. For better, and often for worse, our labels influence our self-worth.

In adulthood we develop certain rigidities that infuse our persona. Our emerging inflexibility isn't something we aspire to but rather is born out of a need to organize our world. While we intrinsically prefer order, manifesting in procedures and structures to manage our overpacked days, it's seldom intended at the onset to define us. The pride we take in identifying ourselves according to classifications such as occupation, geography, or number of family members isn't realized until we consider the limitations of such self-definition.

After I shake hands with another adult, the usual question posed is this: "Oh, and what do you do?"

Every time, this leads me to a small existential crisis, but I always say the answer I think will require the least explanation.

"I'm a teacher," I say. Or, if I think the person asking actually cares, I'll specify with "I teach English and history." Then I prepare for the inevitable grimace or awkward response that this person hasn't read a real book since high school, or fears I've been secretly judging email grammar, or watches a lot of World War II documentaries on TV. Within thirty seconds, my value to the world has been decided and dismissed, casually set aside now that it's defined the boundaries of our current conversation.

Children are at an advantage and disadvantage in this regard, having less to define themselves by. Children don't have jobs or other professional affiliations to serve as identification labels, leaving them without standard openings for introductions or affiliations, that help bring about a sense of pride. This also means they have the freedom to generate more meaningful identifiers based on who they are and what they strive to become rather than a box they may be trapped in.

True self-worth may begin with a close pairing to identity, but over time our esteem is found in our relationships with the world, emphasizing what we give over what we receive. With each advancement of grade, however, it moves them closer to adulthood, where they conform more to our world of labels but further removing themselves from the adventure of self-discovery and ultimately finding purpose or meaning.

Students know how I am labeled as well. They know my name and the subjects I teach, because those details are listed on their schedules. Some of them know labels previous students have given me. But when they ask me what I do, since they're well trained by adults to ask such questions, I don't confirm my labels. Instead, I tell them the truth of who I am.

"I'm a writer," I say.

For half a second, their minds are blown. They always regroup quickly and come back with "Wait. Like, of books?"

As children and adolescents form a more solid but flexible sense of self, they are likely to experience greater value and worth. Solid and flexible may seem contradictory, but they work in tandem like a city skyscraper. The building needs to be strong enough to withstand the elements with the ability to sway slightly with the wind. This allows the building to move with the elements as opposed to against them. Children rely on the role models in their lives, the parents, the teachers, to help them recognize how to go about this process.

"Yes. Of books."

"You mean published books?"

"Sometimes. And of books I'm writing that may never go anywhere."

Around this point in the conversation, they tend to realize they've been distracted from the answer I should have given and will then tell me, "But you're a teacher."

In my twelve years of experience, I've always responded the same way to this because I recognize that they're trying to be good adults. They're struggling to contain me within the box all adults like to set around others.

I smile and tell them, with complete honesty, "I can be both. And, you know, I've never wanted to be a teacher."

It's a thirty-second conversation, which reframes everything.

Due to internal and external influences, we are perpetually making micro adjustments that often become ingrained in our personhood. Children, for instance, who get picked on for being awkward may learn to poke fun at themselves to gain greater volition. In doing so, they may learn how to make others laugh, which builds humility into their makeup. Forming identities means learning to be proud of what we like and learning to accept or change the aspects we don't like. While it's a complicated process, determining what gets assimilated and what motivates us to grow, we can learn to enjoy the discovery.

To survive amidst adults, we learn to work within accepted labels. We learn how to manipulate those labels to keep life from getting too complicated. We compartmentalize who we are. It's safer to share handpicked pieces of ourselves rather than letting others see the whole picture.

Safety is important to educators. We have a "recession-proof" career that we fight to keep hold of. Despite this, we struggle to earn the respect and support of parents, other professionals, and lawmakers, facing conflict at local, state, and national levels as a result. We model ourselves after "great" teachers we remember from school. Nevertheless, we forget their teaching philosophies negatively affect our current students, who can no longer find success in the traditional assembly-line model of education most of us were brought up under. Such limitations are obvious, but many find it safer to accept the label and expectations of a "traditional" educator versus a "progressive" educator. Across all experience levels, some are so focused on securing their safety that they will actively discourage behaviors they perceive as threats—whether that's in how other teachers build relationships with their students; different approaches to curriculum; or even data-driven changes implemented at department, school, or district levels. It's little wonder we may find ourselves trapped in a career that has no hope of balancing the safety we desire with the transformative risks we must take if we wish to revolutionize education.

Crossroads and critical choice points are at the heart of esteem building. When we encounter ego dystonia, or the drives, impulses, and wishes that are deemed unacceptable by others, a decision guided by priorities ensues, knowing we may face judgment or backlash for following our own path. Similarly, when faced with incongruence between external and internal conflicts, such as what we believe and what is expected of us or what we want versus what we need, tension is generated. How we navigate both the tension and the decision either grows or weakens our self-worth.

For a teacher working in a school where disparity of values, for instance, are high but the willingness to confront them are low (due to fear, lack of hope, absence of skills or confidence), self-worth will be jeopardized. Teachers do their best to create their own culture with their students, but a large chasm at the classroom door will make that challenging.

If the school doesn't feel emotionally safe or physically secure, the absence of this basic need will create a void, occupying space where self-worth might have flourished. Knowing that students may be suffering in the hallways, cafeterias, or other classrooms—without any volition to help protect them—leads to feeling defeated. Even if there is no culpability on the part of the teacher doing everything they can to fortify the student, they will still feel defeated where discouraged and disheartened faculty hemorrhage creativity and passion.

The lack of safety may come from rifts between different subsets of the population, including administration and faculty, faculty and students or parents, or between factions within the faculty. It ought to make sense that higher-order needs such as self-worth aren't attended to when the more foundational needs such as safety and security aren't internalized. Supportive and consistent working environments go a long way toward making this possible.

It is a paradox that saps our self-worth and one I struggle with every day. A strange combination of spite and love guides me in this career. I overthink every interaction I have and use my stressed self-reflection to constantly adapt and improve. I focus that same reflective process to help my students grow into better, stronger, more resilient people. I feed their self-worth because, maybe someday, one of them will be strong enough to break the system I was unable to. Often, their greatest strengths are those others will relegate to a dismissive label because it's easier than examining the true complexity of another person, or of acknowledging the variety of skills needed for our society to function.

If we unpack the complex elements of self-worth, we can quantify or at least qualify this ephemeral and universal goal (and it satisfies the aforementioned desire to classify). In our formula, we don't know the precise measurement of ingredients, or how they interact, but we can reasonably find aspects of each tool, skill, or element within each child and adult's esteem.

Growing self-worth encompasses the following:

- ❱ Identity
- ❱ Personality
- ❱ Self-protection
- ❱ Experiences

Identity was previously described as a precursor and a result of self-worth, encapsulated as the beliefs, values, and preferences that define our existence. When those beliefs, values, and ethics coincide with improving the world and respect gained from others, we may find our self-worth growing.

Preferences are important to identity formation because we tend to have more choice, less influenced by our caregivers. They can begin as early in life as a few days into birth, such as the way we are positioned to nurse. Some preferences are instinctive while others grow through trial and error, but all provide us enjoyment that can grow our self-worth, so long as we master the skills of expressing and negotiating.

We described the process by which a stable but flexible sense of self (identity) is formed; however, this is only part of the formula for creating self-worth. How optimistic we are is an example of this intrinsic quality that helps define us. Also shaped by life experience, our outlook helps influence how we see the world and how the world views us. Who we are, including our positivity, will be altered by our experiences at work, so it's critical we attend to how we are being affected by our environment.

I am idealistic and optimistic about my students' potential. I love working with them and seeing them grow, but I do not believe I will stay in this career forever. It's too draining and frustrating. I loathe the bureaucracy and am depressed by the knowledge that reforming this broken system is a Herculean task. I have worked on state-level committees and have been privy to the complicated art of sharing the truth in ways palatable to the lawmakers who provide our funding. I have been fortunate to work within forward-thinking districts and have seen firsthand the backlash they face from the community. Transformative educators constantly fight for their students' best opportunities, but sometimes the most we can do is change our individual classrooms and, if we're lucky, our schools.

Personality refers to our attitude, temperament, and adaptation by which we navigate relationships. As we are rewarded by the affiliation and love from others, based on our persona, we can develop additional esteem.

A personality that is fixed and rigid will be the least likely to contribute to our self-worth. Those on the other end of the continuum, who are open and willing to experiment with change, will find new opportunities for growing self-esteem. Consider the versatility of a child who is an admired football player deciding to take a yoga class.

Exploration outside one's comfort zone grows our self-worth by helping to diversify our personality. The football player is less concerned with image and more interested in trying out something new. The reward comes from the effort and sometimes the result of what we are trying on.

Personality also helps build resiliency, through our embracement of obstacles viewed as challenges. Resiliency is grown through continuous encouragement to learn from the unfortunate events in our lives. The only choices we name mistakes are from situations we don't extract learning from. Everything else comes under the heading of learning.

When our personality helps build a worldview of curiosity, we treat setbacks as chances for rebuilding. Like a bone that heals stronger after a break, so, too, can our personas grow stronger when we face and overcome adversity. So long as the adversity isn't ongoing and without relief, with reserves to endure the distress and with helpful external supports, this is possible.

It has taken me years to accept the truth that burnout will take me from this career. My view may seem fatalistic, but finally accepting it has granted me immense freedom. I no longer worry as much about what "good" teachers do and try to obtain that label. Instead, I focus on the reasons I entered this career in the first place: my desire to help my students and my passion for the subjects I teach. By holding fast to who I am and being comfortable with my limitations as an educator and human being, I've discovered educational liberation.

Self-protection is the method by which we guard against not getting our wants and needs met. When our protections are antiquated, meaning they may have worked better in our earlier years, people may be put off. If our self-protection is flexible—but more importantly we are aware and open about it—we can build our worth.

In order to treat life's setbacks as opportunities for growth, we also need to develop more complex self-protective strategies. Blame and denial are more primitive strategies people are familiar with that don't hold up well with age. Replacing our former approaches with curiosity and acceptance, so we don't need to insulate ourselves from perceived threats, will earn us greater self-worth.

When I step into my classroom, I can focus all my energy on doing what is best for my students, from personalizing their learning and educational goals to implementing social emotional learning (SEL) practices every class period. I can stretch myself to bring in content that makes my students passionate about English and history, from sharing my publishing experiences to organizing guest speakers to comparing the class struggles in The Great Gatsby *to the marriages and careers of Jay-Z and Beyoncé versus Kanye West and Kim Kardashian. This freedom is how I can connect so well with my students. I don't hide who I am or why I care about what I teach. I don't hide my doubts or fears about my future from my students. I choose to teach from a place of truth and vulnerability, and I invite my students to join me for a while on my brief professional journey.*

A different way of looking at defense mechanisms is to view them as contact styles, each of which having a benefit and limitation. Contact styles are the ways in which we attempt to connect with others but with a cautious approach that doesn't allow for full impact. These are examples of different contact styles:

Projector: This person attributes their own thoughts, feelings, and beliefs to someone else. When projectors feel anger or frustration, they quickly make assumptions about the other person. To avoid getting rejected, the projector pushes people away, secretly hoping the others will guess what the projector wants and give it to them. Projectors may inspire creativity in others by focusing on them or intuiting about them in a way that draws out energy.

Reflector: This person keeps everything inside, going over and over their own concerns without confiding in others. Often this person experiences migraines, stomachaches, and anxiety. Reflectors rarely ask for help because they don't want to be let down. Reflectors experience competing energies (forces for sameness and change) as turmoil. However, their thoughtful self-control and diplomacy can yield advantages.

Introjector: This person assumes responsibility for everyone else's feelings and reactions. This person apologizes frequently. This person is often a peacekeeper and a fixer, preferring to quickly smooth over conflicts rather than explore differences.

Deflector: This person is the master of redirection. Deflectors often talk excessively and make self-deprecating jokes to take attention away from themselves. This person rarely examines behavior or feelings and resists feedback from others. This person is likely to only try to get needs met that will require very little conflict and will often redirect any attention received to others.

Swallower: This person chokes down feelings to prevent conflict—a response that may lead to physical problems over time. Swallowers retain information well and are receptive to mentoring and role modeling.

Merger: Mergers take on the attitudes of those around them rather than exerting strong identities of their own. Mergers empathize well with others and tolerate change and uncertainty. The merger has difficulty maintaining a sense of uniqueness but doesn't demand much in the way of supports from others.

Desensitizer: This person guards sensitivities. When others infringe on their boundaries, they react not by limiting contact but through humor or minimizing. By lowering the intensity of situations, this person has some value to groups that escalate quickly. A desensitizer provides balance among those who are more extreme.

Experiences involve the rewards and stressors that contextualize our existence. With purposeful risk-taking, overcoming adversity and hardship, our self-worth will grow. Some experiences are planned while others are unexpected, testing our resilience and adaptability.

Experiences are what arise from our preferences but also from the unexpected occurrences in our lives, which we grow or regress from. Experiences help us to broaden the confines we keep ourselves in, learning the difference between real and perceived threats. We may try a ride at an amusement park we are certain will frighten us, only to find we are thrilled with letting go.

It can be terrifying to teach from this place of personal and professional honesty, but the most meaningful moments of my career have resulted from this active choice. One example came when a former student, now attending my alma mater to become an elementary education major, wrote me a letter at the end of her first year of college. The assignment was to write to a former teacher and discuss what studied teaching methods she'd witnessed me using as well as why she felt a personal connection to my teaching style.

The pedagogical elements she shared were interesting and well cited, but the second half of her letter stunned me. She spoke about one of our last days of school her junior year of high school. She wrote, "Somehow we started discussing mental illness and how it's seen as this taboo thing that we feel uncomfortable talking about, and how wrong that is. . . . That moment when you shared why you decided to get that tattoo on your wrist redefined how I thought about teacher-student relationships. . . . I loved that you were so open with us about your own struggles. I have struggled with depression and anxiety, and I know people who I hold close to my heart who struggle with self-harm and suicidal thoughts every single day. . . . Thank you for being human."

The stakes are high to grow self-worth and all the other psychosocial emotional learnings (PSELs) as they represent the protective factors guarding against trauma, addictions, mental health, and other threats to our personhood. If we view classrooms as human laboratories, where students feel safe to explore new ways of being and relating, they will expand their myopia, explore a greater range of choice in acting, and ultimately feel the reward of both the risk and the outcome, as measured by their self-worth. As perhaps the only adult in their lives with whom they can take chances, rewarding this type of extension will have long-lasting impacts on you and your students.

"Thank you for being human," she wrote. I never realized there was another option. That day in class, when my students asked why I got a tattoo there, on the inside of my wrist, right over the artery, I spoke the truth: "If it's there, I won't want to cut it and mess up the artwork." They nodded sagely, as only teenagers can, and we moved on. It was not a momentous occasion to me because I naively thought that being honest and vulnerable with your students was the bare minimum of being an effective teacher.

Her letter—and her labeling me as human—reframed my views. It made me wonder how we can ask our students to go into the world at the age of eighteen and somehow figure all of this out on their own when they haven't yet learned how to trust in their own incredible potential. It is imperative for them to watch other "responsible" adults struggling to find their own inner peace. Classrooms must be safe enough for students to test their boundaries—both academically and emotionally. Only then will they decide which—if any—limitations and labels they will allow to be placed on themselves, and only then will they be able to determine their self-worth. Hopefully, I'm able to encourage them to pursue freedom and acceptance over safety and tradition for however long I have left in this career. Maybe if I can accomplish this by the time I walk away, I'll feel secure enough to accept the teacher label at long last.

Educators can often appreciate the hidden potential of students, even when they don't recognize it within themselves. As social emotional leaders, we help illuminate the self-imposed limitations interfering with self-worth, such as the early labels we assign ourselves. And finally, it is essential to help teach students how to create opportunities to explore preferences and experiences with the reasonable expectation of emotional safety and physical security.

Key Points

▶ As children and adolescents form a more solid but flexible sense of self, they are more likely to experience greater value and worth.

▶ Growing self-worth involves work around identity, personality, self-protection, and the integration of new experiences.

▶ Children have greater freedom than adults to grow self-worth until they become limited by rigid labels.

▶ Over time our esteem is found in our relationships with the world, emphasizing what we give over what we receive.

▶ Protective mechanisms, such as contact styles, can help or hinder our development of self-worth.

▶ Experiences either enhance or detract from our self-worth, depending upon the quality of the experience and the way we internalize them.

Discussion Questions

Whether using the book for professional development (PD) or within a book group, please consider the following questions to stimulate your own ideas for exploration.

1. Do males or females in my grade tend to have higher self-worth, and why?

2. What are the most important elements of my self-worth?

3. How does identity feed worth and worth feed identity for my students?

4. What are the biggest threats to self-worth for faculty in my school?

5. What are the biggest threats to self-worth for students in my class?

CHAPTER 15

Channeling Aggression Into Constructive Outlets

(Rick Baxter is an elementary teacher in Toronto, Canada.)

I just turned fifty years old, and I have been a teacher for twenty-five years—that's half my life. I have been teaching the past sixteen years in Toronto, and although my teaching career here has been roughly successful, it has also been pretty brutal. The job has left me scarred: I am now not the same person I was as when I started working here. I am lucky to have survived both vitally and professionally. In the past sixteen years I have experienced so much violence, bullying, intimidation, harassment, humiliation, passive aggression, and toxicity. It's been a monumental feat to limit and control my feelings of anger and bitterness, and I am still not through it.

Through our development of a solid but flexible sense of self, we self-reflect, integrating frailties and inequities in need of acceptance of change. We examine personality traits, beliefs, needs, feelings, fantasies, and many other aspects of personhood, helping guide our personal growth work. One of the more hidden aspects of ourselves in need of consideration are our drives, instincts, and impulses.

The two primary drives that migrate into instincts and impulses are sexual and aggressive. The aggressive drive is related to how we deal with conflict, negotiate to get our needs met, and allow for intimacy. Our aggressive drive is responsible for passion and how we advocate for self and others.

But I have survived, and I still go to work, and I am grateful to the people who have trusted me, believed in me, and supported me, because so many have not. This job has scarred me, but it has also strengthened me. It has strengthened my heart; it has strengthened my resolve; and it has made me more compassionate, empathetic, and humble. It has given me hope. But I have had to fight to get here, and so many of my friends and colleagues either didn't make it or have lost so much in the process of simply trying to do their jobs as teachers.

Aggression is largely misunderstood by adults, associated with the most recognizable threat to education. With the ominous threat of catastrophic school violence, we have become hypervigilant to anything evoking fear or concern. Even without this perpetual threat looming, we have for a long while characterized and even generalized the concept of aggression to be synonymous with violence, even altering some consider themselves.

By contributing to this book I have discovered that I am not actually an aggressive person, and I guess for many years I thought I was, but my definition of what aggression is has changed. I am by nature, and by nature I mean by "brain," an impulsive and adrenaline-seeking person. I have an atypical brain that lacks serotonin, dopamine, and adrenaline, and growing up, I participated in many team sports and sporting activities that fueled my absent levels of these feel-good chemicals that most people have a balance of. I learned at a young age that I like—no, I need—to go fast. I still do.

In making violence and aggression mean the same, we have inadvertently stifled the natural maturation process of many young adults who are learning to manage their drives, instincts, and impulses. The process of learning self-control and self-regulation with our aggressive drive is forced to take place in secret and isolation.

Young adults believe they must conceal their aggression, not wanting adults to interpret their fantasy as a perceived threat, leaving young adults alone in the confusing world of their instincts and impulses.

For those young people who grow up in environments where their needs are reasonably met and the world seems relatively fair, navigating their aggressive drive is less shameful, explored out in the open. Through transparency, we come to appreciate that aggression is used to vehemently assert ourselves; generate passionate discourse; and, when necessary, constructively protect ourselves from harm.

Having an atypical brain like mine is useful under stressful circumstances. I have the brain of the hunter, the explorer, the warrior, and the entrepreneur. My type of brain is more useful in times like now, with the COVID-19 pandemic, because I can think very quickly and adjust to changes much more easily than others can. This allows me to innovate and redesign my teaching practice to adjust to the present realities but also to the realities that lie ahead.

Under less stressful times, and working for a very large urban school district, a brain like mine can cause disruption, and I make no excuses for that. Large school districts are notoriously slow to change, and until recently, education in North America, at least, really hasn't changed very much. Because of the static nature, or at least a slower pace of change, it becomes difficult for teachers and students alike, who have brains that are used to processing information very quickly. The slow pace of change can be extremely frustrating and difficult to manage.

For those young people who experience the world differently from the intensity of their drives or perhaps view the world as unfair and don't believe their needs will be met, they are more likely to go underground in this process of experiencing and channeling aggression. For these children or adults, the potential for violence follows a path of suppression, mistrust, and resentment, bottled up and pressurized, waiting for the seal to be broken. With others, their intensity is turned inward, resulting in unhappiness until they can better realize the people and places they more easily fit into.

Thus, I have learned that I do well working in schools that are less static—schools that require innovative thought and application of solutions to support learners who have many challenges and who often express those challenges in school, which is often to the physical and emotional detriment of themselves and those around them.

Understanding environments we will thrive in, along with the difference between these two types of aggression, forms the platforms for this specific psychosocial emotional learning (PSEL). And the starting point for this particular PSEL is the recognition that aggression is a natural and healthy drive, channeled in different directions. If educators can adopt this paradigm, they will more easily guide exploration of this inherently awkward drive into the open.

Writing for this book and working in schools such as these, I have been forced to rethink my understanding of what aggression is. Mostly, being aggressive can be quite damaging to the aggrieved but also to the aggressor. But aggression can also be a useful emotion when applied with discipline and courage. I am not writing this as a researcher but as a teacher who has been working in the field for over twenty-five years in some of the toughest situations I have heard of.

Inclusive aggression allows for meaningful contact, while exclusive aggression assumes the world is hostile and unreceptive to meeting our needs. Distinguishing between the two helps us to understand the life experiences of children and their programming toward overt or covert manipulation. Successful mastery of this PSEL helps us with self-worth and identity formation and protects us from a state of self-loathing turned outward onto others.

Adults may unintentionally exacerbate exclusive aggression because we are afraid, taught to view aggressive and sexual drives as impure and in need of containment. While there is some truth to the importance of restraint, we may go too far in the direction of teaching young people to hide these drives, impulses, fantasies, and thoughts they suspect they will be shamed for exposing.

This job has very nearly killed me, as I have worked in rather hostile environments for many years, and still do. It turns out that I am actually well suited to working in tough schools, and I prefer it, as I find it difficult to tolerate aggression from adults but can empathize and be compassionate and calm when being confronted by aggressive and violent behavior from some of the youth that I work with.

But it has been a long road of recovery, aided by help from professionals, some family, and close friends.

Aggression assumes a bad reputation from our fear and lack of understanding but also because we associate it with being out of control. When we don't make the distinction between a force within us and an action taken, we blend the two. Aggression is a force and violence is an action; they are not synonymous. Fantasy or impulse may be a prelude to violence, but learning self-control and self-regulation prevent implosion (anger turning into depression) or explosion (anger turning into violence).

I moved to South Korea in 1995 to begin my teaching career. At this point in my life, I had no interest in becoming a teacher; in fact, as a student, I was turned off to high school by a difficult experience (for a later time). I made it to university, and after I graduated, I was interested in traveling and paying off my school debt, which didn't actually end up happening until I started working in Hong Kong three years later.

I was twenty-six years old when I began my training in martial arts in South Korea, while teaching English in Seoul. This training transformed my life as I learned how to breathe and how to meditate. In Seoul I trained for ten months with a wonderful group of people, many of whom were highly skilled in martial arts and had military combat training; in fact, as the Koreas are still technically at war, they were also practicing military personnel.

Any martial arts training has breathing as a foundational element. The breath is what connects us to the outside. We bring the air from the outside into ourselves via our lungs—the breath is what connects us to our perceived reality. Our lungs bring air into our bodies and feed our muscles and our minds and our emotions. Deep and purposeful breathing is the only way to have any semblance of control over our environment, and if that environment is hostile, then our breath is the only mitigating factor that will keep someone like me from crossing a line that would inflict regret for the rest of my life.

The warrior fights oneself—never others. The battle is always an internal one. We fight our negative emotions, our hate, and our anger. We do this by breathing. I do this by breathing, as I have for the past twenty-five years.

When we channel aggression into constructive forms, we dismantle the notion we are being violent. For those students who aren't fortunate enough to have a martial arts sensei, we can grant permission and even encouragement to have conversations about our drives and how we manage them. This does not mean ignoring threats but rather invitations for personal exploration so we don't drive youth underground or help them feel ashamed.

Children with inherently stronger aggressive drives or who have grown up in areas where the threat of harm is omnipresent are more at risk from adults who don't teach how to embrace our aggression. Without adequate support for these high-risk students—or worse, we automatically respond punitively—the opportunity for remediation will decay. Our work is to recognize perceived threats based so we don't react out of fear and develop long-term strategies to harness aggression through a more evolved sense of self.

Am I aggressive? In a certain sense I am extremely aggressive, and part of the frustration of working in hostile environments is knowing how aggressive I really can be. But the aggression that I describe is a force of power to help others through their own emotional trauma, and this power of aggression can only be exercised through proper discipline and practice. Thus, I am a role model for my students, and as tough as it is now, and as tough as it was, I am tougher by virtue of my training and my practice—none of which happened without help but by the grace of the people I have been able to learn from.

Aggression is complex, requiring more nuanced exploration of our own drives to better understand those of children. Personal growth and professional development (PD) in this area would be valuable, especially if we can model the journey for middle and high school students who may have no other venue to examine this drive. See Figure 15.1.

If young people believe they have to hide their aggression, for fear of labeling or even reprisal, they endanger themselves in several ways.

When we hide aggression, we do the following:

a. We fragment ourselves. We split the parts of ourselves we are less comfortable with or proud of, causing (dis)integration. The extreme of this (dis)integration is a breakdown of our core selves, including physical and psychological health.

b. We compound the intensity of our impulses or drives. Pushing down or hiding a natural force will pressurize us. If we fill a balloon with helium, it will stretch the fabric until it can no longer contain it. Before that happens, the helium will be forced into a container with less space, making it more potent.

c. We dilute authenticity. As we are increasing the potency of our drive, we are decreasing our own sincerity. We are not showing the world all that we are; we are sharing less of ourselves and becoming resentful for it. As people become less of who they are, the risk of them behaving outside the scope of civility grows.

Figure 15.1

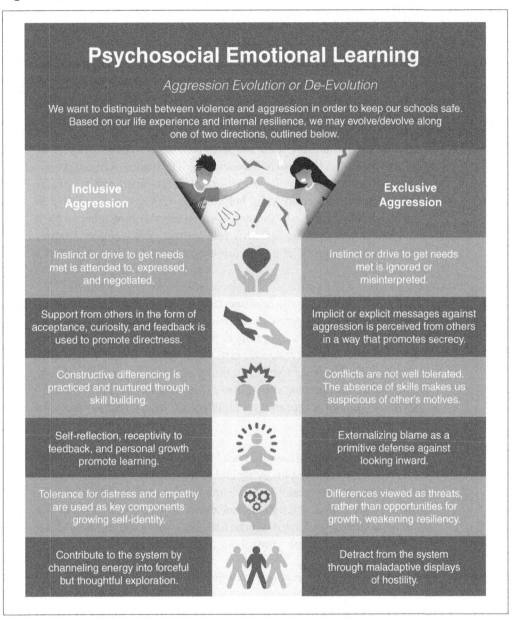

d. We become bullies and victims. As people become less of who they are, they often move toward one polarity or the other. Children who feel powerless and repressed may become victims, or they can seek to increase their volition through drastic measures aimed at helping others feel helpless.

Accepting aggression from students means we can rechannel it and maintain a safe environment. Through training, acceptance, and practice, this rechanneling mitigates the effects of the violence on teachers (mitigates, doesn't negate it; there is still a cost) but also keeps the children safe while they learn to adapt to their own emotional pain. Thus, I am able to be a role model who works under duress, with joy, fatigue, and all the emotions that come with working under extreme conditions.

Acceptance of this biological drive and the importance of repurposing this energy into constructive outlets is a gift for the student who might otherwise assume their role is to be destructive. We attempt to provide this within the rigid adherence of zero tolerance policies, assuming to put students on notice we will not tolerate any form of harassment, intimidation, or bullying, helpful in spirit but sometimes lost in application. Balancing safety and in-depth understanding takes us back to a similar goal of differentiating self-control versus self-regulation within a larger system that has notoriously struggled to protect students and faculty.

The bigger problem for me is connecting with the idea of education as a system—and how systemic violence can really gobble you up and spit you out. I can, in some way, relate to teachers complaining about how difficult teaching is, but it doesn't explain the attrition rate to me. To be a successful and caring teacher in many contexts, one must embrace and practice the warrior spirit, and doing so does not admit aggression but simply an acceptance and willingness to sacrifice for the good of the students.

Getting in touch with our old scripts around aggression, influenced by being on the receiving or giving end of recent anger, makes responding and not reacting possible. If we are cognizant of our biases, working in a climate of safety, we can slow down to be intentional about our intervention. As we all learn to better regulate our emotion, so, too, can we explore and not simply control our instinct for action.

It's very important to respond to conflict and violence rather than react to it, and this is only possible through breathing. The problem with toxic organizations and toxic schools is that often the abuse becomes relentless, and it relentlessly chips away at your ability to respond. I guess some call this burnout. Responding to stress from a position where the mind and the body are connected gives us strength. But as I mentioned earlier, it takes its toll, and working under these conditions very nearly killed me.

Key Points

▶ School is about exploring ideas, thoughts, beliefs and opinions, feelings, and experience through debate, discussion, and dialogue—all requiring energetic contesting.

▶ We are continuously learning how to advocate and negotiate, mindful of the feelings, wants, needs, and boundaries of others.

▶ There are limited resources in our community, and if we don't utilize aggression, we may miss out (i.e., teacher-parent time).

▶ Differentiating between inclusive versus exclusive aggression is key. Inclusive aggression means believing the world is fair and having faith to meet our needs while exclusive aggression does not believe this is possible or likely.

▶ Aggression is natural and healthy, which is important for the following:

  a. Protecting us from harm

  b. Helping us separate and become independent

  c. Growing intimacy and depth

  d. Being part of our identities

  e. Standing up for what we believe

Discussion Questions

Whether using the book for PD or within a book group, please consider the following questions to stimulate your own ideas for exploration.

1. Do males or females tend toward inclusive or exclusive aggression and why?

2. What early childhood lessons did I internalize about aggression?

3. What happens to me when I bury anger toward others?

4. How has technology impacted young people's expression of aggression?

5. How much permission do I explicitly and implicitly give students to express anger?

CHAPTER 16

Developing Tools for Expressing and Negotiating Needs

(Tami Boeve is an instructional facilitator for the Lakeland School System in Memphis, Tennessee.)

I grew up on Long Island, New York, in a hardworking middle-class family. Looking back, I have such fond memories of my childhood and feel that my parents always did everything that they could to meet our needs. Both of my parents are college graduates—both the first in their families. My mother held down the solid nine-to-five job as a medical office manager, which enabled my father to take many professional risks. He was always self-employed and had a variety of businesses, such as a printing company and video stores; he eventually settled into optometry. As a result, our financial situation often felt like we were riding the waves at the nearby ocean beaches.

As we learn to flow with the strong currents of our drives or impulses, improve awareness of our core self, and feel more secure in who we are, we will do a better job of balancing relationships, the source for many of our interpersonal needs, including intimacy, belonging, acceptance, and love. With experience, our recognition grows in how to identify and source these relationships for sustainable and reciprocal reward.

Life is all about creating ecosystems to balance what we give and take from our environment. Our more recent embrace of sustainable farming illustrates this appreciation that what they do today influences next year's crops. As children see themselves as unique beings, separate but needful, they, too, begin to reason like experienced farmers, recognizing the importance of planting seeds to reap the harvest of wants and needs, both for today and tomorrow. As we mature, this become a mutually beneficial process—not simply transactional but meaningful for higher-order needs. We move from seeing others as an endless wellspring of provision to building reciprocity in support of our mutual needs.

As a child, I wasn't truly aware of the now obvious ups and downs of our finances. However, I do remember things in extremes. My mother either took us to the Gap once a week and we were able to pick out several pieces of clothing, or we were eating macaroni and cheese and hot dogs several nights in a row for dinner. One particular memory stands out during one of the troughs in the waves of my childhood. My mother and I had just walked to the grocery store, which she advertised as our weekly adventure. Little did I know that it was because we were down to one car and could not afford another. We were on our last stretch and had just made it to the driveway when one of the brown paper grocery bags that my mom was holding ripped. The sound of glass shattering caught my attention, and I turned around to see a vivid red puddle on the driveway. It was the bottle of spaghetti sauce for our baked ziti, at the time one of our weekly staples for dinner. While I realized this was an inconvenience, I didn't realize how devastating it was to my mother and our family. I remember seeing her slowly crumple to the ground, place her hands over her face, and quietly begin to cry. My instinct was to console her and tell her that I would clean it up. She quickly regained her composure and told me the breaking glass had just scared her and for me not to worry. At the time, I believed her.

As our parental insulation from the shards of pain dissipates, we are encouraged to consider others more fully. This evolution from "I need" to "we need" requires skills for recognizing, expressing, and negotiating needs to satisfy oneself and the other. Mutual benefit also requires holding feelings in abeyance, tolerating distress, and having a secure sense of self to be willing to sacrifice when needed. True generosity, empathy, and altruism are based on this very process.

In the second psychosocial emotional learning (PSEL) in Chapter 7 we explored connecting sensations with feelings, wants, and needs. Understanding what our needs are—the consequences of not having them met, tolerating the displeasure of failure, and the reward of self-worth that comes with accomplishment—leaves us aware but not necessarily skilled in this ongoing operation.

Recognizing, expressing, and negotiating to get our needs begins early and life but takes years to master. When are needs activated, and from what trigger? Are some needs stronger than others, and why? What are the indicators for not having needs met in the short and long terms? How do we translate physical data through sensations into meaningful messages for others about what we need? And what happens when we encounter resistance from somebody we are negotiating with and our needs may not be met?

Years later, as soon as I turned fifteen and was able, I got a job at Roy Rogers, a fast-food restaurant. Getting a job at fifteen was a given. I worked hard and eventually was able to buy a nine-year-old rusty 1982 Volkswagen Cabriolet for $3,400. Not long after, one day on my way home from work, I stopped at the grocery store to pick up several items for my mom—one of which was a jar of spaghetti sauce.

That memory of the vivid red puddle and my mom crying on our drive-way came rushing back. When I got home, I asked her about that day. My mom looked at me and was surprised that I had remembered. She explained that it wasn't about the mess or the broken glass. At that time she was literally counting our change to be able to feed our family of four, and that afternoon she had dropped one of our meals and didn't know how she was going to be able to replace it. This absolutely shocked me. While I realized that we were not "rolling in dough," I had never realized how much my parents struggled to meet our daily needs. They had always kept the work and the struggle behind the scenes. This left a deep and lasting impression on me in regards to several things.

First and foremost, I realized how strong and hardworking and loving my mother was. She never let on how worried she was—or how difficult our lives sometimes were—and instead she made the best of every situation and was extremely resourceful. She made leading our family—even during such difficult and stressful times—easy and enjoyable. My parents were able to meet our needs—or at least be able to make it appear as though they were doing that for us. My brother and I felt like we wanted for nothing and had a wonderful childhood despite our financial struggles. It also left an impression regarding how we choose to advocate for our needs in a way that considers the feelings of others. My mother had done that for our family.

This impression of meeting wants and needs with grace and dignity has filtered into every aspect of my life but no area more as in being a mom and in my professional life as an educator. I truly believe that it has enabled me to not only be successful and effective in my field but allowed me to enjoy my job every single day.

Younger students will learn through alternating. You provide this now, and I'll provide this later. Simultaneous benefit occurs with maturation, in which both parties benefit at the same time. As adults, we learn to benefit from giving and not just receiving. When we feel good about ourselves from meeting others' needs without needing anything in return, we grow our identity and self-worth.

The first step to answering the questions about needs is acknowledging that you cannot recognize needs from your brain. As we explored in the very first PSEL, in Chapter 6, the brain is responsible for protecting us, with simple questions such as "What if...?" and "Should I...?" to anticipate real and perceived threats. The body is the path to understanding needs, illuminated by sensations and feelings that indicate type, strength, location, and impediment.

In Western society, we tend to ignore our bodies, treating our corporal selves as a vehicle to be maintained as opposed to an integral part of the decision-making team. We interpret messages from the body as symptoms to be eradicated, making it impossible to identify, much less act on our needs. If my back hurts, get a massage; if my head hurts, I take some ibuprofen.

Medication is a huge industry in the U.S., based on the overwhelming desire to ease our discomfort. With a decreasing capacity for distress, fueled in large part by our increasing reliance, dependence, and addition on technology, we are losing contact with ourselves. We stop listening and interpreting messages from the body, widening the brain-body gap.

Our growing disintegration means a diluted sense of self and a corresponding decline in empathy. It is not possible to be fully available for relationships when we are fragmented as individuals. The extreme outcome for this breakdown is violence. Children (or adults) who lack faith in the world to get their needs met turn their aggressive impulses inward or outward.

With a deficit of psychosocial emotional competence fueling this breakdown and elevating the risk of self-harm or harm to others, we may appreciate how quick fixes can't solve the complex issues. Prevention and intervention consider etiology before solution, with the epicenter at the intersection of individual wellness and organizational health. Prioritizing all types of learning for children and adults within the organization is our new focus.

Whole child education recognizes the maturation process; as children go from elementary to middle to high school, the complexity of their wants and needs grows. A baby wants comfort from a clean diaper and timely feeding. A preteen still wants the comfort but from a warm bed and more interesting food. An adolescent may want comfort from companionship and the freedom to cook for themselves.

As needs become more complex, so, too, does the task of expressing and negotiating them. A young child may simply need to say please to get what they want, but a middle schooler may have to wait, offer something in return, or simply deal with rejection. Growing complexity requires the skills of expression and negotiation, including our recognition of inherent barriers or resistance.

Fast-forward several years to my first year in college at Vanderbilt University. I was in a freshman "weed out" physics class, and I was literally about to tear my hair out in frustration. For the first time in my life, I could not understand an academic topic. Throughout my K–12 school years, I was a strong and what most would call "gifted" student. While I did have to work hard and study, sometimes more than other students, as long as I had applied myself I did well. I took as many higher-level honors and AP classes as I could, and I graduated with honors. Yet, here I was, eighteen years old, literally failing in class for the first time in my life. I could NOT grasp physics, no matter what I did or how much I studied. I read and reread, worked and reworked problems, but it didn't matter.

There are multiple barriers to expressing one's needs that are developmental in nature. Very young children haven't developed sufficient empathy or tolerance for distress to conduct complex negotiations. This is why early education involves parallel play so children can enjoy the company of others without having to negotiate.

These developmental challenges don't all resolve with age if we haven't successfully navigated the stages early in life. Brain-body imbalance, for instance, makes expressing and negotiating more difficult because we may be less aware our needs exist. Children who grow up imbalanced between brain and body may lose touch with their wants and needs, treating the indicators from the body as symptoms to be treated.

If children are aware of their needs, they may be too afraid to express them or unable to effectively convey this information. A child acting out in class may be labeled as oppositional, when, in fact, self-regulation makes negotiation of needs difficult. The child's strong anxiety turns off other children who don't want to share. In some instances this child would be punished due to behavior without ever addressing the underlying cause.

Barriers of awareness or inability to express a need may look the same from the outside, so exploring the struggle through dialogue is important. "Were you aware of what you needed when you acted that way?" This simple question or suggesting what you suspect the child needed can turn a mistake into a learning opportunity.

I remember calling home and crying to my mom, explaining my physics situation, ready to give up and accept an F for the first time in my life. I was mortified. My mother's advice was to seek outside help from the professor because he was there to meet my needs. She pointed out that it was my education, and I was my own advocate. It sounds silly and fundamental now, but I had never thought of it that way before. In the past I could always meet my own academic needs. As a result of this pep talk, instead of giving up, I was determined to work even harder.

I reached out to my professor and respectfully yet firmly asked for help. I went to every scheduled lab session possible and plopped myself in the professor's office during every office hour available in order to receive extra support. I am sure that I annoyed that professor with my incessant questions, most of which I never did grasp. However, the professor patiently sat with me and attempted to help while he put on a strong and happy face throughout the semester. Similar to my mother, the professor never let on to how frustrated he was with the situation. I received a C in the class, which was my very first. I am convinced that the professor gave me a C just so that he would not have to ever see my face in his office again. I gratefully took it and ran.

Negotiating to get needs met has its own set of barriers—most notably the lack of permission to assert ourselves. Children who grow up in oppressive environments where they are expected to be seen and not heard or children who are given everything they want (possessions) to keep them quiet may avoid negotiating when needs aren't easily met.

Recognizing, expressing, and negotiating our needs can be challenging when the reward doesn't match the effort. The fear of making a situation worse, destabilizing our environment, may cause us to give up prematurely or fail to be creative in our efforts. For those who are comfortable or at least familiar with having unmet needs, they may decide the greater danger is really trying and failing.

Some children or adults don't invest their full selves into the process, not wanting to risk disappointment or rejection. Helping these individuals become more creative or persistent may be met with resistance, important for us to recognize as an antiquated but seemingly vital protective mechanism. Inviting a person to relinquish what they believe is keeping them safe without knowing if they feel secure at the core to tolerate the failure may be premature.

For these situations, we want to help distinguish between somebody not wanting to meet our needs or not being in a position to do so. To help take the perceived loss less personally, we might consider exploring all possible reasons for abandoning our negotiation while giving ourselves credit for the risk-taking.

People don't automatically meet our needs—not simply because they don't care but due to a myriad of other possibilities like not knowing how. Sometimes people need something from us first or don't want to give us what we need. They may have similar fear of fully engaging or not trusting their own needs will be reciprocally met.

Through the development of our negotiating, or self-advocacy, we will need to grow our tolerance for distress even further. If we can endure the upset that comes from not getting what we want, we stand a better chance returning to the negotiation table with that same person or others who witnessed our gracious acceptance of the defeat.

I had learned two valuable lessons as a result of my physics debacle. First, I was my own advocate, and it was okay to ask teachers for help to meet my academic needs, even if they were different from the learners around me. It took me a while to get there, but I was finally able to comfortably admit my weaknesses and struggles. I did it with grace and patience and realized that life and learning is all about the journey. And second, it was the responsibility of the teacher to work hard, to go above and beyond, to figure out what works, and to help students meet their needs. I realized that I was not an inconvenience or a bother to my professor and that it was okay to ask for individual support and attention. These lessons helped to shape and hone not only my philosophy and technique as a teacher but eventually my philosophy and technique as an instructional facilitator.

Manipulation

The process of negotiation to get our needs met involves a range of tactics learned from our family, community, and social media. Negotiation often evokes unpleasantness from others who don't like or are triggered by our methods of persuasion, demand, or bartering. Manipulation is the judgment we apply, evoking strong reactions from people on all sides of the process. Manipulation is largely thought of as a coercive attempt to steal what we want without consideration for others.

Manipulation is not, however, a dirty word deserving of the negative connotation that is frequently misapplied. We grow up hearing that manipulation means coercing another in a way that disregards their well-being. If we are called manipulative, we are offended at the judgment that we get what we want at any cost.

This term has been negatively stigmatized, a misnomer, underserved of its contemporary meaning. How we get our needs met through the differencing process is largely determined by the way in which we manipulate others in our environment, not whether we are manipulating.

In its simplest form, manipulation is our way of using something to achieve a goal, such as manipulating a shovel to dig or a spoon to eat soup. We use humans as well, although our intent has a lot to do with whether a person feels used.

What determines if manipulation is helpful or harmful are two considerations: how overt or covert our process and whether our manipulation adversely impacts others. If a person doesn't feel used, understanding our intent and what may be gained from the exchange, the person may not resist or judge our actions to be self-serving.

Therapists manipulate clients to help expand their perspective, deepen self-awareness, and motivate to create new experiments to promote a greater range of choice. Teachers manipulate students by encouraging new ways of processing information and expanding knowledge. It comes down to our approach, how transparent and considerate of others we are. Also involved are our motivations and caring for the well-being of others that determine our success in manipulating.

In 1997 I got my first teaching job as a fifth-grade teacher in a suburb outside of Nashville, Tennessee. My classroom was an outside portable unit, which other teachers avoided like the plague. However, I thoroughly enjoyed it. We were in our own little world! You would often find my class sitting on blankets and towels in the grass reading and learning rather than being cooped up in our "trailer." I thought it was smooth sailing from that moment on! For the most part, it was. It was an average class, and I had the average first-year teaching experience . . . with one exception. The exception was a student named Chris.

Chris was extremely bright but had one of the most severe cases of ADHD that I have seen even to this day in my career as an educator. I quickly realized that his ability was unlimited, but his focus and attention was not. His previous teachers had all warned me about his attitude and his behavior, going so far as to call him a lost cause. As a first-year teacher, I was appalled and determined to take a different route with Chris. I'm not going to lie; our first few weeks were a complete disaster. Chris would end up frustrated, throwing books, not completing assignments, and sometimes ending up in tears. You talk about rough waters and riding the ups and downs of waves! He was not able to express his thoughts and needs, but instead his behavior became completely impossible and defiant. I kept my poker face on at school in front of Chris, and I am proud to say that I never lost my cool. I often thought of my mom and my college professor and how they would handle this situation. However, I would go home completely exhausted emotionally and physically and shed many tears; my heart was heavy knowing that I was not meeting his needs. I felt like I was simply treading water and not doing what was best for my student. After a conference with his mother, I quickly learned that she was not going to be supportive and assist me in meeting Chris's needs. It was at this point that I started to shift my thinking from academic to personal with Chris, and I thought of every child's basic needs and how he was not able to express them to me.

I began taking small steps to "trick," or manipulate, Chris into being happier, more confident, and eventually more successful. Our first trick was his new classroom position as the official class runner. Since we were in a portable, I was often required to send students to other places, which I did on the typical student job rotation chart. I threw that chart overboard, and the classroom runner became his job and his job alone. This meant that Chris was able to frequently get up, leave the classroom and get some fresh air, and essentially get some of his wiggles and energy out. We even came up with a deal: Every time he was asked to be a runner and leave our trailer, he had my permission to run (not walk like other students) to the building. Not only was he allowed to run but if he felt the need, he had my permission to run laps around our portable before coming back to the classroom to resume his work. Chris was also allowed to stand while working, and I embedded physical activities and breaks into our schedule for every student, such as jumping jacks or quick dance parties.

Chris flourished that year in my fifth-grade classroom, and so did I. This inexperienced first-year teacher had her first experience with developing teacher tools to meet the needs of a challenging student. Years later, Chris reached out to me and thanked me for his "favorite" year in his K–12 school experience. What he remembered most, he said, was my smile and patience and how he felt cared for and eventually confident in my classroom. He told me that after being a student in my classroom, he was comfortable advocating for himself as a learner and asking teachers for help and guidance. He even continued to ask other teachers for opportunities to be their classroom runner! It struck me how similar his feelings were with me and our experiences that year to my feelings with my mother and my physics professor.

We can manipulate others through being passive, aggressive, passive-aggressive, or assertive. Being passive is equivalent to being avoidant, which sometimes means we hope the other will notice our upset and do something to alleviate our discomfort. While this may be transparent, another person may feel used by our lack of explicitness. Being aggressive commonly means trying to overpower resistance. Passive-aggressive manipulation is more subtle, much like trying to get others on our side to help us feel more justified in our stance. Assertive is what we strive for when we are straightforward about our experience and wishes.

This process goes on all day long though we seldom dissect it until a problem erupts. Consider a suburban high school teacher who loved her job, known for being thoughtful and considerate of her colleagues. During an outing with other teachers, she was listening to a phone message at the same time a peer was trying to get her attention. She gestured that she couldn't respond and for the other to wait one minute.

It was a seemingly harmless gesture at the time but one that offended her fellow teacher and resulted in not being spoken to for months afterward. The first teacher didn't know why her colleague was upset, becoming upset at the way she was treated. They would pass in the hallways without acknowledging each other or making eye contact. Sometimes these very simple incidents that could be resolved in minutes, if not seconds, escalate without attention.

In this case, the manipulation was not acknowledging her colleague. The manipulation was a way of conveying hurt feelings and a wish to have her rejection attended to. When the message of silence wasn't recognized as an unmet need but instead resulted in further detachment between the two, the feelings intensified. Over time the feelings became calcified, and the original snub matriculated into a sizable rift.

Perhaps the female teacher who was doing the ignoring was using a tactic learned in her early family life, and maybe it was more effective with those who were familiar with it. It's possible that in this teacher's early life experience she would be ignored by her own mother when she displeased her. She learned through this experience that going to apologize to her mother, even when she didn't know what she did "wrong," was the most effective way to restore peace. Using this same strategy as an adult was instinctive even if it wasn't helpful.

Currently, I serve as an instructional coach for a school district outside of Memphis, Tennessee. My role in meeting needs has shifted from being on the direct path of meeting student's needs as a teacher to meeting their needs indirectly by being their teacher's coach. It is remarkable how similar both of these roles really are. On a daily basis, I am honing my skills and tools as a coach to help teachers not only meet the needs of their students but to reach out for help and support as educators. We then figure out and negotiate how to best help them meet the needs of their students by implementing strategies into their classrooms. So instead of me helping students like Chris through his frustration and tears, I am often helping teachers through theirs. I am now in a position to help teachers learn the lessons that I have learned—to not only help their students but to help themselves.

If we as adults and role models experience failed negotiations as irreconcilable threats, imagine what goes on amongst our students, who lack the skills and experiences necessary to traverse rough terrain. Now imagine what it would be like for a student in the midst of chronic bullying, perpetual ostracism, considerable self-doubt, and a lack of a clear identity. How would this student stand a chance of reconciling differences to get their needs met?

If we further include a detached family system providing no solid grounding and a lack of hope for the future, the potential for extreme reactions takes shape. If this child is triggered by an attempt to manipulate in a way that feels like one more kick to the groin from the world, the response may not seem as disproportionate. A breakdown of negotiating differences devolves into an aggressive fantasy aimed at regaining control in one's life, which sometimes a child will act upon.

Last year, I was assigned to mentor a new teacher to our school; we will call her Mrs. Jefferson. Mrs. Jefferson was a second-year teacher, but her first year teaching was what I would describe as an absolutely horrible experience. Essentially, she was not supported or coached by administration at her previous school, and she left that school feeling like a horrible teacher and an even more horrible person. She was drowning. As part of her improvement plan at our school, Mrs. Jefferson and I were to meet weekly to preview the lesson plans for the upcoming week, and I would often sit in her classroom to observe these lessons. Afterward, we would meet again for immediate feedback and reflection. Mrs. Jefferson was struggling in several areas—most of which were related to self-confidence and classroom management. Our first couple of meetings were what I would consider formal and uncomfortable, with me doing most of the talking. Mrs. Jefferson had absolutely no idea how to react to my support and guidance, and she was not yet comfortable opening up and expressing her frustrations or fears. Previously, she had been judged and reprimanded by administration. She had never had a safe place to go to for support. Over time, we developed a strong bond and trust, and eventually we developed a friendship.

The fortunate students and adults find somebody they can trust to help them learn how to safely and effectively meet their own needs. For those who are less fortunate, the risk can be high. Tragedies like Columbine High School and the countless other incidents of school violence may often devolve when a trusted supporter can't be found. In most cases failed negotiations get resolved without any significantly overt damage; however, we want to appreciate that residual damage is subtle but cumulative.

Trauma-informed or trauma-sensitive schooling is a more commonly used phrase, with an underlying goal to appreciate how seemingly innocuous hurts can mean something much greater for somebody feeling fragile. We may not always see the signs, nor do we always have the time or energy to be on the lookout, making the challenge great. If we can appreciate the process by which people feel harmed and consider the tools the person has and their willingness to use them, we can intervene and diffuse mounting tension.

I remember one particular day as a breakthrough for Mrs. Jefferson. Interestingly enough, it wasn't necessarily a pedagogical breakthrough as an educator. It was a personal breakthrough. After meeting together for a few weeks, Mrs. Jefferson ran into my office, shut the door, and put her head in her hands and began sobbing. She had spent hours planning a perfect lesson, and it had flopped. We all know that this is so common for not just new teachers but every teacher. Her students were not engaged at all and eventually became off task and disinterested. She had put her heart and soul into her work and it had failed, which every teacher takes very personally. Once I was able to calm her down and reassure her that this happens to the best of us, we were able to have a conversation about what had happened. Teachers often struggle with looking outside of their classroom walls for help, and it is a very isolated profession. Mrs. Jefferson had reached a pivotal moment where she was comfortable expressing her feelings, emotions, and weaknesses. She was finally comfortable asking for help.

Throughout the rest of the school year, Mrs. Jefferson and I were able to work together to help her develop her skills as a teacher. Her main focus was how to express the required skills and standards to her students in a way that was most effective for them. More importantly, Mrs. Jefferson recognizes her strengths and weaknesses as a person and as a teacher and is comfortable and can effectively seek out and receive support and guidance. I strongly believe that I was able to help her develop tools to express and negotiate her needs outside of her classroom because of my experiences with my mother, my physics professor, and my fifth-grade student Chris.

One simple act of kindness or understanding can help restore a child or adult's hope that their needs can be met. Helping a person feel less alone so they can reinvest energy for constructive differencing or negotiation to get their needs met is oftentimes enough. Noticing the difficulty for persisting in the wake of feeling let down and providing reassurance you will be by their side, swimming against the current, can be a tremendous gift.

We ride the waves of our lives and experiences just as we ride the waves on vacation at the beach. Our life experiences, both positive and negative, shape the person who we are today. My vivid memories of the broken jar of spaghetti sauce and my mother's strength and grace, my professor's open door in helping me through my first academic roadblock, energetic Chris in my fifth-grade classroom, and mentoring Mrs. Jefferson all have a common thread. These experiences have helped me develop not only my own tools for expressing and negotiating my needs but have allowed me to share these tools with others as a person, a student, a teacher, and now as an educational coach.

Key Points

▶ As children see themselves as unique beings, they can recognize their reliance on others to help meet wants and needs.

▶ You cannot recognize needs from your brain, as this is the role of the body. Not attending to our bodies makes expressing or negotiating less possible.

▶ Children who grow up imbalanced between brain and body may lose touch with their wants and needs.

▶ If a child is aware of their needs, they may be too afraid to express them or be unable to find the right words to convey what they feel or need.

Negotiating to get needs met has its own set of barriers—most notably the lack of permission to assert.

Discussion Questions

Whether using the book for professional development (PD) or within a book group, please consider the following questions to stimulate your own ideas for exploration.

1. Do males or females in my grade tend to negotiate needs more easily, and why?

2. Which one of my needs is most difficult to acknowledge?

3. What is my least effective strategy of meeting a need? How did I learn this?

4. What is my most effective strategy of meeting a need? How did I learn this?

5. What type of person do I have the most difficult time negotiating with, and what does this tell me about myself?

CHAPTER 17

Cultivating Empathy and Advanced Empathy

(Jeffrey Donald is the mindfulness coordinator for Montgomery County Public Schools in Rockville, Maryland.)

When I was a small child, I was accompanying my father in running errands in town. I was raised in a rural environment where farming was a mainstay of the local economy, so fields and orchards between homes was very common. Not far from our home, we passed a walnut grove and noticed a young man eating walnuts off of the ground. I thought nothing of it until the entire neighborhood began talking about a man living in this grove, eating nothing but walnuts as his diet. When my father heard this, he wept. He immediately walked to the grove, insisted the man come with us for a meal, gathered the man's handful of belongings, and brought him home. He lived with us for two years. Later on in my formative years, I asked my father why he felt it necessary to help this total stranger. He stopped his work, turned to me, and looked at me with absolute seriousness—something I knew from experience as a life lesson to come. What he said next changed my life. He said, "There are many types of riches. Always put yourself in the other person's shoes. Then serve them. We are not complete human beings until we serve others. Making a difference for someone else is what makes us rich."

Successful negotiation with others—not simply transactional exchanges of bartering without concern but a truer desire for mutual reciprocity—requires care. Caring and concern for others are the ingredients and result of empathy, a deep appreciation and understanding of another. Most empathy is innate, as evidenced by a toddler who hugs a crying sibling. For others, empathy is slower to develop, sometimes diminished by how they experience injustice in the world.

Through childhood and into early adulthood, we experience life's rewards and defeats, moving us on a continuum between hope and despair. The closer we approach despair, the more difficult it is to maintain empathy, with a self-focus pushing us into survival mode. Why care about others if the world doesn't seem to care about us? While it is possible to understand and care about the feelings of others through our own torment, self-preservation makes it more difficult.

Caring adults who recognize and consider the influence of poverty, violence, and oppression, without accepting them as excuses, help children learn harmony. These savvy educators can pluck the invisible strands that holds us all together, allowing us to hear and feel their reverberations, even when we can't see them. Tension from these strands reminds us to appreciate our similarities and differences, preventing the fabric of our society from unraveling. If we neglect our other senses, only seeing through our eyes where we naturally distort the field with conscious and unconscious bias, we lose vision. In sight we incite, labeling what may seem obvious but lacking a deeper appreciation for all the historical elements creating relevant conditions.

Relying on our sight in neglect of our other senses means we overlook our own myopia, especially dangerous as educators. Through our reflex to judge, we may fail to provide opportunities for building equity, tolerating the pain of unfairness, or growing our resiliency, instead promoting polarization and increasing the likelihood of cementing roles of victims and perpetrators.

My name is Jeffrey Donald, mindfulness coordinator for Montgomery County Public Schools in Rockville, Maryland. My job is to advocate, create, train, and sustain mindfulness practices and programs within school settings as a direct approach to building mental and emotional capacity in schools. Addressing school and community culture as a method to cultivate empathy and compassion is my highest priority. The connection between academic outcomes and social emotional learning (SEL) is undeniable; ask any educator and they will confirm that students cannot achieve true successes in one without the other. They are lofty thoughts and aspirations indeed, but how do I create empathy in others? In order to speak authentically to others, I have to first model this in myself: I need to conquer "the Other" complex.

Understanding the barriers for developing empathy, erected by people and institutions, allows us to design experiments to evolve. School can serve as critical human laboratories where we create and test hypothesis before turning out students into society. Through our design we can ensure consideration of extraneous variables and rushes to judgment. Variables we may not consider can easily be critical determinants that might impact our decision-making. Observing somebody looting during a protest, for instance, may not yield critical data about motivation or circumstance.

How did people learn to get their needs met when they were young? Did they grow up in a food desert or attend a school with low academic standards, propelling their attitude or worldview? We don't know what opportunities took place to develop moral reasoning or care about the feelings of a neighbor, so let us not assign value determination for another. Instead, let us look inward to first appreciate the filters of our own lens and the reasons we see different colors on the spectrum.

I am writing this at a very difficult time in the country's history where we are challenged to look at our differences in terms of privilege and equity and to see the intrinsic value of each soul. My father and mother modeled to me and my siblings how to experience the world through somebody else's eyes, especially if their outer differences stirred up discomfort or displeasure, enriching all lives involved.

Self-reflection allows us to set aside our judgments to travel in the heavy boots of those who think and feel differently than ourselves, using curiosity to help us explore and negotiate our differences. Our depth of understanding for these differences begins with consideration for our own inequities and frailties matriculating into deeper understanding and appreciation. In doing so we resist the urge to judge others, instead becoming curious and interested in the origin of people's feelings and experiences.

A friend of mine shared a very enlightening story with me once. He grew up in a very small town in northern Minnesota where there were literally no people of color. Not a single one. Yet, they managed to find division within their community: the blonds against the redheads. He was the person who taught me about our deeply ingrained Neolithic wiring. He introduced me to "the Other."

People will instinctively look for differences to find comfort in sameness. If you and I can rally together because we think alike, we feel safer to protect against the other who thinks differently. This may be a simpler strategy for those who don't negotiate differences well. It is unfortunate, this brand of pseudo-intimacy, because while the work of differencing is not easy, the rewards are high. By tuning in to the emotions and experience of others, we will create greater depth in relationships, a higher-order need for all humans. With intimacy serving as a potent motivator, people are either fearful or unaware of what they may be giving up.

Self-reflection allows us to target our barriers for being empathic to bring about closeness in relationships. With inward and outward consideration for impediments to empathy, we would have a difficult time recognizing an emerging threat so insidious that we invite it into our lives, watching it take over and believing we are all the better for it. Social media and technology create anonymity and the increased freedom to dehumanize, potentially lessening our instinct to put ourselves in the place of others. Cyberbullying among children, for instance, is made easier because children don't see the immediate reaction of their victims. Desensitization to violence via traditional media and video games, parents enabling their children lessening accountability, and an epidemic of substance abuse all have potential influences on empathy.

Barriers to empathy and the resulting dehumanization of human beings is a cause of racial tension in our society. We become easily polarized when we view life as a competition and others as threats, consuming resources that belong to us as if geography constitutes ownership. "I got here first" is an argument a seven-year-old wields to sit in the passenger seat, recently finding a comeback through reality television glorifying survival of the fittest. Power is intoxicating, but if we define it as the influence over others, we will always have to be watching our backs.

A win-at-all-costs mentality creates an even greater chasm of differences and less concern for how those differences are defended, resulting in stereotyping and discrimination, the antithesis of empathy. Talk shows, third-person shooter games, reality programming, and social media have all helped promote indiscriminate willing, the antithesis of curiosity and caring.

As we satiate our need for power and control, we evolve to a place of empowering others. Without an instinct to dominate or overpower, we become less reliant on external structures to set parameters for our lives. We have greater freedom with a system of checks and balances that doesn't require legal intervention because creation and enforcement of the law leaves too much subjectivity. Legislation is the last bastion of a society when answers can't be found through negotiation, treating people punitively for their lack of ownership.

Paradoxically, the perception of less accountability moves us into a survivalist mentality, leading to a further decline in empathy and relinquishing our pursuit for higher-order needs. Empathy is less necessary in survival mode because we aren't cultivating intimacy; we are using our brain to promote caution. We don't believe we can tolerate greater distress, so we keep risk-taking low.

I have a current example to share that illustrates this inner reflection and dialogue that is essential to the beginning of cultivating empathy.

I had the most honest thought this morning in meditation. I've been watching the riots and aftermath of the George Floyd murder on television and have understandably been deeply disturbed by it. As far back as I can remember, I have known that, as a white person of conscience, I should help Black people with their struggle for justice and equality. It dawned on me today that it's not the Black people's struggle to change their lives that requires change.

What needed to change was me.

We are all racists. Our primitive brains are hardwired to make assumptions, generalizations, and stereotypes faster than we can think about it or even be aware of it. It makes sense. For example, once you've burned yourself with a hot iron, stove, or match, as soon as your eyes perceive one of those things that caused you pain and harm, your reptile brain goes on alert. To survive, we have to be able to instantaneously and constantly assess and ask, "Am I safe here?" We don't have to physically experience every dangerous situation in order to perceive a threat. We can be warned, for example, to look both ways before we cross the street. With enough conditioning, we learn to pause and be careful every time we stand on the edge of the sidewalk, even though we were never hit by a car.

While a segment of the population is moving toward a survival model and feeling victimized, another segment is soaking up power. Another growing threat to a decline of empathy in our classrooms is the trend of entitlement, or the sense that we are deserving of what we have without recognizing privilege or opportunity. Entitlement may become an enduring trait that brings us further from higher-order needs, such as peace and fulfillment.

Entitlement is complex; it's not as simple as children believing they are deserving of whatever they want. It is based, in part, on our declining empathy that leaves children focused on their own wants, helping them to seem indifferent to the plight of others or even the value of earning what they achieve.

Entitlement may also be a self-serving interest interfering with constructive negotiation of differences. Reciprocity is made far more difficult without appreciating the needs of others. For a classroom teacher, children perceived as entitled are difficult to engage with, worsened by our own disgust or indifference. It requires a tremendous amount of patience to work with somebody displaying this trait, which is why we need to be self-reflective to monitor our own distaste. Keep in mind that entitlement varies in degrees from an active belief of "I'm better than" to an unrealized perception of how we exist in relation to others.

I have been unconsciously taught through the system itself, thoroughly and effectively, that anyone different from me, particularly a person with African physical features, is dangerous. Looking, sounding, and acting differently, they are "the Other." I have never actually experienced harm from a Black person; nevertheless, I see one of them, and my primitive nervous system sounds the alarm.

It's embarrassing. I know better.

But it's automatic. I can't help it. And everybody does it.

I have countless Black friends and students whom I love dearly. Worse, I have a brother who is Black. Worse than that, I'm married to a beautiful, proud Black woman. Worst of all, I have beautiful, magnificent Black children.

It still happens. Amygdala hijacked. The Other.

Empathy is a combination of biology, programming, and learned experiences, including the success of other psychosocial emotional learnings (PSELs). Without being in touch with our own bodies (brain-body balance), turning sensations into needs (sensations, feelings, and needs), and without having some sense of self or negotiating differences with others, it's difficult to fully explore the experience of another.

Empathy also requires the ability to communicate what we understand to be the experience of others, referred to as reflective listening. Telling somebody we understand does little to elicit the visceral experience of being understood, unsure how fully we are taking in their experience. Reflective listening forces us to peer outside our own narrow cone, becoming active in the pursuit of growing understanding between others and groups.

Fortunately, what we learn, we can unlearn. My job, in my struggle to end self-absorption and racism, is to bring justice and equality to everyone around me by retraining my mind. This is not only for myself but it is to hold others accountable for their biases and egocentrism. Be the change I wish to see, right?

Beyond my own example, how can I disrupt the systemic lack of empathy in our society? We cannot underestimate the power and influence of the schoolteacher. Schools are where so much more than academics are taught! "Learning to focus, maintaining motivation, and handling the frustrations of sharing, learning and communicating with peers are skills that depend on the ability of the student to understand and manage their emotions. These are basic competencies that are crucial to the success of the student as they progress through the school system" (Broderick, 2013).

Building emotional capacity and culture in schools takes the form of extensive implicit bias, trauma-informed care, mindfulness, and restorative justice training. Although these trainings are available to all, they are not required for students or staff members. The need for this type of professional learning is essential to building thoughtful, whole human beings and should be foundational to the education of all school communities.

In addition to the more commonly known modalities promoting personal growth, there is a lesser-known skill called advanced empathy. Poorly understood even among psychology professionals, this has to do with how we feel about our feelings and the feelings of others. For example, if we feel angry, what's it like to be angry? If we are sad, are we indifferent to the sadness or hopeful to alleviate our pain?

Advanced empathy is a prime determinant for suicide prevention and the assessment of risk for students. If, for instance, a young person has demonstrated some ideation around self-harm, one of the important questions a crisis professional might ask is whether the young person is resigned to unhappiness or is alarmed by the instinct to self-harm. Advanced empathy provides a powerful window into the soul of a distressed child.

Advanced empathy provides great insight into what young people need—primarily the level of support required to help be kind to themselves or others, accomplished through the appreciation of their own experience and that of others. For instance, if young people are sad, are they alarmed by how they are feeling? When support is offered, are they feeling cared for, and is it going to be received? If they resist our warmth, what other feelings, such as fear, are being elicited?

This is a difficult skill because we don't tend to reflect upon our feelings or those of others, especially when focused on academics. Children are even less familiar with the meta-analysis of their own feelings. If the adults will begin experimenting with this skill, it will provide valuable data to grow engagement with students.

Advanced empathy is also speculating on unstated feelings, derived from body language, tone, and our own intuition. This can be more powerful than basic empathy, since children may not be aware of their own feelings; however, the body holds this evidence. You may find this is more effective in relationships that are already established where trust is formed.

The key is to realize that we have reactions to our feelings and others' feelings needing exploration. When we combine empathy and self-reflection, focused on the feeling and what it means to us, we move into a new space where deeper self-acceptance and appreciation for others is possible.

So I have set up an autocorrect feature. When I notice myself feeling uneasy at the sight (or even sometimes the thought) of the Other, I backspace, pause, and remind myself that's not a threat but a human being—God's child, complete with history, feelings, and all of my human characteristics. Black people have waited so long— four hundred years and counting—and have been so incredibly patient for me and my ilk not to do anything extraordinary; just stop misidentifying them as an enemy.

This is the essence of cultivating the skill of empathy, recognizing my process, and willfully changing myself in order to live my highest potential. My teacher said, "If you cannot see God in all, you cannot see God at all." This is where empathy begins. We all have empathy within us, but we must work at it, honing it and strengthening it with practice.

I fail sometimes. We all do.

Here is one more epiphany I had this morning: My feelings of guilt and shame of my failures don't help either; these feelings only serve to make me feel overwhelmed or inadequate to the task of change and self-improvement. Again, autocorrect, backspace, and upload a more productive thought.

Key Points

▶ For students to have successful relationships, they need to recognize and care about the feelings of others.

▶ Empathy may be declining because parents are enabling their children and decreasing their accountability; they are desensitized by violence in the media and video games.

▶ The influence of technology, such as texting instead of calling, and the anonymity of certain social media may diminish empathy.

▶ If we are moving more toward a survivalist mentality, then empathy might serve less of a purpose.

▶ Entitlement and self-serving interests don't help us negotiate conflict or cultivate the deep intimacy resulting from understanding.

▶ Empathy is a PSEL built upon the success of other PSELs, such as balancing brain and body as well as learning to connect sensations with wants and needs.

▶ Without being in touch with our own bodies (feelings and needs), we are without having some sense of self or the ability to negotiate differences with others.

▶ Empathy involves the ability to communicate what we understand to be the experience of others; we refer to it as reflective listening.

▶ Advanced empathy involves how we feel about our feelings and the feelings of others.

Discussion Questions

Whether using the book for professional development (PD) or within a book group, please consider the following questions to stimulate your own ideas for exploration.

1. Do males or females in my grade tend to be more empathic, and why?

2. What are the trends in empathy I'm seeing with students over the past five or ten years?

3. How much of empathy seems to be learned versus innate?

4. Who in my life is least empathic, and how easy is it to feel close with them?

5. What about students who call themselves empaths? How can they be helped?

CHAPTER 18

Deepening Conflict Resolution to Constructive Differencing

. . . .

(Linda Rost is a science teacher from Baker High School in Montana, the 2020 Montana Teacher of the Year, and one of three finalists for National Teacher of the Year.)

The work we do is human work. Our students are on a journey of learning and growth, as we are also on a parallel journey to become better humans. Regardless of our content area, the work of a teacher is to equip our students to begin a lifelong path of growth, learning, and self-discovery about humanity and the world.

In the context of classroom interactions with students, a locus of power and control exists that has often been preestablished in other classrooms through other student-teacher interactions. An imbalance in power can be used to establish classroom norms and protocols, but it can also cause detrimental and harmful effects to students.

Through our negotiation with others to get our conjoint needs met, we experience resistance on both our parts. A natural result of the forces for sameness versus change, resistance is motivated largely by fears of the unknown or perceived threats such as rejection, abandonment, loss of control, and other hurt. When we negotiate to get our needs met, even with a finely tuned degree of empathy, we do so with the possibility of having our needs lost.

As our desire to meet our needs bumps up against the unbending will of another, we experience conflict. When navigated well, this conflict can be aptly described as the exploration of differences. As we explore these differences, we learn more about ourselves and others through contrasts of needs and our styles of meeting those needs.

This requires a solid but flexible sense of self, empathy, and the ability to be self-reflective, appreciating how our frailties and inequities influence our relatedness. For instance, if we know that we are rigid, untrusting of others, we might appreciate that our ability to make contact with others may be thwarted by this self-awareness. Being mindful of our frailty may help us to be more cognizant of our suspicion of others, allowing us to remain open.

This is by far one of the more challenging aspects of being human. Learning how to be at odds with somebody but maintain contact is among the most difficult life tasks. Our starting point is to appreciate conflict as the exploration of difference, so we are no longer threatened by differences but curious about the learning opportunities they offer.

During one of my most memorable conflicts with a student, I can remember staring into his face, at least a foot above mine, screaming at him in a rage I had scarcely ever felt. I was out of control. A staff member came down to the hall to make sure everything was okay. I don't even remember what the conflict was about, and I'm sure he doesn't either, but I'm sure we both remember the feeling we had. I was trying to regain my power and dominance over him, and he was resisting. In the end I succeeded and felt satisfied; he felt defeated. Our interactions were rocky after that, but he never checked the power dynamic again. I realize now, with years of teaching experience under my belt, that there were so many things I did wrong and so many better ways I could have approached the many smaller conflicts that occurred before this one. I also realize how his learning could have been so much better.

Differences are often experienced as threatening because they are perceived as contests, power struggles, or precursors for aggression. Among children, differences summon up fantasies of ostracism and the struggle for belonging. A lack of confidence in the formative years will lead to the suppression of one's own ideas in favor of winning favor with others. In some instances, this can be the start of a downward spiral, ending in self-loathing.

Without learning how to constructively differ, we risk not getting our needs met when simple expression and negotiation fail to produce. Limited resources further require us to conflict with others with dissimilar agendas or who don't keep our interests in mind. Our unwillingness to have conflict will mean fewer needs are met, producing voids. In the extreme these voids may help us to feel powerless to the point of implosion (depression, anxiety, self-harm) or controlling to the precipice of explosion (interpersonal discord, exclusive aggression). When entire classrooms are filled with mixtures of these students and teachers promoting their own agenda through behavior "management," we produce tension.

I first learned about classroom power structures during my first year of teaching while I was also in graduate school. I realized that I needed to be aware of the power structure in my classroom, even though my students may not be. As I studied my students and their learning, I also studied how this structure ebbed and flowed through our interactions. My awareness of it allowed me to consciously shift the power away from me and into the hands of my students to promote autonomy and student-centered learning.

This realization was bumpy, challenging, and ever-evolving. Since my own school experience was characterized with this same power structure, even though it felt wrong to impose it on my students, it was familiar. At the same time, I was a graduate student in curriculum and instruction, and I was experiencing the benefits of student-centered learning, which I had never fully engaged in before. As a learner, I could see how this shift in power structure changed my own learning, and I began to explore it with my students.

Power is a need we tend to stockpile. Since power and control help us to feel safe, we create hierarchies to feed our sense of comfort. Rather than internalizing this need, we siphon power and control through these environmental structures without realizing the impact on students. Some children may be afraid of this perceived power so they won't raise their hand, while others may challenge the authority to usurp the power. We see this phenomenon with teachers working within the power structure of a department or school, deferring to the majority for fear of being labeled as not being a team player.

In systems where unions and district leaders vie for power, resolute parties become firmly entrenched in their position, weakening structures out of fear for seeming weak. The lesson hasn't been learned that true power comes from empowering others through the exploration of differences and not getting one's way. Whether we hold back or become rigid in defense of a position, the absence of constructive differencing becomes the barrier for well-balanced compromise.

My first few years teaching, I can remember conflicts that made my students cry. I made my students cry. I made them cry when their punishment for incomplete homework was to work separately while the rest of the class engaged in enrichment activities that provided better learning opportunities than the worksheets I had assigned for homework. I made them cry when I prioritized the product of their learning over their own learning process. I was trying to satisfy my own ego in the quality and quantity of student work completion over the depth and breadth of their learning.

My own personal dichotomy between the archaic view of classroom power, contrasted with my discomfort of imposing my dominance, provided the cognitive dissonance necessary to shift my ideology. As I slowly started shifting the power to them, conflicts eased, and learning and engagement increased. I started finding ways to quantify this shift. When we engaged in whole class discussions, I recorded how much time was spent in student-led discussion and how much time I was talking and dominating the discourse. I noticed how students responded when I moved between groups during small group discussions.

I can remember one day in the fall when my students were discussing the ethics of abortion. I had been trying to facilitate better student-led discussions so that I wasn't leading the discourse. The discussion became very heated, and finally, students were going back and forth across the classroom, respectfully, one by one, sharing ideas. I froze in front of the class so they wouldn't stop. After several students had volleyed the conversation back and forth a few times, they collectively paused and looked at me. There was fear in their eyes. I asked them why they stopped, and they said they were afraid of getting in trouble. I asked them why they had this fear, but we all knew the answer. This was part of the power training that we had all received as students, myself included. I was starting to understand how it hampered learning and how to dismantle it.

The most toxic part of this dominant classroom power structure is that it is rooted in disrespect for students. Students are expected to comply and to have no opposition in the structures and practices in the classroom. However, they are the most important people in the classroom, and their learning is the most important process. Their input into their learning and our teaching is also some of the most necessary and meaningful.

Judgments Are Simpler

Judgments categorize, label, segregate, and ultimately prevent us from exploring differences that would help us to expand our perspective. Judgments, however, are easy and instinctive; they save time and energy because inward reflection is absent. Because human beings aren't simple and schools represent some of the more complex organizational structures that people dwell in, judgments lack the depth to effectively solve challenging problems.

The dilemma is that judgments are at the core of evaluations where schools base their entire grading system. We may not equate grading with judgment or excuse it as a necessary way of measuring progress, but at the heart of this dynamic it may produce some similar results.

Later in my teaching career, after I had discovered some of these insights from my students, I had a student who struggled in written expression but was a very gifted science student. The student had a natural curiosity and love for science, but struggled in nearly every class because so much of assessment was based in written expression. Since my focus had shifted from dominance to learning, I sat down with the student and asked how he would like to approach the essays that we frequently did for assessments. A new relationship came from that interaction: between us and also between the student and how he perceived his own intelligence and value.

As the student elected to dictate the essays to me as I wrote or typed, he was able to see the ideas unfold and come to life. Before, since the student was unable to put his ideas down on paper, he and everyone else perceived him as less intelligent. Later, this student conducted a research project in my class on our local lake ecosystem after it had been restored following a tornado. The student presented his work to the local county commissioners and attended meetings to take part in the restoration. If I had maintained the typical power structure that this student had experienced before and not taken the time to connect with him, this learning would have never happened. I recently connected with this student, and he told me he was planning on becoming a teacher.

Moving beyond judgment nearly always deepens contact and allows for greater learning. We can observe this phenomenon when it comes to student behavior, driven by a need for belonging. As natural tensions are generated through the course of daily encounters, subgrouping occurs to help rescue people from looking inward. If we can find others who think like we do, we never have to examine our own motivations. Subgrouping divides people into separate factions that disregard others or even builds antipathy.

Differencing is more easily averted when we surround ourselves with people who think and relate as we do. At the surface we defend this position of like-mindedness as having more in common, yet at the core we may realize it's based on fear. Fear of the unknown, of losing power, of feeling alone, prevent us from branching out, maintaining the simpler energy-efficient lifestyle we suffice with.

Judgment is an apparently easier way to resolve differences between others because it's less messy. If a school leader decides one person is right and the other wrong, or both wrong, then verdicts and edicts are handed out, and everybody returns to business as usual. No in-depth exploration of how the issue was generated or what each person did to fuel it takes place. Or consider the busy teacher, reconciling a dispute among the students, not looking at the various systems of influence that catalyzed this problem. Judgments are quick and efficient—but only in the short term.

Another student struggled with behavior problems since grade school. Group work was challenging for this student. One day, I heard a mild conflict during a group activity, and as I turned around, the student was throwing a desk across the room. We were all stunned, and the class immediately looked to me for a reaction. The student stormed out of the room and declared he was going to the office. I had never thrown a student out of my room, and haven't since, but this was not that. The student had removed himself.

My mind was racing as I replaced the desk and quietly asked the other students to resume their work. After about ten minutes, I called down to the office and calmly invited the student to rejoin us in the classroom when he was ready. The student paused on the phone, quietly thanked me, and a few minutes later humbly walked into the classroom. After that moment, something shifted in the student. I can remember the student saying, "I can tell you really want ALL of us to learn, don't you?" That student later conducted a yearlong research project that I facilitated on how computer games can be used to promote learning in science students. Years later, I still have a strong connection with the student.

A consequence of using judgments as a dispute resolution tool is teaching students how to plead their case. If a students know a judgment is coming, they prepare themselves by gathering evidence to support their position instead of looking inward to find culpability. In doing so we are creating a system of lesser accountability, which in the long term can become more destructive because nobody is learning from their actions.

Through decisions based on judgment, there is a winner who gains power and a loser who cries favoritism and rallies support behind the scenes, polarizing students and faculty. A sense of inequity creates bitterness that can sometimes lead to mistrust at best and retaliation at worst. Combine a lack of accountability with a discrepant power differential, and you have a formula for stratification.

Remembering the teacher who felt injured by her colleague who didn't invite her class to join the field trip, we begin to appreciate both the initial groundswell but more importantly the reverberations that follow. The path we take to address our grievances makes a tremendous difference in the health of the school, the relationships we cultivate, our personal integrity, and even our sense of meaning in the world.

Unresolved differences can be insidious, spreading out like a small windshield crack. Over time and repetition, these small cracks can erode the foundation of a school, eventually becoming larger fissures. Without strong leadership to bring attention to the maladaptive process, judgments and perceived threats will become the norm of the school culture. Routine and efficiency become the catalyst for the time-efficient strategy of judging; however, the complexities of human behavior seldom yield as much depth.

Frequently classroom teachers have to quickly assess the situation and determine two things: the cause of the behavior or conflict and the consequences of our response. In other words, teachers have to choose what hill to die on. The cause of the behavior is important in determining the response. These days, I generally have very positive and collaborative relationships with my students. One day, there was a student who, though usually quite spunky and outspoken, was choosing to be disrespectful and confrontational. I quickly analyzed the interaction and realized that if I engaged, like I had with other students in the past, this could escalate quickly. I realized that it could affect the learning of the entire class that day. I took a step back, disengaged, and waited for them to join the rest of the class.

In reality, I was shaken and didn't know how to proceed. I took the lunch period to reflect, then went to the student's classroom during his study hall and asked him to chat in the hall. At this point, I still had no idea what I was going to say. We stood awkwardly in the hallway, and I asked quietly, "What's going on?" My training or school experience might have told me to lecture, discipline, or correct, but the lessons my students had taught me told me the opposite. Right away, the student burst into tears and told me about some significant issues he was having that he hadn't shared with others—issues that were the causes of the conflict. The conflict had nothing to do with me or my classroom. If I had chosen wrong and reacted in the moment, the student would not have had the opportunity to connect and discuss some of these challenges being experienced.

Constructive Differencing

Constructive differencing is intended to prevent splitting, eliminate blame, and promote learning or self-discovery. When faculty and students can approach differences more constructively, they will strengthen the relationships in the school and promote greater adaptivity to adversity. Resiliency will improve, the climate of the school will feel warmer, and students will feel safer, which ultimately creates a more nourishing learning environment.

There are five steps to constructive differencing:

1. Caring

2. Curiosity

3. Conflict

4. Contact

5. Considering

Caring means paying attention to the person—and not just our agenda as well as the method by which we are going about our deliberation. Caring about the other person is a prerequisite for meaningful exchange. If we don't care, we will be more prone to diminishing the other person, serving as a catalyst for degradation in the relationship. Putting aside our agenda in the service of preserving the relationship is a difficult task—when being right or proving our point become figural.

Caring about the other person, in spite of how we may feel toward this person, will help reduce our tendency to personalize the differences. If we resist personalizing, which heightens our emotional or reactive response, we can stay more even in our responses. Remember that this person is a fellow human being, a colleague, and an educator. We may even have disdain for the person, but we must not allow our contempt to contaminate our own integrity and the way we operate.

Another student joined the class midway through the year. The students knew him because he had attended the school the year before and then moved away. I could see right away that the classroom dynamics had changed significantly with the student's return. The student was exhibiting attention-seeking behaviors that were frustrating to the other students, who were committed to learning and working hard in this elective class.

After a couple of weeks, I had two students come by and tell me they were frustrated while doing group work with this student. I also had heard that this student was a challenge in other classes. That day during class, as they were working on a dissection, the student was again acting out. I quietly called the student over to my desk. As the student was walking over, I was racking my brain trying to decide what to say that would actually be different from what this student had probably heard his whole school career. I wanted to say something that would actually cause him to adjust how he was interacting with other students. Should I lecture or threaten?

As the student approached my desk, I was still undecided, so I quietly just told them the truth: "Other students have told me they are frustrated by your behavior. They don't like how you act. You should think about that."

The student looked shocked and took a step back. The student soberly replied with "Okay" and then slowly walked back to the group. After that day, that student showed maturity and restraint. The student collaborated in group activities, and I even saw a shift in the student's learning and work completion. Later, other teachers told the student they had seen a shift in the student's behavior.

Curiosity is all about receptivity to another's perspective, in the service of reducing our blind spot. If we encounter divergence of belief and recognize it as an opportunity for learning and growth, then we diminish the potential threat of disagreement.

Seldom does a person get injured or a does a rupture occur when two people are in exploration mode, because the focus is expansion rather than contraction. We aren't holding fast to some belief but seeking to uncover what may be hidden to us and what fits better in a pedagogical model.

Myopia is a common cause of contraction, because we are only able to see what is right in front of us, extending outward. Myopia doesn't take into consideration the lens by which we look at a particular issue, nor the horizontal or vertical range of our vision. Use curiosity to rebalance our customary 95 percent expressing versus 5 percent receiving ratio. The more we listen, the more we learn.

Conflict is the interpersonal process of exploring the difference, separating debate from dialogue. In a debate, we are purely exercising our cerebral self, bolstering our point of view with evidence and data. If we can redefine conflict as the exploration of differences, tension is brought down to an optimal level that doesn't lead to reactivity.

When we are conflicting, we want to remain respectful of the other and their position. If we approach a point of saturation, risking a breakdown of diplomacy or civility, we might table our exchange for a later point. Recognizing our limitations is helpful in theory but more difficult in practice.

Be mindful of your physiological response, which may include increased heartbeat, shallow or rapid breathing, temperature increase, muscle tension, and a pit in our stomach or throat. When we attend to our physiological response to conflict, we can monitor our degree of intensity in the exchange. Modulating our affect and controlling our behavior all begins with attention to breathing.

I had another student join halfway through the year, and I could tell they were making efforts to find their place within the social structure in the whole school. Their first day, I told them to choose one of the empty seats, and after I had gotten the class started on an activity, I sat down with them to connect and explain the structure of the class. About a week later, I noticed that the new student and the student next to them were frequently talking out of turn and interrupting the class. I walked over and quietly told the student to change seats. The student bristled and quietly said, "No." I was taken aback, and the other students nearby froze.

As with other conflicts that can occur in the classroom, if the teacher engages, tensions can escalate quickly. I can remember walking by another classroom years ago, hearing as the teacher yelled at a student for being tardy. As I passed by, I heard the student, a student of mine, curse at the teacher, and answer the yell in kind. I was shocked at the disrespect from the teacher and the student, especially because the student was never disrespectful with me. Furthermore, I thought about how the interaction affected the learning of the whole class that day and the overall classroom culture—all over a tardy that could have been quietly marked in the computer—and class resumed.

This memory flashed in my mind as I was choosing my reaction. I walked over to the student, knelt down, and quietly told them how their behavior was affecting the learning of them and the rest of the class. They quietly replied that they would not behave in that way anymore if they could choose where they sat. Frankly, I didn't care where they sat. This was about our learning, not about power and dominance. From then on, both students were respectful and considerate of their peers, and I saw an improvement in their learning.

Contact is a concept in gestalt theory based on turning awareness into action in the service of meeting our needs. Contact is a prelude to intimacy, allowing two people to feel closer to each other based on a deeper appreciation of the self and other.

If we remember that intimacy is not a product of sameness, so much as differences, we will stay curious. This means that initial attraction in any relationship is based largely on overlapping ideas, interests, values, etc. However, the depth of that relationship is catalyzed by working through differences.

From the gestalt orientation, there can be no contact through sameness. To truly experience ourselves, we rely on experiences that heighten our awareness. We don't feel our finger until we press it up against another part of our body, such as our opposing hand. Once we have the experience of shape, texture, temperature, etc., in that contextual contrast, we can fully appreciate what it is.

Our finger may seem cold in contrast to our palm. We may feel weakness in that finger that comes from the opposing pressure of the opposite hand. Any information we derive to help us attend to the strengths and limitations of our finger will be found through contact. The same holds true for our exploration of differences. On an island with nobody to talk to, we are limited in how we can grow our perspective. We may use other contextual elements such as nature, or we may go deep into introspection to challenge our own views, but without somebody to dialogue with, our outcomes are limited.

The contact boundary is where information exchange takes place, as a mutual plane of existence that we conjointly form. The ocean meets the beach, and at that point of contact, the shoreline is formed. The beauty of the shore is that it isn't possible without two distinct entities coming together, and it is constantly being refashioned depending upon the forces being exerted.

Considering comes in the aftermath of the exchange. This is a time we reflect on our process of negotiation. Were our needs met? Do we feel a sense of integrity about the way we conducted ourselves? Can we clearly articulate the POV of the person we were talking to? Do we have an understanding of how that person arrived at their perspective? Would the other person likely believe we appreciated and understood their POV?

When we are considering, we are assimilating both the process and content of the exchange. It is very likely we will learn something in the aftermath that might help us shift our perspective or appreciate something about ourselves or the other that wasn't clear during the actual discourse. Returning to that individual to let them know what we have gleaned or what we may have wished to do differently will embolden the relationship and pave the way for future meaningful interactions.

The way that we choose to respond to conflicts with students is so much more than the conflicts themselves. The conflicts are often symptoms of other issues in our lives or the result of our lack of respect for them. I see disrespect for students in other classrooms and in the hallways, and I see students behave differently in other classrooms than how they behave in mine. I see a difference in their learning too.

The priority in our classrooms should not be domination or compliance but the learning and growth of the student. As my priorities have grown and evolved over my career, I have shifted the ways that I interact with and collaborate with my students about their learning and growth.

Key Points

▶ The most common reasons differences are threatening is because they are viewed as contests, power struggles, or a warning for violence.

▶ Among children, differences summon up fantasies of ostracism and the struggle for belonging.

▶ Without learning how to constructively differ, we risk not getting our needs met.

▶ The inability to negotiate may lead to implosion or explosion (exclusive aggression).

▶ Judgments categorize, label, segregate, and ultimately prevent us from exploring differences that would help us to expand our perspective.

▶ Judgments lack the depth to effectively solve challenging problems facing the world.

▶ As natural tensions are generated through the course of daily encounters, subgrouping occurs to help rescue people from looking inward.

▶ Subgrouping divides people into separate factions that disregard others or even builds antipathy.

▶ Differencing is more easily averted with people who think and relate as we do.

▶ Fear of the unknown, of losing power, and of feeling alone prevents us from branching out, maintaining the simpler energy-efficient lifestyle we suffice with.

▶ A sense of inequity creates bitterness that can sometimes lead to mistrust at best and retaliation at worst.

▶ Combine a lack of accountability with a discrepant power differential, and we have a formula for stratification.

Discussion Questions

Whether using the book for professional development (PD) or within a book group, please consider the following questions to stimulate your own ideas for exploration.

1. Do males or females in my grade tend to avoid conflict more, and why?

2. What were the early life messages I learned about conflict?

3. Which parent do I most closely model when it comes to conflict?

4. Who in my life do I feel most comfortable having conflict with, and why?

5. What was a time my relationship with somebody improved because of navigating a conflict?

CHAPTER 19

Anticipating the Consequences of Actions

(Daniel Whitley is an elementary school teacher at Mad River City in Riverside, Ohio.)

One of my most impactful memories from my first year of teaching third grade, which seems like an eternity ago, came from one of our Family Reading Nights. Almost every school has one at least once a year. It is an evening where children drag their parents, or vice versa, back to school for a few hours of games, activities, and lighthearted lessons. The teachers are tired because they have already spent a long day of teaching a group of children, but they do it because they love their students and hope that it can make a positive impact on those at risk students as well as continue to nurture those readers who already love spending time with books.

But something made this evening a little different; one of our parents had a warrant out for his arrest for a violent felony and was on the run. For some reason, he decided to call the police department after our Family Reading Night had started and inform them that if they wanted to find him he would be at our school that evening. So here I am as a first-year teacher, just in my very early twenties and fresh out of college and as raw and inexperienced as I could be watching a group of police officers in body armor search our school. To this day I still have no idea why we didn't simply evacuate the building.

Through all our negotiations with others around wants and needs, we ultimately take actions that impact others. Sometimes that action helps others, and other times they are harmed, not always through malintent. The better we get at predicting the influence our actions have on an individual or group, the more informed our choices become.

We want children to be thoughtful about how they impact others, helping them to evaluate whether getting their own wants and needs will be as important, knowing the risks. Regret is one of the hardest hurts to heal from, and if we can avoid making miscalculations, we can spare ourselves unnecessary grief.

Impulsivity, risk-taking, and the need to fit in are central to not anticipating the consequences of our actions. The need to fit in and be accepted may supersede good judgment and the anticipation of consequences. We are most at risk of poor judgment when we are inexperienced by age or by activity. When we add to this new experience a high degree of importance, the pressure gets even higher.

No college class or even student teaching could prepare someone for how to respond to a situation such as this. I was in charge of doing high-frequency word bingo for a group of third graders, some of whom were in my class and all whom had their wide eyes trained on me to see how I would respond. As an officer searched behind a curtain next to our table, I noticed one of my own students had an increasing look of panic on her face. Thankfully I understood why: Her father had recently been arrested and removed from their home in handcuffs, and this student had been there to witness it all. As her eyes widened and her breathing increased rapidly, I knew I needed to help her, so I did the only thing I could think of: I stayed calm.

I looked at her and asked her how far she was from getting bingo and what she had already filled in. I kept up the lighthearted chatter until the officers had left the room and I saw that her panic was ebbing. Afterward I talked to her mother about what had happened, and I reached out to the school counselor so the student could meet with her to talk about what happened and to come up with strategies for how to help with what was certainly PTSD. But for me it was one of the first moments where I learned how my own actions and decisions could impact my students. My actions in that moment weren't heroic or big or even very creative, but they were my first step to understanding just what an effect my actions, intentional or not, can have on my students.

When we are young, we pay less attention to how our actions impact us much less others. Teens largely live in the moment, looking for excitement or adventure as a way of developing identity and cementing their status among peers. The rebellious ones often gain status from their disregard for others or rules in the pursuit of their own wants. When a teen breaks a rule, challenges authority, or disregards societal norms, they may be rewarded for their defiance, seen as brave and even leaders.

The downside of this reinforcement is that it makes consequences something to deal with later rather than factor it into decision-making. If the time delay between action and consequence is long, the likelihood of learning is less. The longer we wait to take ownership, the more our self-protective mechanisms have a chance to set like concrete, rationalizing or justifying our actions. As an adult responsible for the personal and professional preparation of children, we don't have the luxury of waiting; lessons need to be made in the moment.

To me one of the most frightening things about being a teacher is the possibility of the impact of the mistakes I make could have upon a student. I'm sure that many of you are shaking your head and murmuring that mistakes are simply an opportunity to learn and grow both as an educator and a person. While I agree with you I have found that where I teach the margin for error as a teacher is narrower and the mistakes that you make as a teacher can have dire consequences when it comes to the current and future success of my students in the classroom and in their life as a whole. This is why I have grown to be always aware of how my actions and words can impact my students.

While that may sound dramatic, allow me to divulge the background of my students: I teach at a school that has one of the highest poverty rates in the area. Opioids have ravaged our community, and I have had few students come into my classroom who have not been impacted negatively by the addiction of a parent or family member. The majority of our students live in low-income housing just down the road from our school. Their homes are tiny, shoved together in twos. They are weather beaten and worn down by weather, age, and neglect. Many are infested with bedbugs or roaches; these small friends often travel to our school in a student's backpack or jean cuff.

I give you this background not to evoke a feeling of sympathy or even compassion but to reinforce my first point when it comes to mastering the psychosocial emotional learning (PSEL) of anticipating: Know your student's background. Only then can you anticipate what the consequences of your actions as a teacher can have upon a student.

Even we teachers, administrators, and specialists who are deeply invested in the education and well-being of children have felt the sting of how it feels when a teacher's actions impact us negatively. One of the only memories I have of my senior English teacher was our last day of school before finals. We were going around telling where we were going to go to college and what our career plans were. When it came to be my turn I proudly announced where I would be attending and that I was going to become a teacher. I will never forget her reaction; she laughed and asked if I was joking. It was a painful moment for me. Here was someone I looked up to and respected, letting me know she didn't believe in me enough to accomplish my dreams. The sad thing is that as time has passed this is really the only memory I have of this woman. I'm sure she was an amazing teacher whose opinion I obviously valued, but the only fragment that has lasted all of these twenty-five years is that painful moment. Now as an adult and experienced teacher I hold no ill will toward her. I have found this experience, which was once a motivating mantra for me during my time in college, has transformed into a powerful teaching moment for me as an educator. My forgiveness has flown far more freely toward her over the past few decades—particularly since, as a teacher, I have made my own endless number of mistakes that keep me up at night.

Over my time working in the early child education field I have found that there are several areas that you will need to grow in to master the skill of anticipating how our actions can impact on our students. Like most good lessons in education, all of these areas overlap and build upon each other like blocks.

Life is a constant set of difficult roadblocks put on our path, forcing tough choices at every turn. When deciding between different sets of consequences or prioritizing one need over another, this PSEL becomes especially important. Consider the panic that took place in March 2020, with people rushing to the stores to buy every roll of toilet paper they could get their hands on. People stockpiled essential foods and supplies to take care of their families, without consideration for others.

Survival mode disinhibits our regard for others, believing the fittest and best prepared will endure. In survival mode we neglect to imagine what our actions may mean for the greater community because we feel less responsible for those outside our network and/or don't forecast the implications of our behavior.

A pandemic is not the only time people display indifference with other conditions that lead people toward survival mode. Students who grow up in impoverished neighborhoods, those who have experienced hardship in life contributing to a pessimistic worldview, children and adults who are isolated, loners who lack a support system, and others who have not gotten their needs met due to a lack of empathy or social skills are all at risk.

Even if we do not fit into any of these categories, there are times in our lives when we become resentful or jaded, lessening our concern for others. Going through hard times even when our upbringing was uneventful can lead people into a place of antipathy. We may also be at risk when we misperceive or superficially explore the motives for other people who appear to be disregarding our best interests.

The first and most vital of these areas is experience. I remember when I was a student teacher that one of our students had not shown up to school for several days. When I tried to call, I found that the phone had been disconnected; upon further investigation, the parents had not given us an updated number. This is a common issue in many districts. After talking with our social worker, who was very experienced and beloved in the community, we made plans to do a home visit to see if the child was safe.

As we pulled into the driveway we saw the curtains drawn shut with a snap. As we knocked on the door we were met with a gruff voice asking who we were and what we wanted. As I found out later, the father of the student we were checking on was a known drug dealer, and upon seeing two tall bald men wearing ties and badges, he immediately assumed we were detectives.

This experience of learning how my appearance can trigger memories of negative experiences for parents who come from impoverished backgrounds has helped me to understand how my students' parents view me and how it can impact our interactions. Now I wear a simple polo and khakis with sneakers. The idea is to be dressed up enough to look professional but not in such an intimidating outfit that people of specific backgrounds would be uncomfortable to talk to me. Experience takes time; make sure to surround yourself with educators who you trust and rely on for feedback and advice.

No matter how well intended we are, there will be times when we are judged or criticized unfairly. These hurts will be less painful than the injuries received from those we are closer to. Consider an instance where a coworker or friend said or did something without considering our feelings. When the person who committed such an offense is close to us or thought of as an ally, we find it especially heinous. Our indignance may stop us from investigating whether the person was truly indifferent or maybe it was an oversight. Our lack of comfort with conflict may conjure images of worsening the situation, allowing us to sit back in our passivity and plot out our own retaliation.

We may feel justified in our response; after all, we weren't the ones to initiate such treasonous behavior. We are simply defending ourselves by lowering the bar to enact the ancient virtue of Hammurabi's code. The consequences of our actions seem less important than sending a message of our pain through causing the same hurt to the other. We don't question at these moments whether we have misconstrued the situation or even whether the other deserves an opportunity for recompense.

The development of self-awareness and self-reflection is part of this growth as well. Self-reflection is one of those parts of a teacher's growth that I have never found particularly pleasant or enjoyable. In the past, one of the biggest mistakes I have made myself as a teacher is to neglect this practice. It is easy to tell yourself that your teaching is fine and doesn't need improvement or to evolve. Or it is equally easy to slip into the other side of this mindset of "I am a horrible teacher, and all I do is make mistakes."

The problem with both of these viewpoints is that they are wrong. No matter how experienced we are as educators and no matter how perfectly planned out our lessons are, there is always room for improvement. Likewise, no matter how inexperienced or raw we are as teachers, there is always something good to take away from our teaching if we are passionate and pour ourselves into it.

There are many ways to self-evaluate, but my favorite two methods are videotaping my lessons or having a trusted colleague observe me teaching. When I do this, I always ask for both areas where I can improve or grow as well as what I did that was successful. This balance of positive and negative feedback is vital because no one can improve when all they hear are compliments. On the flip side, only hearing about your mistakes will eventually lead to viewing yourself as a failure. Neither mindsets are healthy on their own.

Attribution theory provides additional value in this PSEL, teaching us that we are more likely to blame a person's persona for their mistake while we hold situations at fault for our errors. For instance, our friend Jenny didn't enter her grades on time because she's lazy while we missed the deadline because there were too many demands on our time. The same holds true in reverse that we credit ourselves for successes, but a win for others is viewed as fortuitous.

If we recognize this tendency in ourselves and our students, we may find opportunities to test the theory. Hypothesis building through the scientific method will serve a dual purpose of academics and social emotional learning (SEL). Through this testing we hope to grow our sense of self and esteem as we expand our perspective about people and life, also allowing us to become better teammates within our department, grade, and school.

This is a perfect lead-in to the third area and the one that I believe is the most vital of all when it comes to learning the art of anticipation, which is collaboration. The relationships that I value the most in this world, besides those of my family, are the ones that I have developed with my teaching team. In fact our bonds are so strong that we consider each other as family. These teaching teammates are people who I would trust with my very life. The trust we have developed is why I am comfortable asking them for feedback and advice for everything from lesson development to classroom management.

I know we may not always have the advantage of working with people who fit this criteria for us, but if you do happen to be one of those lucky people who work with a wonderful team, fully invest in them. If you do this, not only will you have a support group who can help you grow and develop into a teacher who is prolific at anticipating but you also have the chance to have something bigger than teaching: you can develop friends for life.

Collaboration also extends to administration and the guardians and parents of students. I am thankful to work with a principal who is a true leader and visionary. He is supportive and insightful and has helped one of the poorest schools in the area transform into one of the highest performing. I am grateful for his insight and mentorship because it certainly has helped mold me into the teacher I am today. I know that not all administrators are this supportive or perhaps they aren't someone you are comfortable approaching for advice. In that case, worry about controlling what you can control, and try not to worry about what you can't. You can't force relationships where they won't grow. Look for someone else in your building or district who you trust and can ask for advice. Build that relationship, seek that wisdom, and use it to help develop and grow as a teacher and in your ability to anticipate.

Relationships with parents and guardians can be tricky at times. They are often the child's biggest advocate, and they can also at times be difficult or have unrealistic expectations or even no expectations at all for their child. The parents are, however, the people who know the child best and are therefore the greatest resource for learning how to best reach and anticipate the child's academic and emotional needs in and out of the classroom. I have found openness and consistent communication with guardians to be the key to establishing a positive relationship between myself and the adult or adults in the child's life. Creating a team attitude between yourself and parents is vital to the success of the child as well as the key to your success, anticipating the needs of that child and, by extension, the family's needs as well.

Self-reflection helps us to integrate our inequities, developing our identity and building self-worth, thereby raising our empathy and anticipation of consequences. This process helps us work closely and cooperatively with others. Depending upon how skilled we get in both the intra- and interpersonal skills will influence our day-to-day and moment-to-moment decision-making.

A high school sophomore who lacks popularity but knowingly diverts social time into studying may be doing so intentionally. She has adequate social skills and a healthy list of friends to spend time with but elects to stay in on a Friday night to get work done. She has an upcoming test and wants to lessen her stress for the upcoming week. Even though she may be referred to in less-endearing terms by her peers, her decision is well thought out.

Contrast this with a same-aged peer who impulsively jumps into a random pool during the freeze of winter to impress his friends. His desperate need for approval interferes with reasoning and anticipation of consequences, putting himself in danger. We attribute these missteps to impulsivity but need to consider the complex underpinnings of this behavior.

The art of anticipation is a difficult one to master. It takes time, patience, experience, collaboration, and often sacrifice on our part. Nevertheless, it is a skill that is vital to your success as a teacher and even more importantly your student's success and well-being. It is that ability that separates the great teachers from the good ones.

The most effective way of developing this developmental sequence of esteem, identity, self-reflection, empathy, and anticipation of consequences is through the emulation of these pillars for psychological health. Educators who believe in and operationalize these ideals will more easily model and convey the importance of students to join in this personal growth journey.

Students and educators who learn to anticipate the consequences of their actions will have an easier time mastering the last PSEL, a critical final element for the creation of a healthy organization and a foundation for becoming a contributing member of society.

Key Points

▶ Through all our negotiations with others around wants and needs, we ultimately take actions that impact others.

▶ The better children get at predicting the influence our actions have on an individual or group, the more informed their choices become.

▶ Impulsivity, risk-taking, and the need to fit in are all responsible for young people who don't anticipate the consequences of their actions.

▶ Children who want to fit in and be accepted may not prioritize sound judgment.

▶ Teens often live in the moment, looking for excitement or adventure as a way of developing their identity and cementing their status among peers.

▶ When a teen breaks a rule, challenges authority, or disregards societal norms, there is often a reward for defiance, seen as brave and even a leader.

▶ Attribution theory teaches us that we are more likely to blame a person's persona for a mistake they make while we hold situations at fault for our errors.

Discussion Questions

Whether using the book for professional development (PD) or within a book group, please consider the following questions to stimulate your own ideas for exploration.

1. Do males or females in my grade tend to anticipate consequences better, and why?

2. When did I start anticipating the consequences of my actions: as a child, teen, or adult?

3. How much do I consider this PSEL now versus when I began teaching?

4. What are the most effective ways of helping impulsive students anticipate consequences?

5. What has the anonymity of social media done for this PSEL?

CHAPTER 20

Modeling Ownership and Accountability

(Kevin McCormick is a principal in Racine, Wisconsin.)

As a new classroom teacher, as well as changing career paths, I was flooded with a multitude of new responsibilities. As I prepared to begin the school year, I was excited to meet my new students, build my classroom, and get to work. With my father being a teacher, I believed I had an "inside track" to understanding the role of teacher and mentor. I had worked with children in the past, but this setting was nearly entirely new to me. This was going to be a lot of fun.

As the final of the psychosocial emotional learnings (PSELs), it's the most influenced by the ones that precede it. If a person isn't tolerating stress well, for instance, the level of ownership and accountability may suffer. We don't want to appear weak, and so we cover up our inadequacies (instead of integrating them) by deflecting blame. New situations or ones without clear parameters, including unexpected life changes and chronic stressors, can erode our confidence and tempt us to be less culpable.

My prior experiences working with children were as a playground leader during the summer and a youth sports coach. While the role of each of these had some structure, they were really about informal learning and having fun, with limited ownership and accountability. This is the same approach I initially brought to classroom instruction.

During my first year of teaching, I was confident I could develop positive relationships with students, ultimately leading to academic success and social emotional stability for my students. I knew my kids came from diverse backgrounds and varied home support systems, but I didn't quite understand the level of need represented in my classroom or my school. I began to realize the impact that teachers have on children—most of it being unseen or unspoken. As we moved through the beginning of the year, I realized this was not a "hobby" or "summer job." The level of responsibility I faced became clearer.

Needs and wants are the driving forces for everything we do, so the more skilled we are using our social emotional tools, the more likely we are to climb higher on the diamond (remember Maslow's hierarchy reimagined). As our level of responsibility grows to meet our own needs and shape the process for others, the more pressure we will feel. The stakes are high, and the idea of failure means influencing the lives of young people in sometimes dramatic ways. The most effective ways of being certain we will do right by our students is to work parallel to them on our PSEL to model the process, which in this case is about taking responsibility.

One of the first realizations I had during the first quarter was that I had to take ownership of my practice and my students' growth. I had never realized the significant role a teacher plays as a mentor, confidant, mandated reporter, instructor, and growth agent for students. As I started to feel the weight of the needs that my students brought to school, I had a couple choices: I could continue my loose, somewhat casual approach to teaching and learning, or I could accept the responsibilities of being a teacher and "own" my work and dedicate myself to developing a deeper understanding of the practice of teaching. I chose to take ownership of my work and my practice. This was a foundational shift for me and my growth as a professional educator.

As we take greater ownership in our personal and professional lives we fuel our other PSELs, including self-worth and identity, forming a self-sustaining loop. This is how we decrease our reliance on our external environment to become more self-sufficient. Our parallel work with our students also forms the basis of deeper intimacy, the type of relationship that students label as most meaningful to them.

Through this shift in attitude and perspective, I became accountable to my students and their academic and social emotional growth and well-being. I found that as I grew, they grew—not all at the same rate but still measurable. Through my conscious and intentional actions the classroom setting became more accountable, and students began to respond with their own ownership, pride in work, and accountability. By no means was the setting perfect, but it became a place where my students and I could grow together by owning our choices, habits, and practices.

It is interesting to me that I was always one who was concerned with accountability, but it wasn't until I was accountable for others that I understood the magnitude and impact my actions, preparation, and follow-through could have on others. This initial experience provided an opportunity for me to grow personally and professionally. Developing accountability and ownership in students is one of the greatest learning experiences a child can have. I believe that being able to understand and accept these principles is one of the greatest lessons we can learn ourselves and teach our students.

Through the entire process of psychosocial emotional and moral development, children require consistent models to acquire these elements of healthy maturation. Of particular importance for modeling is the willingness to take responsibility for one's thoughts, feelings, and actions. Observing adults engaged in this work will help children feel emotionally safer and more physically secure in their environment, learning an important life lesson that we conserve valuable energy when not deflecting blame, while promoting greater self-worth for being accountable.

Taking ownership of our thoughts, feelings, and actions is critical for becoming a contributing member of society. Whether it's elementary schoolchildren who acknowledge forgetting to do their homework or high school adolescents who violated a code of conduct, the development of a healthy community depends on this type of integrity.

During my time as a district-level administrator, I was responsible for evaluating, supervising, and coaching principals at all levels. This experience and level of responsibility was new to me. While I had done the same for teachers, I was now being held to a different level of accountability.

When students don't anticipate the consequences of their actions, they are less likely to take ownership. These students may feel regretful about what happened, try to justify their behavior, or make excuses. Perhaps their self-worth isn't developed enough to withstand the shame that comes with being fallible, or they risk losing a poorly established sense of self.

Teachers want to resist the urge to blame in order to create an environment of ownership, and parents want to resist insulating their children from being responsible. Educators who investigate wrongdoing and/or use punishment as a means of keeping order will find compliance through fear as opposed to the internalizing of this PSEL.

Parents who give in to the temptation to rescue their children from what they suspect is unjust blame will likely diminish ownership and accountability on the part of the child. These same parents may find combative relationships with educators, further undermining confidence in their children being treated well, reinforcing their instinct to protect.

Many schools and organizations as a whole are set up to encourage rescuing, which promotes fragmentation in the system. Parents who reflexively want to protect their child or the educators who reject this form of enabling aren't appreciating the systemic influence created by a largely evaluative system, which encourages competition, sometimes without the balance of good sportsmanship.

The structure of the evaluation system was such that I was faced with uncertainty, lack of clarity regarding process, and follow-up and team support. I was essentially alone. With minimal to no mentorship or coaching and very little feedback, I experienced doubts, ambiguity, and lack of understanding of what I was accountable for. Being in this situation, I found I did not feel as though I had ownership of my responsibilities and results. I was simply following directions. Part of this uncertainty came from my own insecurities and from working in an environment driven by fear. The combination of these two pieces led to more insecurity and more hesitation on decision-making, communicating, and sharing new ideas. For me, emotionally and mentally, this was a recipe for disaster, which I only realized after a couple years in this role.

It's understandably difficult for parents who believe their children are being treated unfairly, whether it's through the often used strategy of group discipline or resulting from a perceived dislike of their child. The instinct to exculpate their sons and daughters from this real and/or perceived unfairness taps into their own moral imperatives and instincts to defend.

We know that group punishment is often a sign of desperation from a teacher who doesn't know how to decrease an undesirable behavior, and it's within a parent's right to explore this with the child's teacher. An undesirable consequence is the adversarial relationships that pit student against teacher, placing administrators in no-win situations. School and district leaders don't want the ire of the parent community but need the investment of their educators, a primary source of tension seldom discussed openly. This tension may have harmful effects on all levels of the school system.

During this time period, I became less directly involved with decision-making, and my participation in discussion, planning, and action steps became less and less. A result of this was that I became numb to potential consequences for inaction and lack of communication. I would go to work on a daily basis not knowing what to expect, fearful I may see a phone number pop up or an email that would strike fear in me, resulting in even further distancing myself from the responsibilities in front of me. I was scared most of the time. I thought I was doing good work, but I really wasn't.

Openly challenging an educator, going into investigative mode, or outright aligning with the child is less likely to produce accountability, but this isn't the primary objective of the parent. Parents often become overly concerned with perceived fairness of how their child is being treated rather than how to encourage good citizenship. The opportunity to promote self-advocacy or constructive differencing is lost behind the outrage of real or imagined inequality. We want to remember, however, that even when a person feels justified in the defense of self or other, the very act of doing so takes us further away from ownership.

When we consider the importance of social emotional learning (SEL), we might look at these seemingly unfair situations as opportunities to help promote the child's ability to navigate these situations on their own. Depending upon the age of the child, their existing skills, and the severity of the situation, we make determinations on what type of support to provide, hopefully considering the long-term impact and not simply the immediacy of the situation.

One of the instances of not accepting ownership and being accountable for my actions was the time I failed to complete the task of finishing several evaluations of principals. What started as a lack of confidence and clarity turned into outright ignoring my responsibilities. I was hiding and running from the work I was responsible for. I continued to ignore the work until a deadline for sharing the information was approaching. The lack of follow-through on my part was eating at me and caused a great deal of stress for me at work and at home. I acted as though everything was going well, but I was escaping the truth in various ways through eating, drinking, having a short temper, being in denial, getting angry, and isolating myself. All of these things helped me to avoid ownership and ignore potential consequences.

Educators can make it easier for parents in making these decisions on how or when to intercede, with one critical piece of information. A parent who knows the classroom teacher is continuously modeling the PSEL of ownership, advocating and espousing the value of looking inward before making assumptions, will feel more trusting in the process, recognizing the teacher's agenda of personal growth.

This shared value is more difficult in communities where surviving is more likely than thriving, because a Darwinian attitude of self-interest will make accountability seem less important. In the larger society where it's even considered advantageous to disempower others and point fingers, we may find it harder to instill this belief system. Holding on to the ideal that modeling ownership and accountability is the most powerful form of learning an educator or parent can do must have the support of the full ecosystem.

This comes in simple forms like saying you are sorry to show children how to apologize. It can be done through acknowledging when you didn't leave enough time to get something done or didn't follow through as promised. Adults can model through sharing their own frailties and inequities to demonstrate how to introspect and then use those limitations in conjunction with the behavior they are taking ownership for.

For the sports fan who watches collegiate or professional athletics on television, you might be familiar with the postgame interview by the coach or star player. When we hear these key figures putting the responsibility on their shoulders, we feel good about them. We trust they emulate ownership so they can expect the same of their players. Conversely, those who blame are not likely to last long in their positions and don't inspire their team.

After the deadline had come and gone, I realized that by not addressing my responsibility, the consequences could be worse. So I organized my thoughts, was honest with myself, and called my supervisor to let him know I had only partially completed a few of my evaluations. This was both a surrender to the burden I was carrying as well as a moment of liberation. I almost immediately felt relieved as I accepted ownership of my inaction. For me, this was more about me owning my work and understanding I was accountable to the system, my supervisor, the principals, and myself than finishing the work. While the consequences I faced and accepted were not disastrous, this was a significant event that began to change my perspective toward my work as well as opened the door to a deeper understanding of the scope of my influence and authority within the system I was working.

The relief that comes with unburdening oneself isn't easy to quantify but enormously reinforcing. As human beings continuously seeking peace through balancing what we give and take in our small and larger communities, letting go of fear to acknowledge our wrongdoing is powerful. We can feel instantly lighter when we announce to the world that we were wrong, violated a norm, or unintentionally hurt somebody. We will build our capacity for distress through this unburdening as we realize the world rewards more than punishes honesty.

Whether it's a learned reflex from living in survival mode or a reaction to placing too much pressure on ourselves to be infallible, the task of taking ownership is challenging for people of all ages. From the child who fears punishment to the adult who fears embarrassment, we have to fight against the urge to self-protect. When we have grown the prerequisite of self-confidence through reflection and exploration of our frailties and inequities, we are better positioned for this life-changing PSEL.

By owning my mistake and by understanding the consequences of my actions, I began to see and accept things in a new way. By placing so much pressure on myself through unrealistic expectations, fear-driven productivity, and a lack of ownership, my work was superficial and short-term oriented. This is when things changed.

For those who put too much pressure on themselves to seem perfect or perhaps more accurately described as avoiding the appearing of imperfection, the pressure to avoid scrutiny can be detrimental to one's mental health. Thus, understanding the polarity for not taking ownership is important to explore, as it's responsible for a growing segment of the student population suffering from mood disorders. When kids hold themselves too accountable, espousing standards that are rigid or perfectionistic, they run the risk of developing schemas and attitudes generating everything from worry to anxiety.

These are the children who believe in doing the "right thing," achieving academically at all costs to their well-being, and not being forgiving of themselves for mistakes. Some adults share this mentality, which can be reinforced through being seen as a trustworthy, decent human being with high integrity.

The pressure to seem perfect represents a smaller segment of the population, but for these individuals, ownership needs to be separated from personalizing. A child isn't responsible for the actions of the group, and a teacher isn't responsible for the attitudes of a class. We can influence but without making it our fault.

One of my first steps was to connect with the principals involved to complete the evaluations and to address the delay in finalization. While I was a respected leader by many principals, this was a humbling and somewhat embarrassing experience. This was one unforeseen consequence I had to accept. As I moved forward and came out of the depths of uncertainty and insecurity, my confidence began to grow, and I became more about action than words. While I have always been good with words, this was no longer about how well I could write or speak; this was now about taking action and owning my work. This transformation from an ambiguous existence in the education system to a focused and driven mission was life changing.

Moral Reasoning

Through this PSEL, it can be helpful to incorporate understanding of moral development, which influences our ability to anticipate the consequences of our actions and take ownership. Lawrence Kohlberg (1958) is considered a pioneer in this field, expanding on the original work of Piaget from 1932. Moral reasoning may be viewed as a component of the larger goal of character development.

Character development has been a topic of conversation since the mid 1940s with a resurgence in the 1990s and early 2000s; however, it had difficulty gaining traction. Dewey (1944) wrote, "It is a commonplace of educational theory that the establishing of character is a comprehensive aim of school instruction and discipline."

Two reasons for the difficulty in successfully implementing character education across the country are the basis for which these standards are developed and the murkiness of terms like *ethics, values, morals,* and *conduct.* There were concerns around the influence of religion and the principle role of the school, confounding the debate. Some argued that academics would be diluted and others that families were being usurped of their authority.

The absence of an agreed-upon process to cultivate shared values has been a sticking point in schools and society as a whole. As we will consider later, the answer may lie in the support of philosophy, which can support multiple lines of character development without a need for standardization or prioritization of values.

For the purposes of understanding accountability as an important social emotional target, we can still draw from moral reasoning and the developmental work that grounds this evolution in theory. Being accountable and taking ownership lies at the intersection of psychosocial emotional and moral development, forming the basis for character development.

Kohlberg identified six stages of development within three levels, including preconventional, conventional, and postconventional moral reasoning. At the preconventional level (generally nine and under), we have developed our own personal code but are able to adapt to the standards of a group.

If you are an elementary school teacher, you likely set forth rules at the start of the school year or perhaps ask the students to generate the rules. This is similar but also different. Morality is not simply about rules but more about an ethos that guides our behavior and decision-making. We don't take something that doesn't belong to us because it's a rule but also because it doesn't feel good to us.

Many children will answer the question "Why should we give something back that doesn't belong to us?" with the response that we could be punished or perhaps that the person who lost it might be worried. This is where we begin to differentiate a child who is internalizing morality as opposed to simply following rules or avoiding punishment.

Many children or adults don't have a personal code of morality. Instead, our moral code is shaped by the standards of adults and the consequences of following or breaking their rules. Authority is outside the individual, and reasoning is based on the physical consequences of actions.

Remember from earlier how the external application of shoulds comes in the form of rules, but the goal is the internalization of these messages and is how we form our moral development. If there are too many rules in a school, we may be slowing down the development of moral reasoning by increasing dependence on the shoulds of others. Developing our own moral imperatives through mediums such as philosophy is helpful.

Schools may also benefit from creating safe spaces for children who have violated a boundary or disrupted school operations, with opportunities for self-reflection. How did their fear of not getting a need met increase their desire for self-protection? How did their maladaptive strategy for getting what they want impact others or the whole? How come their own shoulds didn't get activated, and what reasoning was used to justify their actions? This is how moral reasoning is promoted as an adjunct of PSEL.

Children are also learning that right and wrong may be a matter of perspective, and there can be multiple views on a single topic. We can hasten this process by posing situations and dilemmas to children in order for them to work individually and in groups to come up with their own separate and collective viewpoints.

At this age, children may defer to the groupthink, so it's important to help put them in situations where they can feel free to consider options that may not align with the majority. When children can ultimately come up with their own set of moral guidelines, you can introduce the idea of taking responsibility but allow them to define how this will work. Remember that the more ownership of the idea generation, the more likely the child will hold themselves to it.

With adolescents and young adults, we are open to internalizing the values and attitudes of figures we hold in high regard. We may not always look deeply into the actual behavior of these individuals, such as idolized sports figures, but at least we are using targets to aspire to. This presents opportunities for educators to help students research whether purported values are lived values.

Not only did this new ownership define my work but it began to more clearly define me as a person. Over the course of the next several years, I continued to reflect on my work, inquire with confidence, and embrace my work as an educator of students and adults. I also developed the strength and courage to own up to the responsibilities I had to myself and to my loved ones.

I believe the key to my experience of ownership and accountability revealed itself when I began to veer off track in my professional life, which was a symptom of my lack of social, mental, and emotional preparedness for the work placed in front of me. I shrunk out of fear and ambiguity and took the path of least resistance. This resulted in consequences of various magnitude and impact.

As we become more established adults, judgment is based on self-chosen principles, and moral reasoning is based on individual rights and justice. Consider a teacher who doesn't believe that standardized testing is a good use of time or a fair evaluation of student progress, yet they work in a system that demands it. How that adult resolves that dilemma is part of the long-term goal of being accountable—both to one's integrity and to the institution we are affiliated with.

As a result of a great deal of work to address my emotional and mental health with the same vigor as my physical well-being, I have increased my capacity to own my actions and understand the potential consequences. This allows me to make better decisions, ask questions with confidence, and understand multiple perspectives without losing my own voice.

It is important that I share that my experience was made possible through the support and guidance of several individuals. For me, one of the consequences of not being prepared mentally and emotionally for ownership and accountability was the development of an "I can do this alone" mentality. This belief led me deeper into the muck. Once I realized it was okay to trust others, share responsibilities, and be honest with myself, all aspects of my life, including my work as a leader, improved dramatically.

This type of social contract means that individual rights and interests may sometimes be sacrificed for the greater good, which may be considered the pinnacle of moral development. Sometimes it's one's own rights that are yielded in the service of this greater good—and, beyond that, if the individual disobeys established laws and one's own rights in favor of this greater good.

Educators can use lessons around equity and equality to help students explore the limits of their moral development, providing hypotheticals around fairness and discussing American heroes who may have made difficult decisions that led to their own peril. Educators might even use contemporary issues such as catastrophic school violence to help students consider their own internal conflicts between self-preservation and the betterment of their community.

Key Points

▶ Through the entire process of psychosocial emotional development, children need models to help them learn to take responsibility for their thoughts, feelings, and actions.

▶ Children who feel more secure within themselves and safe in their environment advance along this journey more easily.

▶ Taking ownership of our thoughts, feelings, and actions is critical for becoming a contributing member of society.

▶ Whether it's an elementary student who acknowledges forgetting to do homework or a high school student who violated a code of conduct, the culture or integrity of a system depends on this type of integrity.

▶ When students don't anticipate the consequences of their actions, they are less likely to take ownership.

▶ Teachers who resist the urge to blame in order to create an environment of ownership will be more successful.

▶ Parents tend to rescue their children—a likely way to reduce ownership and accountability. Helping children learn how to navigate differences and introduce solutions is key.

Discussion Questions

Whether using the book for professional development (PD) or within a book group, please consider the following questions to stimulate your own ideas for exploration.

1. Do males or females in my grade tend to take more ownership, and why?

2. What lessons in accountability do I recall from my childhood?

3. When was a time I didn't take ownership, and why?

4. If I have children, how do I promote this PSEL?

5. What is a teacher's role in promoting values and morals?

Human Evolution and Psychosocial Emotional Learning

When initially engaging in personal growth work, we may be healing from old wounds or attempting to uncover the source of our unrest. Without distress we may take our psychological and physical health for granted; thus, exploring the complexities of psychosocial emotional growth is not a common practice outside of parenting or therapy.

As educators with the solemn and honorable mission for developing the lives of young people, we are morally if not ethically responsible for engaging in our own personal growth, parallel to what we ask of our students. When we prioritize this work, we will be more successful in our jobs and our lives. When the entire faculty takes part, we can build incredibly dynamic schools to teach and learn within.

As we absorbed from the courageous narratives of our fifteen educators from around the country, our success is tied to effort and not outcome. We cannot control what life throws at us, so reward is best measured by our process. Nobody can take away the hard work we invest into evolving as human beings or the pride associated with modeling this lifelong journey for those we vow to instruct.

And before this expedition begins, our biological and genetic predisposition helps to form our personality type, determining our stamina and moral compass to navigate us down this long path. Some embark with a full backpack or unusually high endurance while others get lost or fatigued early.

With the proper guide to incentivize, to equip us with the right tools, we can overcome these obstacles. Our fifteen courageous educators disclosed their own journeys they built careers upon. In spite of life's unfairness and the voids left from unmet needs, people can still thrive.

Through lessening our dependency upon inconsistent caregivers and equitable opportunities to evolve, we overcome the limitations of biology and persona. While the intensity of needs may follow us into adulthood like an endless well of despair—like not feeling accepted by our childhood peer group, producing adult codependency—we can overcome. When skills become instincts to meet our needs and overcome challenges, we grow our resiliency. With manageable degrees of stress and opportunities to advance, we may reduce our reliance on the protective mechanisms that trap us in survival mode.

Figure 21.1

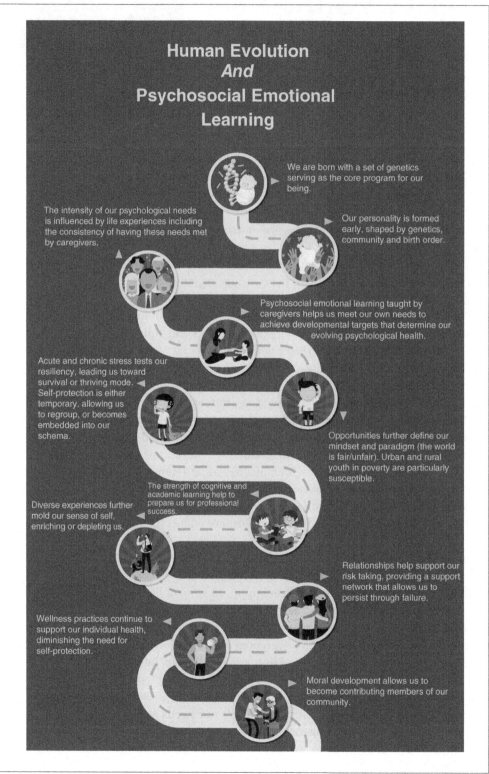

Look for the companion workbook due out soon, translating these complex tools into a workable framework for your classroom and school.

Opportunities from caring educators within supportive school cultures, to experiment with recognizing and meeting our needs, are invaluable. If school prepares us through diverse experiences to lead us out of our myopia or early life conditioning, we feel more hopeful to achieve beyond what our backgrounds may have predicted.

Without these rich experiences and supportive relationships to expand our thoughts and deepen our feelings, both chronic and acute stress place us at greater risk for succumbing to mental health problems, including trauma, anxiety, depression, and addiction.

If our school provides wellness opportunities to improve our physical health and psychosocial emotional learning (PSEL) for our psychological health, we may see our community as a fair place to reinvest our energy. Synergistic relationships within our school will form the basis for organizational health. Whole school health is the result of whole child education and the investment in our most precious human resource: educators.

Evolving educational ecosystems through PSEL is the future for all of education but will require a recommitment of time and energy to propel us into this new era of instruction. The challenges we face to recover and advance forward means a sustainable fuel source for those on the front line. The investment will pay dividends for many generations. See Figure 21.1.

Appendix A
Road Map for Psychosocial Emotional Learning

. . . .

Psychosocial emotional learning (PSEL) forms a network of interactive skills, dynamics, and calibration tools to advance our personal growth work. The more proficient we get at utilizing these PSELs, the more likely we are to minimize the use of protective mechanisms and get our needs met. Consider the following infographic to map this intricate network:

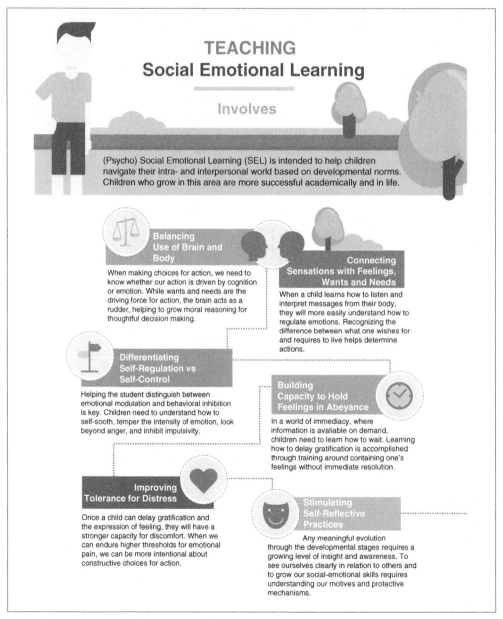

Helping Integrate Inequities and Frailties

Human beings of all ages use defense mechanisms or protective strategies to insulate themselves from fear of rejection, shame, hurt and other unpleasantness. As we learn to own all aspects of ourselves, includingour less favorable, we don't need to hide.

Evolving Identity Formation

The most significant goal for all children is the successful navigation of their psycho-social stages of development. As children understand who they are and what matters to them, they can relate as a separate entity instead of being a follower.

Growing Self-Worth

As children and adolescents form a more solid but flexible sense of self, they will feel greater value and worth. Through this process they require outside influences helping them to build efficacy for their effort and intention to be their best.

Channeling Aggression into Constructive Outlets

Aggression is a natural and healthy drive, which gets channeled in different directions. Inclusive aggression allows for meaningful contact, while exclusive aggression treats the world as hostile and unreceptive to getting one's needs met.

Developing Tools for Expressing and Negotiating Needs

As children see themselves as unique beings, they can recognize their reliance on others to help meet wants and needs. This requires skills for recognizing, expressing, and negotiating needs to satisfy themselves and the other.

Cultivating Empathy and Advanced Empathy

For students to have successful relationships, they need to recognize and care about the feelings of others. If they can tune into their experience of feelings, they will move toward greater ownership and the ability to take actions that consider themselves in relation to others.

Deepening Conflict Resolution to Constructive Differencing

Learning how to be at odds with somebody but maintain contact is among the most difficult tasks of a human being. As we appreciate conflict as the exploration of difference, we are no longer threatened by differences, but curious about the learning they offer.

Anticipating Consequences of Actions

Through our negotiations of wants and needs, we ultimately take actions which impact others. The better children get at predicting the influence of their actions, the more informed their choices become. Greater intentionality of choices is key for relationship building.

Modelling Ownership and Accountability

Through the entire process of social-emotional development, children need models to help them learn to take responsibility for their thoughts, feelings, and actions. Children who feel more secure within themselves and safe in their environment learn this more easily.

Appendix B
Next Steps

· ·

We want to separate ourselves from other books—the ones with immediate impact but fade over time. Instead, let us continue the work by engaging in conversations, holding each other accountable, and building a community to support educator wellness. If you would like to visit a dedicated web page where we can further our momentum for individual and systemic growth, here is what you will find at www.teachercoach.com/PSELbook:

▶ Submit your own PSEL story, and be featured on the TeacherCoach website, where others can learn from your experience. With or without anonymity, take part in the movement for greater transparency around the humanity of educators. Together we can promote greater attention to educator health and wellness.

▶ Vote on the most challenging PSEL. With data, we can more easily determine what help is needed and where. Contributing to our research helps shape future offerings and promotes the work of educator health among decision makers.

▶ Take the Educator Health Pledge to hold yourself accountable to self-care. Information on educator wellness week and other valuable information on physical and psychological health will be made available for our special audience of readers.

▶ Promote our work on social media through hashtags such has #PSEL, #TCPSEL, and/or #PSEL4Teachers and likes to help us bring this work to those in need. Receive a coupon code for any training.

▶ Through the TeacherCoach blog, you can provide guest posts and commentary as well as stay current on the latest topics from our content experts. If you don't have a dedicated district portal, you can join our home portal to access the blog: https://home.teachercoach.com/

▶ Build your community through contributing blog posts and discussion groups to bring personal growth work to life in a supportive environment.

▶ Check out our fifteen contributing educators from around the country who courageously shared their personal and professional stories to bring life to the book. For those who are not anonymous, feel free to reach out and share your reaction with them.

Be on the lookout for *Whole School Health and Psychosocial Emotional Learning Workbook*, which is due out soon. In this book, we will explore the application of these principles and how they can be applied in the wake of the post–COVID-19 world crisis.

References

American Cancer Society. (2020). Cancer facts & figures 2020. Retrieved from https://www.cancer.org/research/cancer-facts-statistics/all-cancer-facts-figures/cancer-facts-figures-2020.html

American Psychological Association. (2017). APA's survey finds constantly checking electronic devices linked to significant stress for most Americans. Retrieved from https://www.apa.org/news/press/releases/2017/02/checking-devices

Bates, C. (2002). *Pigs eat wolves: Going into partnership with your dark side*. Saint Paul, MN: Yes International Publishers.

Broderick, P. (2013). *Learning to breathe: A mindfulness curriculum for adolescents to cultivate emotional regulation, attention, and performance*. Oakland, CA: New Harbinger Publications.

Bump, P. (2018). Eighteen years of gun violence in U.S. schools, mapped. *The Washington Post*. Retrieved from https://www.washingtonpost.com/news/politics/wp/2018/02/14/eighteen-years-of-gun-violence-in-u-s-schools-mapped/?amp;utm_term=.692766ea01f4&noredirect=on

Campbell, T. C. (2014). Casein is a carcinogen. Retrieved from https://nutritionstudies.org/provocations-casein-carcinogen-really/

Centers for Disease Control and Prevention. (2015). Expected new cancer cases and deaths in 2020. Retrieved from https://www.cdc.gov/cancer/dcpc/research/articles/cancer_2020.htm

Collinson, S. (2020). Trump officials deflect blame for U.S. death toll, escalate reopening push. Retrieved from https://www.cnn.com/2020/05/18/politics/trump-us-death-toll-blame-reopen/index.html

de Brey, C. (2018). Indicator 5: Teachers threatened with injury or physically attacked by students. Retrieved from https://nces.ed.gov/programs/crimeindicators/ind_05.asp

Dewey, J. (1944). *Democracy and education*. New York, NY: The Free Press.

EcoWatch. (2015). 84,000 chemicals on the market, only 1% have been tested for safety. Retrieved from https://www.ecowatch.com/84-000-chemicals-on-the-market-only-1-have-been-tested-for-safety-1882062458.html

Felt, L. J., Robb, M. B., & Gardner, H. (2016). Technology addiction: Concern, controversy, and finding balance. Retrieved from https://www.commonsensemedia.org/research/technology-addiction-concern-controversy-and-finding-balance

Gestalt Institute of Cleveland. (1988). *Becoming a better intervener*. Unpublished manuscript.

Hanushek, E. A., Peterson, P. E., & Woessmann, L. (2013). *Endangering prosperity: A global view of the American school*. Washington, DC: Brookings Press. Retrieved from http://hanushek.stanford.edu/publications/endangering-prosperity-global-view-american-school

Hastings, M., & Agrawal, S. (2015, January 9). Lack of teacher engagement linked to 2.3 million missed workdays. Retrieved from https://news.gallup.com/poll/180455/lack-teacher-engagement-linked-million-missed-workdays.aspx

Hastings, M., & Agrawal, S. (2015, January 9). Lack of teacher engagement linked to 2.3 million missed workdays. Retrieved from https://news.gallup.com/poll/180455/lack-teacher-engagement-linked-million-missed-workdays.aspx

Jacob, A., & McGovern, K. (2015). The mirage, confronting the hard truth about our quest for teacher development. Retrieved from https://tntp.org/publications/view/the-mirage-confronting-the-truth-about-our-quest-for-teacher-development

K–12 Education Team. (2015). Teachers know best: Teachers' views on professional development. Retrieved from https://k12education.gatesfoundation.org/resource/teachers-know-best-teachers-views-on-professional-development/

Kohlberg, L. (1963). *Moral development and identification*. In H. W. Stevenson (Ed.) & J. Kagan, C. Spiker (Collaborators) & N. B. Henry, H. G. Richey (Eds.), *Child psychology: The sixty-second yearbook of the National Society for the Study of Education, Part 1* (pp. 277–332). Chicago, IL: National Society for the Study of Education; University of Chicago Press. Retrieved from https://doi.org/10.1037/13101-008

National Child Traumatic Stress Initiative. (2020). Understanding child trauma. Retrieved from https://www.samhsa.gov/child-trauma/understanding-child-trauma

Scherz, J. (2019). *Educator wellness survey*. Unpublished survey.

Schwartz, S. (2019, July 16). Teachers support social-emotional learning, but say students in distress strain their skills. Retrieved from https://www.edweek.org/ew/articles/2019/07/17/teachers-support-social-emotional-learning-but-say-students.html

Sutcher, L., Darling-Hammond, L., & Carver-Thomas, D. (2016, September 15). A coming crisis in teaching? Teacher supply, demand, and shortages in the U.S. Retrieved from https://learningpolicyinstitute.org/product/coming-crisis-teaching

Speck, D. (2018). Third of teachers have mental health problems. Retrieved from https://www.tes.com/news/third-teachers-have-mental-health-problems

Strauss, V. (2013, February 21). U.S. teachers' job satisfaction craters—Report. *The Washington Post*. Retrieved from https://www.washingtonpost.com/news/answer-sheet/wp/2013/02/21/u-s-teachers-job-satisfaction-craters-report

Sharot, T. (2011). *The optimism bias: A tour of the irrationally positive brain*. New York, NY: Pantheon/Random House.

TED. (2009, October 7). *The danger of a single story; Chimamanda Ngozi Adichie* [Video file]. Retrieved from https://youtu.be/D9Ihs241zeg

Will, M. (2018, May 30). Nearly half of public school teachers are satisfied with their salaries, data show. Retrieved from https://blogs.edweek.org/edweek/teacherbeat/2018/05/teacher_salary_job_satisfaction.html? r=95960808

Will, M. (2017, October 30). Educators are more stressed at work than average people, survey finds. Retrieved from http://blogs.edweek.org/teachers/teaching_now/2017/10/educator_stress_aft_bat.html

Index

A SAGE Publishing Company

Helping educators make the greatest impact

CORWIN HAS ONE MISSION: to enhance education through intentional professional learning.

We build long-term relationships with our authors, educators, clients, and associations who partner with us to develop and continuously improve the best evidence-based practices that establish and support lifelong learning.

Solutions you want. Experts you trust. Results you need.

AUTHOR CONSULTING

Author Consulting

On-site professional learning with sustainable results! Let us help you design a professional learning plan to meet the unique needs of your school or district. www.corwin.com/pd

INSTITUTES

Institutes

Corwin Institutes provide collaborative learning experiences that equip your team with tools and action plans ready for immediate implementation. www.corwin.com/institutes

ECOURSES

eCourses

Practical, flexible online professional learning designed to let you go at your own pace. www.corwin.com/ecourses

READ2EARN

Read2Earn

Did you know you can earn graduate credit for reading this book? Find out how: www.corwin.com/read2earn

Contact an account manager at (800) 831-6640 or visit **www.corwin.com** for more information.

Made in United States
North Haven, CT
11 October 2021